# Long Rein

**Also by Jay Hovdey**

*Inside Horse Racing*

*Whittingham: The Story of a Thoroughbred Racing Legend*

*Cigar: America's Horse*

# Long Rein

## Tales from the World of Horse Racing

By Jay Hovdey

With a Foreword by William Nack

DRF PRESS

Published by
Daily Racing Form Press
708 Third Avenue, 12th Floor
New York, New York 10017

ISBN: 978-1-932910-30-8
Library of Congress Control Number: 2014935930

Cover photo by Vicki L. Vinson
Cover image, detail of "John Henry" at Santa Anita Park,
lifesize bronze by Nina Kaiser
Back cover photo by Marcie Heacox
Cover jacket, illustrations and text designed by Chris Donofry

Printed in the United States of America

*For Lorelei*

*"You live through time, that little piece of time that is yours, but that piece of time is not only your own life, it is the summing up of all the other lives that are simultaneous with yours. . .It is, in other words, history, and what you are is an expression of that history, and you do not live your life, but somehow your life lives you, and you are, therefore, only what history does to you."*

*—Robert Penn Warren*

*"I keep telling people there are more things to the racetrack than horses."*

*—Charles Bukowski*

# CONTENTS

# FOREWORD

As a boy growing up in Southern California, where the sun shines bright on ball parks, football stadiums, and racetracks alike, Jay Hovdey spent many a glorious day at the side of his father, Orvil Hovdey, happily ensconced in such far-flung sporting venues as Dodger Stadium at Chavez Ravine, the Los Angeles Coliseum, and all the racetracks within reach from Del Mar to Hollywood Park to Santa Anita.

"The night before our racing excursions," Jay would later recall, "my dad would drive me to this seedy flophouse of a hotel in downtown Anaheim and keep the motor running while I darted inside to buy the *Racing Form*."

For young Jay, in fact, nothing quite equaled the days passed with his father at those teeming California racetracks of the 1960s. They were together at Hollywood Park in '65 when one of Jay's boyhood heroes, Native Diver, whipped Hill Rise and Colorado King in the Hollywood Gold Cup. They were there for three consecutive runnings of the Strub at Santa Anita, the first one featuring Bold Bidder's smashing triumph in the race, when he broke the course record for ten furlongs, and the last one starring Most Host as he pulled off his stunning upset of the mighty Damascus, another of Jay's favorites.

"I remember being very quiet all the way home," he would recall.

These were the racing moments, shared with his father, that set the racing hook in the boy and inspired his lifelong romance with the world of racing, the incomparable world of the Turf.

And so it is no wonder, in this exemplary collection of his best racing columns and stories, that the most heartwarming tale of them all—the story revealing the source that fed and nurtured his passion for the game—is Jay's tribute to Orvil Hovdey written in July of 2006, the one acknowledging all those races that they saw in their shared past.

"If you've been looking for someone to hold accountable for what you've been reading here, it's too late," Jay wrote in his lead to that *Racing Form* column. "Elvis has left the building. The end came for my dad—the man who put the pen in my hand—early Tuesday evening, 83 years, four months, and a few days after he hit the ground running in a dry, cold corner of Montana prairieland that went by the name of Outlook."

By July of 2006, of course, Jay had long been among the most eminent turf writers in America. He was by then the executive columnist of *Daily Racing Form*, as well as the winner of four Eclipse Awards for excellence in turf writing. Two years after its formation in 2010, Jay would be inducted into the Joe Hirsch Media Roll of Honor at the National Museum of Racing in Saratoga Springs, the equivalent of Thoroughbred racing's Hall of Fame for racing writers.

As an American turf writer, Hovdey traces his literary pedigree in tail-male back to the most esteemed practitioners of the craft—from Joe Palmer, Joe Estes, and Joe Hirsch to Charles Hatton, Steve Crist, and Red Smith—and this volume of his *Daily Racing Form* columns bears vivid testimony to his rightful place in that lineage. What colored his tribute to his father is what touches his profiles of every subject in *Long Rein*, from his obituary/appreciation of Charles Clay, the groom of Sunday Silence, to his stories of the many Thoroughbreds he has seen and esteemed for their speed, their will to win, and their unflagging courage under fire—such as the grand mare Zenyatta, the star-crossed Lost in the Fog, and those two hickory-tough geldings, Kona Gold and Best Pal.

And that, as is apparent one story to the next, is Hovdey's deep affection for the running horse—for those qualities that ennoble him, raise him, and define him as a Thoroughbred—and his abiding love for the sport and for the game as it is played from shedrow to the jocks' room to The Jockey Club. Above his desk, Hovdey has five photographs of horses hanging on the wall, and among them is Best Pal, a kind of spiritual descendent, in Hovdey's mind, of the great Swaps, Native Diver, Cougar II, and John Henry.

Of Best Pal, he wrote:

"There are horses who jump the rails and worm their way into our hearts and minds. They set up shop for good. They help define the game. They give people a reason to show up every morning, muck stalls in the dark, and brag about being a citizen of the Thoroughbred racing world."

This whole book is full of lyrical tributes to Thoroughbred racing and some of the finest horses—and most memorable figures—to have graced its stage.

Here Jay raises a toast to them all. With a wink and a nod to Orvil for starting him on his way.

—William Nack,
author, *Secretariat: Making of a Champion*
January 30, 2014

# INTRODUCTION

"Whatcha doing, Daddy?"

She was six, standing at my shoulder and looking at the blank page before us on the computer screen.

"Thinking," I replied.

"Thinking?" she said. "I thought you were supposed to be writing."

Busted.

"If you're thinking about writing, you're not writing," David Milch reminded us, over and over, as we considered the various twists and turns in the scripts for *Luck*, the show about horse racing Milch created for HBO. Although it lasted only one season, *Luck* was my master class, a chance to distill in those nine episodes all that I had experienced inside the ropes of Thoroughbred racing into a story line here, a scene there, a few lines of dialogue that might light a spark.

By a rough count, since the fall of 1998, I have written in the neighborhood of 2,500 columns and a bushel basket of long-form features for *Daily Racing Form*, horse racing's publication of record. In these pages, 81 of those pieces have been selected and arranged in a manner that hopefully makes sense. Some of them have required a brief author's note to remove any unnecessary, dangling suspense, while keeping in mind that they were written in the moment, for their time. And there has been a handful of corrections made so as not to compound an original error.

In many ways, the game has changed considerably in the decade and a half embraced by their datelines. Still, the themes are universal, the horses are the heroes, and the men and women who work with them count themselves as blessed to be along for the ride.

"Writers are the custodians of memory," wrote William Zinsser, author of *On Writing Well.*

They are also the file clerks, the dispassionate witnesses, the sympathetic ears. Zinsser is right, though. Writers are unemployed without memories. We root around in people's heads, seducing their trust, then spill the take onto the page in a selfish, shameless act of pure ego. When it works, everybody wins. I love writing about horse racing in the same way I love watching the train heist from *The Wild Bunch*, the sound of Chet Baker singing "Let's Get Lost," or the sight of my wife, Julie Krone, teaching children how to ride. All are intricate, subversive puzzles with deeply satisfying payoffs.

As to the title of the book, when a jockey puts his or her horse on a long rein, they have committed themselves to a steady gallop at the horse's own pace. They are in for the long haul, taking in the view, content to let others fire and fall back along the way. I beheld my first byline in high school and never saw anything so cool in my life. After that, I did not set out to spend my career writing about the fates and follies of racehorses and their keepers. It only ended up that way...and lucky me that it did.

There is a custom that introductions like this one should offer a list of grateful acknowledgments. Where to begin? My mother for the gift of an *American Racing Manual* for my 14th birthday. Dan Smith, who did a fine book with Bill Shoemaker, for my first job at the racetrack. Joe Burnham, the peerless cinematographer, for challenging me to write in pictures, sounds, and colors. *Daily Racing Form*'s Steven Crist for putting me on the payroll, with the exhortation, "Do what you do."

A writer is helpless without a good editor. Thank goodness I've had some first-rate caretakers along the way, including Tim Capps, Tracy Gantz, Robert Henwood, Cathy Laws, Gerry Strine, John Cherwa, and Ray Paulick. In order for the selections in this book to see the light of day, they first had to pass muster with Rich Rosenbush and Irwin Cohen of *Daily Racing Form*, who kept the bar high. And then there is Frank R.

Scatoni, my own Maxwell Perkins, whose creative work in shaping this collection earned my everlasting appreciation, although I believe he also got paid.

"One day I will find the right words, and they will be simple," wrote Jack Kerouac, when he wasn't wandering the road.

I'm still looking for the right words to describe the intoxicating complexities of Thoroughbred racing, the mix of blood sport and ballet, of ridiculous risk and giddy reward. Until then, until those simple syllables hit me between the eyes, it is my privilege to share in these selections my love of the game and my admiration for the people and the horses who play it.

—Jay Hovdey
February 21, 2014

# Long Rein

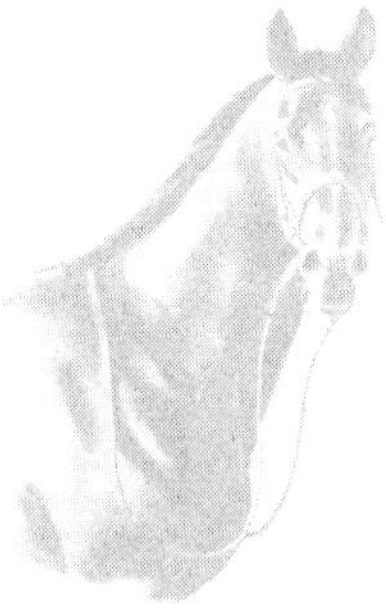

One

# HORSE HEROES

*"Come on in here," said Henry Moreno. "She won't bite."*

*This was funny, since one of Moreno's horses already had bitten me the summer before when, as a careless rookie on the racetrack circuit, I had taken my eye off the ball long enough to let a young colt named Quote grab a mouthful of my upper arm and give it a friendly squeeze. The bruise he left behind spent the next week changing through a rainbow of sickly hues.*

*Moreno wanted me to get a closer look at a mare named Sangue, which everyone pronounced "sang" and translated from its Latin root as nothing less than "blood." I already knew how good she was, which was very good indeed. Now I'd find out if she ate meat. But Sangue was accommodating and allowed her trainer to give me an intimate tour of the professional Thoroughbred in full: the angle of the shoulder, the density of muscle, the powerful housing for her heart and lungs. She tolerated the visit with a wary eye, then turned as we ducked under the webbing at the front of the stall, as if to say, "Next time bring carrots."*

*Being a good racehorse is an accident of birth. Staying a good racehorse is a tribute to good luck and the hard work of all the people involved. Don't get me wrong. Fast or slow, colt or filly, they all eat the same sweet feed and dream the same horsey dreams. Over time, though, personalities seem to emerge in harmony with their accomplishments: the grouchy John Henry, the imperious Cigar, the crowd-pleasing Precisionist.*

*The good ones included in the following pages have landed there not only because of what they did as racehorses, but also for what they represented when they were standing perfectly still. The sport was a better place because of them, and I was lucky to be allowed in some of their stalls. But don't let a trainer kid you. They all bite.*

## BEST PAL

*November 27, 1998*

There are photographs of five horses hanging on the wall over the desk at which this is being written. Best Pal is one of them.

That means Best Pal is thought of nearly every day in this household, and will continue to be as long as there is a wall and a desk. I have a feeling we are not alone.

Some great horses strike a brief flame. Once in a while they come to mind, bright and vivid, like the memory of a first date, or an earthquake. Others entertain us for long and satisfying careers. We come to think of them as part of the gorgeous scenery, and when they leave, the color in the scenery fades.

Then there are the horses who jump the rails and worm their way into our hearts and minds. They set up shop for good. They help define the game. They give people a reason to show up every morning, muck stalls in the dark, and brag about being a citizen of the Thoroughbred racing world.

When Best Pal went to his knees and died on Tuesday morning, it was the first time he knuckled under to anything. He was a horse of complete and unflinching integrity. When he won, the planets were properly aligned. When he lost, he was never scorned. In the lineage of California's greatest native icons, Best Pal was the spiritual descendant of Swaps, Native Diver, Ancient Title, and Flying Paster. In the past 30 years, only two horses have rivaled Best Pal's public adoration on the California stage. They were Cougar II and John Henry.

When Best Pal emerged from Ian Jory's shedrow at Santa Anita in the fall of 1990, fresh from his effortless sweep of three stakes at Del Mar, he was wearing black bell boots, a green saddle towel, and a small crescent-shaped scar between his eyes. Seems that late one night, bored and full of 2-year-old vinegar, he decided to pick a fight with his stall. It was a draw.

"Gives him sort of a piratical air, doesn't it?" Jory said in fond admiration.

That was the perfect description. Best Pal was a buccaneer. He was a man-size horse with the attitude to match. Even at rest, it was clear Best Pal was always thinking about something. His next race. His next meal. Your next move. He roamed through three different barns on his way to more than $5.6 million in hard-earned swag over seven memorable calendar years. Never mind the list of horses who came and went during Best Pal's days. He was there to greet them at the door and still pouring drinks when they left.

John Mabee, the man who bred and owned Best Pal, came under criticism for shuttling his horse from Jory to Gary Jones and finally to Richard Mandella. But if Best Pal knew the difference, it never showed. Each of the three men will swear to this day that Best Pal trained them more than the other way around.

"He was like one of those people who wouldn't let you get close, but you knew he liked you anyway," Mandella said Tuesday upon hearing the news.

"He was one of those horses who was so smart, who did everything just right, you know they're going to be a good horse," Jory said. "You never had to show him anything twice."

Best Pal did some of his very best work for Jones, winning the Santa Anita Handicap, the Hollywood Gold Cup, and the Pacific Classic.

"Damn." Jones was floored. The world was suddenly dark. "A heart attack? It's like losing part of the family. He was my main man. The best I ever had. He lived a full life, but I thought he had a lot of years left."

It is to Mabee's everlasting credit that he and his wife, Betty, retired Best Pal the moment he ran that inexplicably bad race in the 1996 San Pasqual Handicap. They did not need to see another. Best Pal had never lied to them before, and he wasn't kidding then. They took a big hunk of his earnings and set up a living trust to care for him in perpetuity. They turned him out in his own grand paddock at their Golden Eagle Farm in north San Diego County. The Mabees encouraged visitors, and they let him lead the parade to the post for the past three runnings of the Pacific Classic at Del Mar.

In the photograph over this desk, Best Pal has just returned to the cheers of the Santa Anita crowd after winning the San Antonio Handicap in February of 1995. It was his last big win. Chris McCarron is reaching down to give him a hug, and the smile on his face is one of utter gratitude and delight. Best Pal lived only 10 years. But for those of us lucky enough to get in his way, he provided some of the best years of our lives.

~~~

## SMARTY JONES

*June 1, 2004*

In order to run in the Belmont Stakes, and thus take their places in history as winners of the Triple Crown, such heroes as Secretariat, Affirmed, and Seattle Slew were required merely to go out and play hard in their own backyard. They already lived here, at Belmont Park, and by Wednesday of Belmont week their earlier business trips to Louisville and Baltimore had become distant memories. They were home, surrounded by familiar smells, sleeping in their own beds.

Smarty Jones, on the other hand, has become the ultimate road warrior. He keeps a bag packed and the tank full, with toll change handy and bottled water in the back. If the Teamsters ever want a mascot, Smarty's their guy.

On Wednesday he was at it again. The drive from Philadelphia Park to Belmont Park took 2-1/4 hours and covered about 90 miles, although it wasn't quite as simple as that. This time, Ronnie Bradford's spiffy Cedarlane Farm van carrying Smarty Jones emerged from the Philadelphia Park stables at 9:35 a.m., preceded by three motorcycle police (Bensalem variety) with lights flashing and sirens ablare.
~~~

A couple of unmarked police vehicles fell in behind, followed by a small but dedicated trail of media and a handful of groupies on wheels. Overhead, TV news choppers whined like very large, impatient cicadas, as the motorcade made its way past a line of honking, waving fans, all of them waiting patiently to use the road when Smarty was finished with it.

Past Hooters, past The Pantry, past a Holiday Inn, the impromptu parade reached the part of the Pennsylvania Turnpike that runs behind the Philadelphia Park backstretch. In the distance, a banner hung: "Look Out NY, Here Comes Smarty." Enough said.

Unlike California and its Western neighbors, East Coast states are all about the size of a generous Wal-Mart parking lot. After leaving Bensalem, it was therefore necessary for Smarty and Co. to pass through at least three different enforcement jurisdictions, although I looked down once to switch the radio from NPR to ESPN, so there might have been a fourth.

After blocking off two key ramps and negotiating a toll plaza—"Break a leg, Smarty!" yelled a theater-going tolltaker—the Pennsylvanians turned the show over to New Jersey State Police. The ride continued unfazed, with Smarty Jones passing the next hour cruising at around 58 m.p.h and counting the cars on the New Jersey Turnpike. Then East Rutherford loomed, and traffic began to clog the vast, chemical splendor surrounding the Meadowlands.

There are, amazingly, no less than four distinct choices for Exit 14, and you'd better be sharp or you will end up committing your route to the depths of the Lincoln Tunnel, rather than the more stately George Washington Bridge.

In the distance, the skyline of Manhattan brought Woody Stephens to mind, and his favorite warning to invaders, something about the buildings getting taller once the Hudson was crossed. But what would he know about winning a Belmont? Or five?

"In my 64 years on this earth, I have never seen anything like this," said Bill Foster, the John Servis barn foreman, who was in his usual spot riding shotgun in the van. "This is an unbelievable experience."

At that point, the horse van in which Smarty Jones was riding was being escorted by one NYPD squad car, two New York State Police vehicles, and another from the Port Authority. A fifth official car—is there an MTA?—joined briefly and then peeled away.

"It's like traveling with the President," Foster said.

A word here might be appropriate about following a horse van into New York City. Once over the bridge and into the Bronx, traffic began to rise like an evil tide and the honking horns returned, although something tells me they weren't for Smarty Jones. New York drivers abhor a vacuum, so tailgate your motorcade buddy like the paint on his rear bumper. And if you want to keep the target in sight, get ready to blow off at least one toll stop with a tale of woe and be prepared to commit any number of minor, though enforceable, moving violations.

Soon, though, the procession reached the Throgs Neck Bridge—hey, there's Fort Schuyler!—and spilled onto the relative serenity of the southbound Clearview Expressway, which came to an abrupt end in Queens Village. That meant Smarty got to cruise past Our Lady of Lourdes Catholic School, as well as the shops and dwellings along Hillside and Springfield. We camp followers resisted the temptation to shout, "Do you know who this is?" since it takes a lot more than a police-escorted horse van to raise a New York eyebrow. A few minutes later he was at the Belmont stable gate.

The last time Smarty Jones vanned to the city was in January for the Count Fleet at Aqueduct. Seems like an age ago, but for the horse, it felt the same. As Smarty's van drove into the Belmont stables, a left turn was required at Secretariat Ave. beforc he could arrive at Barn 5, where Secretariat himself was stabled in the spring of 1973. It has been said that the thrill is not in reaching the destination, but in taking the journey. Maybe Smarty Jones is a horse for both.

*(He wasn't, as it turned out, but not for lack of trying. Smarty Jones was caught in the final stages of the mile and one-half Belmont by Birdstone, a colt who had finished far back in the Derby. Still, Smarty Jones had done enough to be voted 3-year-old champion of 2004. The Belmont was his last race.)*

# CIGAR AND FRIEND

*April 29, 2002*

They are blasphemous, unholy heretics, representing all that dare question the worship of the Triple Crown. And here they were together, nose to nose through a steel grate, thick as thieves and sharing a private joke.

Cigar and John Henry have led remarkable lives of great accomplishment and celebrity. They did not need the Kentucky Derby, the Preakness, or the Belmont Stakes to get them there. Their claim to everlasting fame was built over the long haul, crafted from hard work and consistency at the highest levels.

In May of 1978, when John Henry was 3, he was 3 for 17 and had just been sold to Sam Rubin to race in New York. Then, at Belmont Park on June 1, John Henry made his first start on turf, winning by 14 lengths. Nine days later Affirmed won the Belmont Stakes and the Triple Crown.

In May of 1993, Cigar was 3 and in California, training at San Luis Rey Downs. To that point he had made one start. On May 1, Sea Hero won the Kentucky Derby. On May 9, Cigar won a maiden race at Hollywood Park.

John Henry has been in racing's Hall of Fame since 1990, his first year of eligibility. Cigar, eligible for the first time this year, now will be enshrined alongside ol' John. Between them they earned nearly $16.5 million, in addition to 11 Eclipse Awards and Horse of the Year titles in 1981, 1984, 1995, and 1996.

They also live right across the breezeway from each other in the Hall of Champions at the Kentucky Horse Park, just north of Lexington. It is a happy coincidence for the thousands of visitors each year who show up expecting to see a few nice horses and go home bragging that they got to brush close to the very best.

There was a crowd of about 75 on hand early Tuesday afternoon, when 12-year old Cigar made his public debut as a bona fide Hall of Famer. He is the first one on stage during the Horse Park's daily Parade of Champions, something that John Henry, who waltzes out second, accepts grudgingly.

Of course, John Henry does everything grudgingly. At the age of 27, he was already a national treasure and a world-class grouch. Now he's a medical miracle as well. He has bounced back from an operation that removed 18 feet of twisted intestine earlier this year, which, in the words of Hall of Champions assistant director Tammy Siters, "had about a 7 percent chance of success."

"John stands a very small but nasty 15.1 hands, and he lost about 150 pounds," Siters told her audience. "But now he's rearing, bucking, and trying to kill people again."

That is good news, especially to Cigar, who has a relationship with John Henry that manifests itself as a weird stew of hero worship and schoolyard smack, as in, "Hey, old man, I got your Arlington Million right here. Do the words 'Dubai World Cup' mean anything to you?"

"When John went to the clinic, Cigar stood at his stall door and stared across at John's stall for days," said Cathy Roby, who runs the Hall of Champions. "Then, when John returned, he wouldn't go into his stall until he'd stopped to say 'I'm back' to Cigar."

While Bill Mott trained him for Allen and Madeleine Paulson, Cigar was a hard, lean gladiator, tolerant of both extensive travel as well as a chronic foot problem that would have stopped most horses cold.

Now he is a horse in full, a robust 1,350 pounds. He eats three pounds of sweet feed each day, a healthy ration of timothy hay, and all the Starlite peppermints he can chew and swallow.

Cigar lives in the roomy, paneled stall once occupied by Forego, who died in 1997. He spends his nights out roaming his private paddock, but his favorite time of day is late afternoon, when the draft horses finish their duties pulling Horse Park tour carts and walk home along Cigar's far fence line.

"He loves to give them a hard time," Siters said. "He'll lay back, then make a run right at them and stop at the fence, acting like he's never seen horses like them before. Who knows what he's thinking?"

"He gives himself a lot of exercise," Roby noted. "And he's been very healthy, knock on wood. He did pull a hip muscle once that needed attention. And because he's so active, we have a chiropractor work on him regularly.

"He's also the world's biggest ham. Last year an ESPN crew came here. He ran around, rolled, reared, then came up to them as if to say, 'You get that okay? I can do it again.' "

Siters led Cigar from the sunlight back into the Champions barn and up to John Henry's stall. She was hoping for a Hall of Fame moment. John Henry was staring out his back door.

"C'mon, John," Roby pleaded. "Come over and see your pal."

John Henry did not budge.

"Okay," Roby said. "Have it your way. Stay there."

John Henry turned slowly and shuffled to the grate, then sniffed at Cigar's offered nose. Cigar's breath was minty fresh . . . and Hall of Fame sweet.

~~~

## LOST IN THE FOG

*September 17, 2006*

Greg Gilchrist was kneeling in the straw at the front of stall number six on the side of his Golden Gate Fields barn facing the shores of San Francisco Bay. He had his cellphone in one hand and Lost in the Fog's right front foot in the other as he briefed his stable veterinarian, Don Smith.

"His temperature's 102.2, doc," Gilchrist said. "That's up a bit from when we took it last. He's got some filling in his left hind that I'm not too happy about. But I can't feel any pulse in his feet at all, and there's no distended veins, so maybe all he needs is a little Bute."

Gilchrist snapped his phone shut and stepped across the shedrow as assistant trainer Karen Long kept a good grip on Lost in the Fog's halter. When she let go, the colt took a nip in her direction.

"Hey, that's the meat over there," Long said, nodding toward Gilchrist. The trainer held up a right hand bandaged at the base of the thumb.

"He got me yesterday," Gilchrist said. "Got me good, too. The feeling is just now starting to come back. But that's okay. When he stops wanting to bite me, then I really worry."
~~~

There is nothing but heartsick worry these days among the people closest to Lost in the Fog, the Eclipse Award sprint champion of 2005 and the most popular horse to come out of Northern California since Seabiscuit. In August, inoperable malignant tumors were discovered in his spleen, near his kidney, and just beneath his spine, spirit-numbing news that has turned a Thoroughbred fairy tale into a medical nightmare, wracked with complications that keep Gilchrist and his staff on constant alert.

"It's liable to be like this from now on," Gilchrist said as Lost in the Fog reached for his water bucket. "Just one little thing after another. His immune system has got to be affected by the chemo, and that means he could catch any little thing that comes along. But I won't quit on him, at least not until he's ready."

It was Thursday, less than a week after Lost in the Fog had received his first chemotherapy treatment at the UC Davis equine clinic, and Gilchrist was listening to a phone message as he waited for the morning sun to break through so Lost in the Fog could graze on a lonely patch of grass, just a short walk from the Gilchrist barn. Gilchrist broke into a smile as the message played.

"There were four of us together in Vietnam, in the 82nd Airborne—me, Greg Gatlin, Patrick Beale, and Wayne Worley," Gilchrist explained. "We vowed that if we made it home we'd get together every year at Super Bowl time no matter what. And we have.

"That message was from Greg in Ireland," Gilchrist said. "They just scattered Patrick's ashes over a whole lot of Irish countryside, just like he wanted, and now they're trying to drink up all the Guinness they can find. I'd be with them, too, if it wasn't for Lost in the Fog."

But then, a horse like Lost in the Fog tends to reorder priorities. More than just a stakes-winning meal ticket or a lovable barn character, he raised the emotional stakes. Owner Harry Aleo beams like a proud father whenever Lost in the Fog is mentioned. Russell Baze looked upon his most famous mount as a fellow artist and collaborator in high drama. Gilchrist treats Lost in the Fog like the younger brother he never had.

"I remember being at Pleasanton, and going weak in the knees when they told me what they found at Davis," Gilchrist said. "They wanted to put him down right away. But I said whoa, let's at least give him a chance. We owe him that much."

A few yards away, beneath the shedrow, Lost in the Fog was out of his stall and walking around under a shimmering white cooler adorned with Gilchrist's royal blue "GG" logo.

"It's amazing he looks as good as he does," Gilchrist said. "Then, he's always been a healthy horse. In fact, I've never had a horse with blood so rich. He'd always run a red cell count in the 11.5 range, on a constant basis, compared to the normal count down around 9.2. A horse will store more blood and read higher when they're excited. But that wasn't it with him. I guarantee you that right now, as sick as he is, I'm running horses who don't have as good a blood count as he does."

A few minutes later, Lost in the Fog is grazing, with Gilchrist at his side, shaking his head in amazement.

"I know there's times he must feel just rotten," Gilchrist said. "But here he is, enjoying the grass and the sun, and you wonder what kind of horse can be this brave."

At the very least, he's a horse who could win 11 of 14 starts, including the first 10 races of his life at eight different tracks in California, New York, Florida, and Arizona. His last victory came in the Aristides Handicap at Churchill Downs on June 3, his last start was in the Smile at Calder on July 15. The tumors were discovered a month later.

As a fallen star with a national following, Lost in the Fog has touched the same sympathetic chords played since last May through the ongoing ordeal of Kentucky Derby winner Barbaro, as he continues to recover from the severe injuries he sustained in the Preakness Stakes.

"This office was filled with baskets of carrots and apples, flowers everywhere, and a big pile of cards," said Rowena Gilchrist, the trainer's 92-year-old mother, who wears a Lost in the Fog ball cap and keeps her son's office neat as a pin. "Look at this, what this lady sent from Novato, with the carrots and cookies."

It read: "Mr. Gilchrist. Please accept this basket I made for Foggy. The statue is of Epona—the Celtic goddess of the horse—she is for healing and has been holding vigil in my home for Barbaro."

"Here's another one," offered Patty Prospero, Gilchrist's significant other, as well as the Golden Gate paymaster. "This man from Indiana even wrote a poem."

It was a simple verse, a four-stanza ode to Lost in the Fog entitled "Don't Bet Against Him," accompanied by a note that read, in part:

"Dear Mr. Gilchrist & Mr. Aleo—I would like to express my admiration for both of you as you support the Fog in his recovery. You didn't leave your comrade on the field of battle and all of the supporters are grateful."

Across the Bay Bridge, in one of San Francisco's oldest neighborhoods, Harry Aleo sat at his desk at Twin Peaks Properties, on 24th Street between Noe and Castro. He likes to call the place "the Noe Valley Archives," and the clutter is rich with the bric-a-brac of local history. The predominating theme, though, is all Lost in the Fog.

"You know, he never had a chance to run his best race in his prime, as a 4-year-old," Aleo said. "But the Aristides, at Churchill Downs—it's heartbreaking when I think about it. He's growing that tumor, now the size of a football, underneath his spine, and he still comes through and wins that race."

Aleo picked up a thick manila envelope, filled to overflowing.

"I must have gotten a hundred letters from people, all over the country," said Aleo, the 86-year-old son of a grocer who famously turned down millions in offers for Lost in the Fog. "It's all so comforting. I answer every one of them—how could you not?

"A lot of people have suggestions about what we should do," Aleo went on. "I'll pass them on to the vets. There was one from a psychic healer who said that the horse didn't like his name, that we needed to change his diet, and that he needed to be out in a field.

"Then there was one from a lady in Florida, who had a kid that had cancer. She went and prayed to St. Michael, and promised if her son lived she would build a shrine to the saint. Her son lived and the shrine was built. She went there and prayed for the horse, then dipped a swab of cotton into the holy water, touched the shrine and had it blessed by the priest, and sent it to me to put on the side of his stall."

And did he do it?

"Damn right I did," Aleo said.

Aleo is no more anxious than Gilchrist to prolong Lost in the Fog's ordeal.

"My father died of lung cancer," Aleo said. "Tough old dago. He swore to the end it was the chemo and radiation that was killing him.

"We give these next two chemo treatments for Fog a chance and then let them measure the tumors," Aleo said. "If they haven't been reduced, no more chemo. We'll just try to keep him comfortable. But when he starts to hurt, and stops eating, we'll know it's time."

Back at the barn, later in the afternoon, Gilchrist and Long were breathing easier after Lost in the Fog was administered a shot of butazolidin. Within 20 minutes, his temperature had dropped a half a degree.

"Two days ago he had a pretty bad day," Gilchrist said. "He walked for a little while and then just laid down in his stall. After a while he started lurching, and his gums went white, like some kind of awful colic. Then before too long he was up again, acting like nothing happened. I'm not sure I want him to go through too many more days like that.

"But he'll tell us," the trainer added. "He'll know. In the meantime, he's getting steroids, chemotherapy, homeopathic treatments, and 14 million people praying for him. He's even got a woman who comes out here every morning and plays him classical music. I'd say he's getting about every chance."

*(True to their promise, Gilchrist and Aleo would not let Lost in the Fog suffer needlessly. Three days after my visit, the colt was in desperate pain and unable to stand. He was euthanized, a champion to the end, and his ashes were buried under a tree on the farm of his birthplace in Florida.)*

~~~
~~~

# YOUR HOST

*April 5, 2000*

It has been half a century since Your Host won the Santa Anita Derby. Back then it was worth $136,900. On Saturday it will offer a cool million. Unfortunately, the horses have not improved proportionately.

But that's unfair, because even today Your Host might be treated like the hottest thing this side of Dubai Millennium. In 1950, he was nothing less than a Hollywood star, complete with a personal press agent.

A record crowd of 65,542 showed up on Santa Anita's opening day, December 26, 1949, to witness Your Host win the California Breeders' Champion Stakes. By the end of January, after watching Your Host win the San Felipe Stakes, Calumet Farm's Jimmy Jones was caught wondering aloud if the West Coast darling might not be "ten pounds the best 3-year-old in America."

Even John Longden, a man notoriously hard to please, was tempted to place Your Host in the same neighborhood as Count Fleet when it came to carrying speed over a distance of ground. The 1950 Santa Anita Derby did nothing to change his mind. Your Host led 11 opponents through every step of the 9 furlongs, won by 2-1/2 lengths, and cooled out before Longden could catch his breath.

"He ran with his head real low," recalled Longden, 94 now and a five-time winner of the Santa Anita Derby. "You don't like 'em to do that, but with him it didn't matter as long as he got there first. That's what counts."

Your Host descended upon the bluegrass that spring with all the subtlety of an avalanche, borne by a private railroad car adorned with a sign that read, "Kentucky Bound, Derby Winner, 1950." Easterners, such as author William H. P. Robertson, recoiled at the sight, pointing out "the lack of restraint characteristic of certain other announcements from filmland."

Guilty as charged. Your Host was bred by Louis B. Mayer, the head of MGM, at his farm in Perris, California, and was purchased for $20,000 by Mayer's son-in-law, studio exec William Goetz. The courtly Harry Daniels was his trainer, and Tuffy Morlan, the legendary exercise rider, became the colt's boon companion.

Your Host gave his fans plenty to love. Even though the son of Alibhai was raised on the blue-blooded side of the tracks—his grandsires were English Derby winners Hyperion and Mahmoud—circumstances made him closer in spirit to the Little Rascals.

As a foal he injured his neck, and thereafter carried his head at an angle. His groom insisted that the colt's right eye was set higher than his left, although no one bothered to measure the groom's legs. Your Host had nicknames like "The Twister" and "Ol' Sidewinder," yet his action was smooth and fast.

Fast enough, in fact, to set a Keeneland track record for 7 furlongs in his first start outside California, after which, in the words of racing writer Joe Palmer, "Local spectators promptly walked the plank."

Translation: Your Host went off the 8-5 favorite in the 76th Kentucky Derby, opened up two lengths early, caught pressure from Mr. Trouble, but still led the field at the head of the stretch. At that point Longden felt the air leave the balloon, and Your Host faded to ninth, while Middleground went on to beat Hill Prince.

After the race he was considered just another California flash in the pan. But the flash refused to fade away. On November 23, 1950, Your Host ended his 3-year-old season with a flourish at Hollywood Park in the Thanksgiving Day Handicap, defeating 1949 Derby winner Ponder and eventual 1950 Horse of the Year Hill Prince in a three-way photo.

Your Host's transition to his 4-year-old season was seamless. It took a world record by Bolero to beat him in the 7-furlong San Carlos, then he won the Santa Catalina Handicap under 130 pounds. The Santa Anita Handicap was on the horizon, but first came the San Pasqual, on January 13, 1951. Your Host was moving to the leaders on the far turn when he clipped heels and fell, fracturing his right shoulder and forearm.

You could have heard a two-dollar ticket hit the ground. Moonrush went on to win the race, but no one really cared. All eyes were on the far turn, where Tuffy Morlan was racing on his pony to help his fallen friend. Historian B. K. Beckwith recorded Morlan's reaction.

" 'There he stood,' Morlan said, 'broken and in horrible pain, but his funny, cockeyed head was up and he whinnied at me. It was the first time he had ever asked me for help, and I could do nothing but take him by the head and weep.' "

Dry your eyes. There's a happy ending. Your Host was badly damaged but saved, and he somehow managed to sire 139 foals. Among them were Miss Todd, Social Climber, and Windy Sands, the sire of Santa Anita Handicap winner Crystal Water.

But most of all, Your Host is worth remembering because he was tough enough to live. And because he lived, he also sired Kelso.

~~~

## HALLOWED DREAMS

*July 15, 2000*

Hallowed Dreams was shell-shocked. Every time a horse walked past her stall, the little filly would act like a country kid dropped cold on the corner of Hollywood and Vine. She couldn't sleep. She would hardly eat. And she sure as heck couldn't train, which is why she was brought to Evangeline Downs in the first place.

Lloyd Romero wracked his brain. The $15,000 he paid for the filly was starting to look like a shaky piece of business. Finally, the trainer told his assistant, "Go get that new pony and put him in there with her. Maybe that'll calm her down."

So there you have it. Blame it all on Buck, the big paint gelding who convinced Hallowed Dreams that life at the racetrack wasn't so bad after all.

Nearly two years later, with Buck still at her side, she is the toast of Cajun country and the star of her state, with 15 wins in 15 starts and a date with number 16 on Saturday at Louisiana Downs.

If Hallowed Dreams wins the 6-furlong Dixie Miss Stakes—just like she won the Laurel Lane, the Tellike, the Elge Rasberry Memorial and a dozen other races most people outside Louisiana never heard of—her streak will land like a melon on pavement right alongside the modern records of Citation and Cigar.
~~~

Citation, Cigar . . . Hallowed Dreams? The mind reels. How will the game survive?

"It doesn't matter where she's been winning," said Bill Mott, the man behind Cigar's 16-race streak. "If she's been over there 15 times and got the job done 15 times, she's pretty special. You run into different circumstances that allow you to get beat all the time, and you've got to overcome them."

Pampered as a princess, Hallowed Dreams has become a fairy-tale kind of character, one that could pop up only in a Harry Potter novel or something spun by the Brothers Grimm.

Except for the fact that this fable is as real as the nervous nausea that hits assistant trainer Selina Bremmerman like clockwork every time Hallowed Dreams runs. It's as real as the second chance the filly has provided jockey Sylvester Carmouche, whose career was once derailed by scandal. And it is every bit as real as the $2 million Lloyd Romero said he turned down for Hallowed Dreams, offered the week before she won the Fantasia Stakes against fellow Louisiana-breds for number 15 on June 25.

"How much better can I live? And can you tell me I'll ever have another one like her? I don't think so," asked Romero, a larger-than-life character who was played by Walter Matthau in the 1978 movie *Casey's Shadow*.

"Besides," Romero added, "why would I sell her now when she could be worth more to somebody if she breaks that record?"

Finally, Romero was speaking a language the rest of the racing world could understand. The practical aspects of turning down seven figures for a 3-year-old daughter of Malagra out of a Brother Machree mare are hard to fathom. But the man must be admired for rolling the dice, even as he is criticized by some for keeping Hallowed Dreams in Louisiana.

"Maybe someday we'll run someplace else," Romero said. "But last time I checked, those airplanes fly both ways."

Hearing this, Johnny Gaspard just shakes his head. He is partners with Romero in the ownership of Hallowed Dreams, but Gaspard makes it clear that it is the trainer who calls all the shots.

"I can't stand my trainer," Gaspard says, and you believe him, with his deadpan poker face, until Romero walks by and lets one fly in Gaspard's direction.

"Hey, white trash. Who you talkin' to?"

Then you start to get it. These guys were raised on match races between rails and $500 sidebets. They cut each other very little slack and most strangers none at all. They are not from California. They are not from New York. And they couldn't care less what people in Los Angeles or Long Island think about what they're doing with Hallowed Dreams.

Romero does not pretend Hallowed Dreams is anything more or less than a talented sprinting filly who still has room to improve. She is a dark bay with a drip of white between the eyes and a low stocking on her right hind, with a ladylike head and shoulders that belie her powerful hind end.

"That's where she gets her speed," Romero noted. "And she's got that beautiful, straight hind leg."

On Saturday, Hallowed Dreams will be facing a few new shooters, but she has yet to step up to graded-stakes company, she has never run beyond 6-1/2 furlongs, and her earnings so far come to a fairly modest $347,000 and change.

Still, not even a cool $2 million could buy all the good times and bragging rights that come with a streak that began back on May 20, 1999, when Hallowed Dreams broke her maiden by eight going 4-1/2 furlongs at Evangeline Downs.

From there the legend grew, until her backyard track hung out a sign that reads "Home of Hallowed Dreams," and fans began to travel the length and breadth of the Pelican State to watch her run. Six for six at Evangeline. Five for five at Louisiana Downs. Three for three at the Fair Grounds in New Orleans. And a perfect day at Delta Downs last February 26, when she won the Southern Belle Classic by 7-1/2.

Except for the inconspicuous "Lloyd J. Romero Farms—Erath, La." painted near the front, the four-horse Sooner van in which Hallowed Dreams travels is virtually anonymous. There are no police escorts—like those that accompanied Cigar in his heyday—and no banners that announce "The Hallowed Dreams Express!"

"Where I come from," Romero said, "you don't want to be doing things like that, rubbing it in. That'll come back to bite you later on for sure."

Selina Bremmerman agrees. She is a careful woman, protective of both her filly and her trainer, with a deep vein of worry that emerges every time Hallowed Dreams puts her streak on the line.

"I'm not concerned about her winning," said Bremmerman, 34, who was born and raised in New Orleans and formerly married to jockey Charles Bremmerman. "I worry about her getting bumped off stride, taking a bad step, hitting a hole in the track."

Bremmerman started with Romero seven years ago as a groom and now helps him run the barn. They have become close friends as well as colleagues, and their simpatico shows. As she prepared for the Fantasia last month, Romero looked on with a combination of admiration and amusement as Bremmerman arranged tack, checked bandages, and watched Hallowed Dreams for the slightest twitch that seemed out of the ordinary.

"She won't leave that filly alone," Romero said with a grin. "But watch how the filly looks at her."

Right on cue, as Bremmerman briefly ducked out of the barn, Hallowed Dreams pressed against her webbing and gazed longingly down the shedrow. All she could see was the big red and white mug of Buck in the adjacent stall.

"Where Holly goes, Buck goes," Bremmerman explained. "They're the same age, and you can't get them apart. They even have to kiss before she goes her separate way to be saddled."

Sylvester Carmouche, at the age of 41, needs Hallowed Dreams every bit as much as the filly needs Buck. They have now won 13 straight together, dating back to July of 1999, and it is a blessed relief for Carmouche to see his name in a different kind of headline. The lanky native of Lafayette lost 8-1/2 years of his riding career to a suspension for trying to rig a 1990 race in the fog at Evangeline Downs. Romero was among those who went to bat to get Carmouche reinstated.

"That was a whole different person back then," Carmouche said of his transgression. "I'm so grateful to be riding the filly that I can't stay away from her. I visit her every morning, gallop her when Mr. Lloyd needs me, just to be around her."

"He paid his debt," Romero said. "People got no business calling him the 'fog jockey' any more. He's the man who rides Hallowed Dreams. And he's got the mount until he takes off."

"That will never happen as long as I'm alive," replied Carmouche.

Hallowed Dreams entered this world at the farm of Mike and Ann Kennington, just outside of Shreveport, on March 17, 1997. A year and a half later, by then under Romero's care, the filly was beginning to give off special vibes.

"We were watching her breeze for the very first time," Bremmerman said. "She was bullet fast. Lloyd said, in just a joking manner, 'We might have a shot at Personal Ensign's record.' "

It should come as no surprise that Romero is predisposed to think of greatness in terms of Personal Ensign. His son, Randy Romero, rode Personal Ensign through her career of 13 starts and 13 wins, a record achievement now eclipsed—numerically at least—by Hallowed Dreams. Romero does not pretend his filly is in the same league.

"To me, Personal Ensign was the best of the best," Lloyd Romero said. "So every time we break a filly, get one going, what comes to my mind is Personal Ensign."

You mean, the same way Junior Griffey comes to mind when your kid hits his first line drive off the tee?

"That's right," Romero said. "This filly breezed fast, not even knowing how to breeze. That thing about Personal Ensign's record, it just came off the top of my head. But you got to dream big, you know."

When Hallowed Dreams needed a rider for her third race—the $120,000 D. S. "Shine" Young Futurity at Evangeline Downs—Romero took a shot and asked Randy to ride. The father and son have not been close, but there was no law against a good horse trying to break the ice. Besides, there was a further family tie. Romero's father-in-law, the late Clyde McKean, trained Pacific's Dream, the dam of Hallowed Dreams.

"I had to say no," Randy said. "I had announced my retirement, and I had commitments in Kentucky."

The Futurity was on July 3, 1999. Hallowed Dreams won by eight. Randy Romero retired two days later to take the book of the promising young jockey Marlon St. Julien. Any regrets?

"Yeah, well, I don't know," he replied. "If I rode her that day I probably wouldn't have quit riding. But I'm happy for all the people with the filly."

It was a little after five o'clock on a hot Shreveport afternoon, a half hour before post time for the Fantasia, when Bremmerman jumped aboard Buck to accompany Hallowed Dreams and stable lad Justin Jeansonne to the paddock. When it came time for the pony to step aside, Jeansonne turned the filly's head toward Buck, and they brushed noses, just as natural as a wave good-bye. After that, number 15 was a six-length breeze.

"Look at this," said Romero as he walked through the crowd after the Fantasia, shaking hands like he was running for mayor. "Louisiana is family, and she belongs to Louisiana.

"They say she should be running for more money, more money," Romero added. "Let me ask you this: How much does it cost to bury you? About $5,000. And I got that."

*(The winning streak ended in her next race, after which she won seven more in a row. In 2002, Hallowed Dreams retired to the life of a broodmare, with a record of 25 wins from 30 starts.)*

~~~

# PRECISIONIST

*August 3, 2003*

John Russell fished around in his considerable vocabulary and settled on the word that best described the racehorse named Precisionist.

Russell called him "glamorous."

That he was, striking from every angle, his chestnut coat aglow like sunlight on lacquered redwood. Precisionist was both large and graceful, classically constructed, a dreamwork of selective Thoroughbred breeding. In the words of the wiseguy on the rail, Precisionist looked fast just standing still.

Starting Monday and from now on, the career of Old Glamor Boy will be on display at the Hall of Fame in Saratoga Springs. Precisionist will be
~~~

inducted—along with a class of 2003 that includes Dance Smartly, Sonny Hine, and Mike Smith—at the National Museum of Racing on Union Avenue. The public is welcome to the ceremony, which is only right, because Precisionist was every inch a crowd-pleaser.

When he was good, he was very good. When he was bad, he was just being Precisionist. Those who were at Hollywood Park on the evening of December 18, 1983, will never forget the sight of a washed-out, wild-eyed Precisionist dragging trainer Ross Fenstermaker and groom Allison Sgroi all the way around the clubhouse turn, on the way to the paddock for the Hollywood Futurity.

It was Fenstermaker's job to keep the pot from boiling over. The record speaks for itself. In 36 starts between the summer of 1983 and November of 1986, Precisionist won 17 races and came within one victory of becoming 1986 Horse of the Year.

As it was, Precisionist was a champion sprinter who also won such mile and a quarter races as the Strub Stakes at Santa Anita and the Swaps Stakes at Hollywood Park. And while most of his success took place in California, Precisionist had the good sense to cultivate a New York following by winning the 1985 Breeders' Cup Sprint at Aqueduct and the 1986 Woodward Stakes at Belmont Park.

Fenstermaker gets paramount credit for the care and condition of Precisionist. But everyone knew it was Fred Hooper who called the tune of Precisionist's ambitious campaigns. When Mr. Hooper said run, his trainers usually answered with "where" and "when."

Hooper, an Alabama road-builder, bred Precisionist at his Florida farm from a mating of his Kentucky Derby runner-up Crozier and the Forli mare Excellently. By the time Precisionist came along, there already had been one Hall of Fame horse in the Hooper family. Susan's Girl, a three-time champion, was inducted in 1976.

Susan's Girl had seven different trainers during her five seasons of racing. John Russell took her through 31 of her 63 starts and was responsible for two of her championship campaigns—in 1972 and 1973—when her 14 stakes victories included the Kentucky Oaks, the Acorn, the Santa Margarita, the Gazelle, and the Beldame.

For her final eight starts, Susan's Girl was trained by Ross Fenstermaker, and he did not let her down. She won the 1975 Delaware Handicap, the Matchmaker, the Spinster, and her second Beldame.

Russell returned the gesture with Precisionist, although the circumstances were dramatically different. When the 7-year-old Precisionist arrived at Russell's Hollywood Park stable, in the spring of 1988, the red horse had not raced in 18 months. He was carrying a screw in a broken ankle. And he had proven to be infertile after two active seasons at stud.

For a trainer, this pretty much describes a no-win situation. Russell's first thought was justified. "You just wondered where this was going to go," he said.

At first, it went wrong. On the day of the comeback, in a one-mile race at Hollywood Park, Precisionist broke like a bullet, stumbled, and threw Chris McCarron. Russell swallowed his tongue.

"Chris hung onto the reins for about the first 30 yards, being dragged along, but trying to keep Precisionist from being a loose horse," the trainer recalled.

"By the time Chris finally had to let go, Precisionist was 10 lengths behind the last horse," Russell went on. "He caught them in the middle of the far turn, drew off and won by himself, literally. And he was loving it, having the time of his life."

Class lasts, and Precisionist, despite his age and his repaired ankle, made a final impact that survives to this day. He won two stakes that summer of 1988 at Del Mar, setting a track record for a mile in one of them, and went on to hit the board in three other stakes, including the NYRA Mile. He even ran in another Breeders' Cup Sprint and was a respectable fifth, beaten barely two lengths by Gulch on a sloppy track at Churchill Downs.

"By then his ankle was starting to bother him," Russell said. "Although the way he ran, it probably didn't make a bit of difference to him. He just put it out of his mind."

Precisionist did not need that last campaign to earn his place in the Hall of Fame. As icing, though, it was decidedly sweet.

"I really don't feel I played any more than a minor role in his story," Russell added. "But it was a pleasure to be around him. And, yes, he was glamorous. I've always thought Precisionist and Secretariat were the two prettiest horses you ever saw."

If that is the case, Precisionist is right where he belongs.

~~~

## BARBARO

*January 31, 2007*

Above and beyond his skill as an equine surgeon with only a handful of peers, it is to the everlasting credit of Dr. Dean Richardson that at no point during the last eight months did he lead anyone to believe that the Barbaro story was going to turn out all right.

Certainly, there were times when Barbaro's condition appeared better than it did the day or the week before. And for the sake of those around him, Richardson sometimes allowed himself to think briefly of the glass as being half full. But as the man who was charged with Barbaro's ultimate welfare—the human who spoke for the horse—Richardson never backed away from the grim truth. Saving Barbaro was always a longshot.

Still, it was a longshot worth betting, worth emptying the wallet. Only the hardest of hearts would broach the slightest recrimination for the heroic attempts to save Barbaro's life. When the end came, early Monday morning at the New Bolton Center, it was a result of Richardson and the Barbaro family making good on a promise they made long ago.

"If we couldn't control his discomfort," Richardson said Monday afternoon, "we wouldn't go on."

And so Barbaro thus becomes racing's Lady Di, worshipped beyond his worldly accomplishments—even though they were substantial—and remembered as larger than life even in the face of his mortality. In a snap poll taken of AOL users Monday morning, 71 percent of more than 52,000 respondents indicated they would remember Barbaro as "a survivor," while just 15 percent cited his Kentucky Derby victory as his everlasting imprint.

Horses have gone down in public before. But it was Barbaro, a child
~~~

of the modern communications era, who galloped helter-skelter through websites, cable channels, and chat rooms, landing more often than not at the center of mainstream media outlets.

The grief, therefore, is vertically integrated, beginning with those closest to Barbaro—owners Roy and Gretchen Jackson, Richardson and his staff, the team of trainer Michael Matz, jockey Edgar Prado—then coursing through the hearts and minds of anyone associated with a racehorse, on to those who are enchanted by the racing game, to the millions upon millions of horse lovers, and then spreading to the vast, non-racing public who responded to Barbaro's plight like no racing story since the days of Ruffian.

Standing just offstage, their heads lowered, are Richardson's colleagues in the veterinary profession. Two of the best were asked to share their thoughts.

"It's a sad day," said Dr. Greg Ferraro, a surgical pioneer and director of the University of California-Davis Center for Equine Health. "This demonstrates that even when people do everything right, and are willing to persevere, you can do a lot—a lot more than we used to be able to do even 10 years ago. But as perfect as we like to think our work can be, we're not there yet. When something like this happens, we certainly learn what our limitations are."

"Barbaro had the best shot he possibly could have had," said Dr. Wayne McIlwraith, former president of the AAEP and director of the Orthopaedic Research Center at Colorado State University. "He went to a good surgeon who was the most experienced in using the locking screw plate. He was done in a timely manner. All his aftercare was excellent. There was nothing missed, and no expense was spared. The owners didn't put a price on anything. It just shows how severe it was to deal with.

"Before Barbaro, the general public did not know that equine orthopedics is just the same as human orthopedics," McIlwraith went on. "We've come a long way in terms of getting fractures reconstructed better, so that they're bearing less weight on the other leg. But laminitis remains a terrible, terrible disease. We've got to throw more money at it, there's no doubt about it. But because it's an equine specific problem, the only funding is going to come from equine sources."

Ferraro could not have agreed more.

"It's almost like the easy things have been solved," Ferraro said. "Now we're down to the real hard stuff, and laminitis is a very difficult thing to understand and control. It's not for want of trying, either. But we've got to keep going. Every piece of knowledge builds on the knowledge before it. You've got size and weight to deal with in a horse, and that foot jumps up to bite you post-surgically every time you turn around."

The ultimate challenge for the racing industry is not to allow Barbaro's death to be in vain. If this does not light a fire under laminitis research, nothing will. Barbaro may have been the perfect poster child for the need to find solutions, since he was nothing less than the perfect patient, ready to accept all current technology.

"Some of the things Barbaro did were amazing," Ferraro noted. "He told them when he wanted to get into the sling. Told them when he wanted to get out. Never fought with them coming out of anesthesia. Cooperated and tried hard no matter what they wanted to do with him. He had such a close relationship with Dean, I guarantee you that when he walked in there early this morning, the horse looked him in the eye and said, 'I've had enough. It's time.' That's when I look at euthanasia as a gift we give them."

Barbaro is at peace now, although he was never really allowed to suffer. Even so, Richardson confessed to second thoughts.

"I'm sure I made mistakes," Richardson said. "That's how you learn."

Ferraro answered that simply, and spoke for many:

"He makes you proud to be a veterinarian."

~~~
~~~

# FRANKEL

*September 24, 2012*

"There he is," said Teddy Grimthorpe, pointing in the direction of two horses cantering up the Warren Hill gallop. "He's the one trailing."

And there he was. Frankel. The Horse of Horses, perfection on the hoof, cantering along under his regular morning rider, Shane Featherstonhaugh, at a middling pace behind his older half-brother, Bullet Train.

The pair of them were having a routine bit of exercise on a routine morning beneath the dramatic canopy of a late summer Newmarket sky. There were no crowds, no television cameras, none of the trappings of Frankel's widespread celebrity. Just Grimthorpe, who serves as Juddmonte Farm's racing manager, and the Cecils—Henry and Jane—along with a couple of lucky American visitors who thought it would be cool to be able to say they saw the great horse in the flesh.

"He won't knock your eye out," we were warned by more than one knowledgeable British racing friend. "But the more you look at him, the more you will understand."

This was not hard to believe. No horse ever could be a physical match for the reputation assembled around Frankel. At that particular moment, about a month shy of what was likely to be his final race on October 20 in the Qipco Champion Stakes at Ascot, the 4-year-old Frankel was unbeaten in 13 starts over three seasons, nine of those victories in Group 1 events, including the last eight in a row. His *Timeform* number of 147 was the highest since the ratings began in 1948, while his *Racing Post* rating was a more conservative but no less dizzying 142.

The British press, noteworthy for their descriptive excess, ran out of superlatives after Frankel's 11-length victory last June in the Queen Anne Stakes at Royal Ascot. It was, from all angles, his 4-year-old answer to the sensation of his wire-to-wire explosion to win the classic 2,000 Guineas at Newmarket the year before.

"But this was not just Frankel's finest performance," wrote *The Guardian's* Greg Wood after the Queen Anne. "It was possibly the best single performance by any horse, on any track, since three Arabian stallions were imported into Britain to found the Thoroughbred breed in the early years of the 18th century."

Such giddy praise tends to be both contagious and off-putting. Since June the predictable backlash has bubbled up from contrarians intent on curbing fans' hysteria and placing the colt in some kind of rational perspective. His six-length win in the Sussex Stakes at Goodwood on August 1, went the story, was little more than a paid workout, and to many it had become clear that keeping Frankel undefeated had become the point rather than testing him to the fullest extent of his potential.

Then came the Juddmonte International Stakes on August 22. At just over 10 furlongs, the International would be Frankel's first try beyond a mile. He won by seven, beating Breeders' Cup Turf winner St Nicholas Abbey, among others, in a tour-de-force that inspired Marcus Townend of the *Daily Mail* to write:

"The extra two-and-a-half furlongs Frankel raced over for the first time, which had asked questions about his stamina, merely provided 528 extra yards for the crowd to cheer him home."

For all his considerable ability, Frankel has earned his matinee idol reputation based not only on what he has won and how often, but how he has done it. There is considerable sizzle to this steak.

"He's the first horse in my experience of racing in Europe that has developed a truly significant following," said the *Racing Post's* Julian Muscat. "Last year the crowd for the International Stakes at York was nineteen and a half thousand. This year the crowd was 31,300."

Muscat spent a good portion of his career with the *Times* of London chronicling the exploits of the world's best Thoroughbreds. He was at Del Mar when Cigar tried to win his 17th straight, at Lone Star for Ghostzapper's Breeders' Cup, and at both Santa Anita and Churchill Downs when Zenyatta faced males in the Classic.

"Frankel has got a truly extravagant action," Muscat said. "He looks different to other horses when he runs. And because he's very exuberant he tends to win by a long way."

In the wake of the Juddmonte, Marcus Armytage of England's *Daily Telegraph* took a crack at getting to the essence of Frankel's excellence.

"Generally a horse's ability is limited by his whereabouts in the speed-stamina spectrum," Armytage wrote. "Horses have either one or the other…or, in the case of middle-distance horses, a blend of both but, until Frankel, never lots of both. What makes him unique is his ability to go a top-class sprinter's pace over distance."

But all that's on the ground. It is the feeling Frankel leaves in the air that sets him apart, a buzz that lingers long after he's home and dry, packed off back to Newmarket.

"You take a horse like Sea The Stars," said Muscat, referring to the once-beaten 2009 European Horse of the Year. "When he beats a Group 1 field by half a length fairly much in hand, the first-time racegoer isn't going to get it. They expect the champion to put away his field. Watching Frankel do his thing is almost like watching a driver dominate a Formula 1 race, or Michael Johnson run the 400 meters."

European ratings are based on the subjective identification and evaluation of a horse's very best performance. Frankel earned his 147 in the Queen Anne and will carry it into the Champion Stakes. Epsom Derby/Arc winner Sea-Bird had a 145, Brigadier Gerard a 144, Mill Reef a 144, Sea The Stars a 140.

In reality, however, the great ones are held as great because of a cumulative effect. The impact of a single, brilliant performance pales in the face of Brigadier Gerard's 17 wins in 18 starts over three seasons, of Cigar's 16 victories in a row over nine different tracks, of Zenyatta's 19 straight triumphs going from last to first before her kamikaze run fell just short in her final start.

And now Frankel, with a record of 14 for 14 on the near horizon. Here he was walking calmly down the path, having a break before another canter up Warren Hill. Partially covered by Cecil's monogrammed, black, red, and gold striped exercise sheet, the bay colt there before us, with black mane and tail, four short white stockings and distinctive star, was neither dramatically tall nor especially long. His forearm, though, was huge, his hindquarters imposing, while his neck, head, and shoulder were set at angles that would defy criticism from the most discerning analyst.

"The only thing I can liken it to, in a funny sort of way, was when I went once to the Forum in Los Angeles, not long after Bruce McNall had bought Wayne Gretzky," Teddy Grimthorpe said. "I'd never been to an ice hockey game, so the people I went with asked if I wanted them to point out Gretzky. I said, 'If I can't spot him myself it will be very disappointing.'

"Then this guy came out and just glided around the rink—just effortless," he added. "Frankel has that sort of beauty of motion, rare and remarkable."

Frankel is a son of Epsom and Irish Derby winner Galileo out of the Danehill mare Kind. He was bred and raised in England by Prince Khalid Abdullah's Juddmonte Farm and named by the prince for his primary American trainer, Robert Frankel, who died in November of 2009 at age 68 after a year-long battle with cancer. Frankel trained Juddmonte's only American classic winner, Empire Maker, along with a host of Juddmonte champions and major stakes winners that included Marquetry, Honest Lady, Flute, Wandesta, Ryafan, Sightseek, and Beat Hollow.

Racing writer Brough Scott was asked if the typical British racing fan understood the reference when Frankel burst onto the scene. He laughed.

"Well, they tended to know the reality show star, didn't they," he said, referring to Frankel's daughter, Bethenny Frankel, from the cast of *The Real Housewives of New York City*.

"As far as Bobby, people in the business knew, of course," Scott added. "But ordinary persons, no. And the pity is they still don't, really, because now the name is so comprehensively identified with the horse. But in a way it is rather wonderful he—Bobby—was immortalized in this way. They truly got it right."

In fact, there have been two other Thoroughbreds registered with the name Frankel. The first, a foal of 1957, raced in Japan without distinction, while the other was a California-bred foal of 2001 whose sire, the Juddmonte runner Tinners Way, was trained by Bobby Frankel to win back-to-back runnings of the Pacific Classic. The Cal-bred Frankel raced six times, all at age three, and for the last time in an $8,000 maiden claimer at Bay Meadows, in which he broke down while on the lead and was vanned off the track.

"I remember training a horse named Frankel, but I don't remember much more than that," said Mike Puype, the second of three trainers to handle the Cal-bred Frankel. "I don't know if any other horse named anything will be as good as this Frankel though."

By now Frankel and Bullet Train had gone by a second time—along with the other 50 or so horses in the set—giving Henry Cecil the chance to describe the challenge Frankel presented in his first year as a racehorse.

"He'd want to pull hard all the time," Cecil said. "If he was going to make it, he needed to learn that it had to be the rider who said go, not him."

Cecil was wearing a dark blue cap and quilted jacket, both adorned with the stylized "Frankel" logo under which a variety of merchandise is being marketed for charity. The trainer spoke in a whisper because of the throat cancer he'd been fighting, to that point, with three sessions of chemotherapy.

"It wears you out, and I have one more treatment," Cecil said. "But I'm hopeful. The scans have looked good."

The challenge presented by Frankel gives Cecil plenty of reasons not to dwell on his physical condition. The colt's tearaway style as a 3-year-old nearly got him beaten in the 2011 St. James's Palace Stakes at Royal Ascot when he opened up a huge lead that dwindled to three-quarters of a length at the wire. Cecil and jockey Tom Queally learned from that experience.

"What he needed was a lot of work," Cecil said. "A lot of work."

That work was applied at the sweeping variety of training facilities available to all the centrally located Newmarket stables. There are the several synthetic strips—with names like Long Hill, Side Hill, Warren Hill—along with the vast Limekilns turf grounds and the racecourse tracks at nearby Newmarket.

Cecil insists Frankel is the best he's ever been around. This from a man who, over the past 43 years, has trained the winners of 25 English classics and earned 10 English training titles. Cecil's admiration for the colt seems boundless, but he is protective as well. While acknowledging the public's adulation, he bristled at the fantasy league attitude that wanted to see him run more often, in more countries, over more ground.

"You listen to that and you won't have a horse," Cecil said. "They've never trained a racehorse, or ever ridden one for that matter. What would they know about where he should run?"

The Champion Stakes will be Frankel's ninth straight appearance in a Group 1 event. This is not exactly dodging a challenge.

"Everybody has always wanted more," Grimthorpe said. "They wanted him to run in the Arc. Someone told me he should have been running over six furlongs to prove he was good at that. My reply is that if you haven't made up your mind about him yet you haven't been watching. The racing professionals I've talked to—or at least the ones who offered me their opinion—say they've never seen anything like him."

Brough Scott, whose long and respected career as a racing journalist and author has had the benefit of his early experience as a professional jumps jockey, has observed Frankel with both a raised eyebrow and an open heart. Unlike many of the fans and media who have rushed to anoint the colt the "greatest ever," Scott would prefer to first establish a few ground rules.

"When Mill Reef won the Arc in 1971 it was a breakthrough, a real benchmark for greatness," Scott said. "He wasn't necessarily the greatest but you were going to have to measure up to that.

"Of course Frankel fits with all the benchmarks of greatness, and he will be the benchmark for all milers in the future," Scott added.

The class system is alive and well in British racing, where sprinters, milers, middle-distance runners, and stayers each have their own pew in the cathedral. If the point is identifying the best horse to have ever run in the British Isles, good luck and fair sailing, Scott says. It takes more than a 147 posted by Timeform, a company now owned by the promotionally aggressive Betfair, to define greatness.

"Racing is not just how fast they go," Scott noted. "It's measured against other things, and Frankel simply hasn't been subjected to the tests that all these others were. And that's not being a curmudgeon. That's a fact.

"Brigadier Gerard's mile performance beating Mill Reef in the Guineas is, I believe, something unique," Scott continued. "Frankel's Guineas was very exciting. Nobody's seen anything like it. But the fact remains, and I know it's not his fault, that Frankel has never had the opportunity to beat a Mill Reef."

Nor will he. With a purse of $2 million, the mile and a quarter Champion Stakes—centerpiece of the Qipco Champions Day extravaganza of five rich races—will attract the best of whatever is left of the middle-distance division. As to its being Frankel's final race, his people defer to Abdullah for any official proclamation, and that word will not come until after the Champion is run.

"The competition at Ascot will be against history, against fate," said Scott. "Will something go wrong, will he lose a shoe? Will the stalls bang him? Will Queally get stuck on the rail?"

Which is to say, it's still a horse race, and the anythings that could happen are too numerous to consider. Seattle Slew lost at Hollywood Park, Cigar lost at Del Mar, Zenyatta lost at Churchill Downs. It is not for those races they are remembered, and they are considered among the best.

"No one's ever done it like Frankel," Scott said. "That might be enough, and moreover that should be enough. Anyone asking for more is asking the impossible."

Teddy Grimthorpe agreed.

"Whatever it is, it will be a very emotional day," Grimthorpe said of October 20. "In one way or another he's dominated every single one of his races, and he's dominated our lives. It's hard to imagine life without him."

*(With a victory in the Champion Stakes over difficult, heavy ground, Frankel came to the end of his racing days with a 14-for-14 record. He was retired to stud with great fanfare, and as 2014 dawned, his babies were hitting the ground.)*

Two

# TO THE SWIFT

*In 1996, on a magical night in a faraway land, composer Burt Bacharach, the man who wrote "The Look of Love," watched in awe as his brave runner Soul of the Matter finished a valiant second to Horse of the Year Cigar in the first running of the Dubai World Cup. Overcome with emotion, Bacharach dashed down the grandstand steps and through the crowd to greet the exhausted Soul of the Matter upon his return.*

*At the Breeders' Cup Championships at Churchill Downs in 2010, the groom who took care of the French champion Goldikova would not be contained. As his beloved mare raced to the lead in the final furlong of the Mile, he burst from the confines of security personnel and ran down the dirt course, waving his leather strap and screaming, "Allez! Allez! Allez!"*

*At another Breeders' Cup, this one in 1984 at Hollywood Park, trainer Neil Drysdale beamed with pride at the sight of Princess Rooney's domination of the Distaff while his wife, Inger, stood on a chair cheering with abandon, then suddenly lost her balance. I know this because she fell on me.*

*As dramatic art, a horse race is disproportionately weighted in favor of the last act. I guess this should be expected when you pack weeks, sometimes months, of anticipation and preparation into a brief, increasingly desperate orgy of barely controlled chaos, what sportswriter Roger Kahn called "animated roulette."*

*The outcome is everything, for everyone involved. But the opening scenes set the tone, just as holding hands can lead to a night to remember. And, like one of those nights, the taste of a good horse race can linger long after the prices have been posted.*

*The selections that follow offer a sampler of those moments—of a horse from New Mexico winning the Kentucky Derby, of a sure thing blowing the Triple Crown, of a single trainer dominating racing's biggest day—providing proof enough that in a horse race anything can happen, and probably will.*

## WAR AT THE SHORE

*July 25, 2001*

Juan Soto, a tall man they call "Juanito," reached one arm gracefully across Kona Gold's neck and gave the old horse a hug. Kona Gold submitted to the display of affection as if it had been offered a thousand times before, and it probably had. After all, he was 7-years-old, and Soto has been in his stall for most of those years.

On this particular day, though, in the peace and quiet of the Del Mar test barn, there was something reassuring about Soto's gesture. Kona Gold had just been asked for every ounce of his strength in order to beat Caller One by three-quarters of a length in the $200,000 Bing Crosby Handicap, and now it was over. The old man could rest, at least for a little while, until he was needed again.

The game does need Kona Gold, needs him desperately. And if you doubt that, you were nowhere near Del Mar last Sunday afternoon when Alex Solis brought Kona Gold back to the cheering crowd, then took him 50 yards up the stretch so that the fans on the grandstand apron could pay tribute to their hero. Kona Gold responded with an impatient shake of his head, as if to say, "What did you expect?"

"Did you see that? Did you hear them?" Bruce Headley, keeper of the treasure, was still weak-kneed with pride a half hour after the race. "I can't remember anything like that. I've still got goosebumps."

Headley, who both trains and owns part of Kona Gold, goes back a long way in California racing, back to the late 1940s, when he and a lad named Willie Lee Shoemaker were among a bunch of kids just learning the ropes at the old Suzy Q Ranch east of L. A.

Headley has seen a lot of West Coast crowd-pleasers come and go. Swaps, Cougar, John Henry, Best Pal—they all were able to reach outside the rails and into the hearts of the people in the stands. Kona Gold is treading these days in the spiritual footsteps of Native Diver, who played to large, grateful California crowds through the mid-1960s.

In fact, the 2001 running of the Crosby summoned memories of a Native Diver moment from 1965, when the younger Viking Spirit tried to knock the king off his throne in the Los Angeles Handicap at Hollywood Park. For most of the 7 furlongs, they raced together—the black Diver and his chestnut challenger—until they hit the line, spent to the depths, just a neck apart in world-record time. The neck belonged to Native Diver.

The Crosby had all the ingredients for the same brand of great theater featuring the two best sprinters in the land. The 4-year-old Caller One entered the ring for trainer Jim Chapman aglow with robust health, his huge hindquarters flexing beneath skin stretched tight. Kona Gold, longer than his opponent and a duller shade of bay, traipsed around the paddock with Soto at his side, calm in the face of another day at the office.

As expected, Caller One led from the start, and from the quarter pole to the eighth pole the younger horse threw an :11.64 furlong at Kona Gold that should have broken his spirit. Most horses would have cracked under the pressure of the chase.

"I thought the old man was beaten," said a Caller One backer, staring at his losing tickets. "Then his heart kicked in."

In the shadow of the wire, when the outcome was obvious, Solis rose in the saddle and shouted in jubilation, then switched hands and pumped his stick in the direction of Caller One and Corey Nakatani. A gentleman to the core, Solis was acting way out of character. But then, horses like Kona Gold tend to shake loose our deepest emotions. Under the circumstances, Solis was not required to apologize. His explanation was sufficient:

"I got excited."

He was not alone. After the race Kona Gold found himself in the middle of a mosh pit winner's circle, seemingly populated by everyone who ever knew owners Irwin Molasky, his son Andrew, and their partner Michael Singh. Kona Gold remained serene, and dry as a bone.

"He doesn't sweat," Headley explained. "He's a non-sweater. Can you imagine the system of capillaries and internal circulation he must have to compensate for that, as hard as he runs?"

No question, Kona Gold is a remarkable beast. And so is Caller One. Since they are both geldings, this is their life. If we are lucky, they will meet again and again, at the very least in the Breeders' Cup Sprint at Belmont Park in October. To this point the advantage is 2-0 Kona Gold, but as the town sheriff said when comparing the speed of two gunfighters, "You'd hate to live on the difference."

"That horse is unbelievable," Chapman said later, in appreciation of Kona Gold. "Watching him in the spit box after the race, it was like he didn't do anything. And his legs look like the legs of a 2-year-old. I've got to get three or four more years out of my horse before I can even begin to match Headley."

Lucky us. We get to watch them try.

~~~

# LOOK WHO'S LAUGHING

*May 4, 2003*

As this is being written, it has been 24 hours now since Funny Cide won the 129th running of the Kentucky Derby. A cautious peek through the tightly drawn curtains of a motel near the airport revealed no river of blood running down Phillips Lane, no plague of toads raining down upon Standiford Field, no beasts running loose in the streets, committing unnatural acts. Louisville had not been consumed by fire.

This was a surprise, although a pleasant one, since the conventional wisdom had just been shattered and replaced with a heresy so rank as to bring a curse upon the land. Or at least in the Lexington area, center of the nation's breeding industry.
~~~

A Thoroughbred racehorse named Funny Cide, foaled in New York and later relieved of his testicles, had just captured America's greatest prize. To hear the reaction, it was hard to decide which was more astounding. New York is where you grow apples and blueberries and precocious little Broadway babies, not Thoroughbreds. And the last time a gelding won the Derby, Herbert Hoover was a household name.

Of course, such statistical anomalies can be explained away. Larger foal crops compared to those of the mid-20th century mean more of everything, including geldings good enough to win the Derby. Three times in recent memory an altered male has finished second, and none were closer than Cavonnier in 1996, who lost by a lip to Grindstone. It was an event trying hard to happen.

As for New York's sudden emergence as a cradle of Derby glory, let's get real. The breed has become so thoroughly cross-pollinated through accommodating statebred requirements that a good horse can turn up with almost any kind of stamp on his passport. This Derby winner came fully equipped with the bloodlines of Mr. Prospector, Seattle Slew, and Sea-Bird, all part of Funny Cide's family tree.

It was a strange enough Derby anyway, with Kid Rock seemingly ready to assume the role of grand marshal and spiritual heir to Matt Winn, and Iraq war protesters on the march downtown, where they staged a mock Derby between Empire Maker and Peace Rules. The outcome was not hard to predict.

And yet, if a poll were taken and everyone was asked to cite the most outlandish twist to the results of Derby 2003, the answer would have nothing to do with gender or birthplace or choice of a particular prep race.

No, the stunner was the identity of the trainer, and no one was more stunned than the trainer himself.

At the age of 65, respected by his peers, Barclay Tagg can be forgiven if he thought the highest rewards of the game were about to pass him by. Certainly, his credentials were as good as any trainer would want. After a fling with jump riding, he climbed down from the horse and apprenticed himself to such icons as Jonathan Sheppard and Frank Whiteley. Based in Maryland, not far from his Pennsylvania roots, Tagg tended to get the most from what he was given. Sometimes they were good enough to win on the national stage, like when Miss Josh won the Gamely at Hollywood Park, or Royal Mountain Inn took Belmont's Man o' War.

Tagg is also an unrepentant pessimist, although "realist" might be more to the point.

"I am a pessimist," he conceded, offering a self-deprecating smile. "I'm not proud of it, but I am."

How could the job make a person otherwise? A trainer with a bounce in his step and a perpetual grin must be written off as either simple-minded or self-delusional. Guys like Bobby Frankel, Richard Mandella, and Allen Jerkens earned their scowls in battle. The enemy, as Tagg articulated in his post-Derby interviews, is the breed, and what is required.

"It's a daily occurrence with all these Thoroughbreds," Tagg said. "Things go wrong with them so easily. They're very, very frail, and we ask them to do a lot. We ask them to carry weight and run 40 miles an hour, and train every day, and live in a small stall full of dusty straw and hay. It's contrary to what nature really set them up for.

"So you think you might have a big, fat, shiny, good-looking horse that's working beautifully and running beautifully, and you set him all up for something like this"—the Kentucky Derby—"and any day you walk in there at five o'clock in the morning and feel his legs, there could be something wrong with him. That's it. You just stop the whole thing. It kind of numbs you after a while."

Funny Cide tested Tagg's pessimism to the limit. In the weeks between his second-place finish to Empire Maker in the Wood Memorial and his date in the Derby, he literally did nothing wrong. There was never an oat left in his tub, never a wrong turn on the track or a warm spot where a cold, hard ligament should be. In the end, Tagg had to concede. Maybe this time it was meant to be, and when it happened, it was, in Tagg's words, "wonderful, just wonderful."

Now it's on to the Preakness.

"It's unnatural, to run a good horse back in just two weeks," Tagg said. "But I guess we'll have to just bite down and do it. Nothing seems to faze him. Last night after the race he was bouncing around his stall, ducking down and grabbing for my leg, trying to bite me. You'd never know he just ran a mile and a quarter against the best 3-year-olds in the world."

At least he sounded optimistic.

*(Funny Cide won the Preakness with authority, setting up a try for the Triple Crown in the Belmont Stakes. Alas, he was beaten on a dreary, rainy day in New York, which made Barclay Tagg feel bad for about as long as it took him to remember that he had won the Kentucky Derby.)*

~~~

# VOLCANIC

*July 4, 2007*

There is a time, and this may be it, to close the books on what a particular horse means in terms of historical significance, to end the quibbling debate, and to simply savor the rich meal he has served.

In winning his third consecutive Hollywood Gold Cup last Saturday, under circumstances that roused the hardest hearts, Lava Man secured once and for all his place among California's greatest Thoroughbred competitors. Ancient Title and Best Pal may have been better from the start. Candy Spots, Snow Chief, and Hill Rise spread their message far and wide. And it was Swaps, with no argument, who towered over them all.

But in terms of stubborn consistency, on home ground mixed with familiar sights and smells, Lava Man has few peers. His adamant refusal on Saturday to allow a tricky combination of pace, surface, and weight spread get in his way in the 68th running of the mile and a quarter Gold Cup added another layer to a legend that is now 25 months running.

During this stretch—a virtual eternity in modern racing—Lava Man has won 13 of 15 California starts. He might have been 15 for 15, too, were he not ridden into the ground in the 2005 Pacific Classic (he was beaten only three-quarters of a length), or had he not come upon the emerging grass star After Market, trained by John Shirreffs, in the more recent Whittingham Memorial.
~~~

It was Shirreffs again last Saturday who provided Lava Man with an opponent ripe for upset. A.P. Xcellent is a 4-year-old colt owned by Stan Fulton who is just now living up to his $750,000 yearling price, perhaps due, in part, to the contradictory messages sent by his ever-quarreling grandsires, Seattle Slew and Exceller. Whatever signals A.P. Xcellent was channeling from his genetic code, he was coming off a game third in the Californian and looked the part of a good horse going to the post for the Gold Cup.

"He does look good," agreed Shirreffs as he eyed the field from the rail. "And he's been doing great. But once the gate opens, it's a whole different game."

It is a game played to near perfection by Lava Man and his regular companion, Corey Nakatani. They have been together now since November of 2005, when Lava Man tore through the sole of his foot on the rough sand during the Japan Cup Dirt. Since recovering from that blood-splattered trauma, they have won 10 of 13 as a team.

For the Gold Cup, Nakatani and Lava Man had to deal with A.P. Xcellent and Mike Smith's free-wheeling lead, including an opening half of :48.75, along with an eight-pound advantage in the weights. It was also Lava Man's first race over Hollywood's synthetic surface.

"That didn't concern me as much as the pace," Nakatani said. "I had a feeling, as loose as the track was, horses weren't going to be changing positions too much. So I basically had to make it a two-horse race, and put him in a position to strike. But I listen to him, not the other way around."

There was a point, in midstretch, when it appeared as if A.P. Xcellent would outduel Lava Man on his own terms. Then, in the shadow of the wire, Lava Man's nose went down when it counted most.

"What a gallant effort, for both horses," Smith said. "They really duked it out, like the last round, really throwing it down. My horse fought back so hard you could almost hear him grunting. But that Lava Man, what a tough old dude. When a horse digs in like mine, usually that outside horse will fold a little, and that's what I needed him to do. But he didn't do it. Lava Man ended up wearing me down at the end."

In winning his third Gold Cup, Lava Man mirrored the achievement of

Hall of Famer Native Diver in 1965-1967. Like Native Diver, who lost his only start outside California, Lava Man never was meant to travel. Failures in Tokyo, Miami, New York, Louisville, and Dubai have pretty much closed the book on such ambitions. although the fact has mystified his connections—trainer Doug O'Neill and owners Steve, Tracy, and Dave Kenly and Jason Wood—to the point of preoccupation.

"That is very hard to understand," said Leandro Mora, O'Neill's chief assistant, who did the honors for the Gold Cup while his boss was out of town. "I have traveled with him. He has been happy and trained good. So I don't know. But you know, good horses are welcome to come to Lava Man instead of us chasing them every time."

Mora may have something. Think you've got a good horse, a real good horse? Let him fly West and try to beat Lava Man, dirt or turf, any time of year. Lava Man might not be a national hero, but he's a monster in his own cave, and to get to races like the Santa Anita Handicap, the Pacific Classic, and the Hollywood Gold Cup, you've got to go through him.

"The fans out here, cheering him on, it just takes your breath away," said Jason Wood, as Saturday's race began to sink in. "We're fortunate enough to be a part of it. But even if we weren't, we would appreciate it, because we would be one of those fans."

~~~

## TIZNOW AND FOREVER

*March 7, 2001*

Boy, did Frank Stronach miss a great day.

Stronach, of course, is the high-profile chairman of Magna Entertainment Corp., the Canadian company that owns and operates Santa Anita Park. On Saturday, Santa Anita dusted off its greatest treasure and presented the Santa Anita Handicap for the 64th time.

Boy, did Frank Stronach miss a great race.

If Stronach had been at Santa Anita Park last Saturday, he would have seen people waiting at the gates, long lines at the tellers, and the infield
~~~

crowded with families—all a testimony to the true power of a Thoroughbred star. Well-targeted advertising and a gift for the fans helped lure a few non-believers to the park. But by the time the big race came along, the reason for their excitement was crystal clear.

More than 34,000 strong, they came to see Tiznow.

If Stronach had been there, he would have loved the atmosphere in the garden paddock as Tiznow and his 11 sidekicks filed into the walking ring. Only a horse with the presence of Tiznow, the reigning Horse of the Year, can keep a crowd in such a buzz.

They cheered when Jay Robbins gave Chris McCarron a leg up on the Horse of the Year. They yelled encouragement as Tiznow made his way through the tunnel and onto the track. They bet him down from 8-5 to even-money in the time it took for Tiznow to go from the post parade to the starting gate.

And with a quarter of a mile to run, they loved the sight of McCarron sneaking his trademark peeks beneath his arms and between his legs. At that point, there was nothing chasing Tiznow except the specter of his loss in the Strub Stakes and the nagging reminder of the patch on his right front foot.

"He's absolutely cantering!" cried Trevor Denman as Tiznow's massive shadow began to obscure Wooden Phone on the final bend of the turn.

"Chris McCarron is waiting, waiting, waiting!" Denman was really rolling now. "Now he pushes the button, and Tiznow takes the lead in the Big 'Cap and goes for home!"

Frank, you had to be there—camped out with the fans on the apron terraces, or up in the stands, rising to your feet as part of a joyful congregation, screaming at Denman's cue. "Now he pushes the button!" And just like that, as Tiznow drew off to win by five, racing in California was born afresh.

Michael Cooper, watching the replay of the Handicap on a small monitor, mumbled, "I wish it was that easy," but only a few people heard.

Cooper, who bred the champion and owns him with the family of the late Cecelia Straub-Rubens, is painfully aware that Tiznow is anything but a push-button horse. He is a 4-year-old Thoroughbred with the mentality of a linebacker. A chow-hound who would wolf down his bedding if sawdust came in flavors.

The frustration over Tiznow's foot was magnified by his otherwise glowing health leading up to the Handicap. Every time Robbins beheld his horse, he saw a 10-furlong monster crying to run. Then his attention would shift to that spot on the inside of the right front foot, where the acrylic patch was attached to the hoof wall. How many of us truly understand the science behind epoxy bonding? Some things must be accepted on faith, if they are accepted at all.

"He's the only horse in the barn with a quarter crack," Robbins said. "The last one I had was probably two years ago."

If there is any justice, he will never have one again.

Had he been at Santa Anita on Saturday, Frank Stronach undoubtedly would have presented the trophy for the Santa Anita Handicap, then he might have glimpsed Jay Robbins briefly slip away from the ceremony after Tiznow was unsaddled and led out of the winner's circle. Robbins, a man who stores a lot inside, needed one more piece of contact, however brief. He reached up and centered the reins, letting his hand linger briefly on Tiznow's sweaty brown flank.

Some things seem preordained. Tiznow always was going to win the Santa Anita Handicap. Getting there was the challenge, and Robbins paid the price with a string of hard days and sleepless nights. Even on the morning of the race, the trainer had detected a trace of warmth in Tiznow's problem foot. There was no throbbing pulse—a sure sign of something amiss—but it was enough to put Robbins on edge.

And so, after holding his breath for nearly two minutes, Robbins was able to enjoy the final 50 yards of Tiznow's Santa Anita Handicap. His chin quavered with the release of tension, and his voice was barely a croak as he whispered the first thing that came into his mind:

"I'm going to sleep for 10 hours tonight."

He deserved to, because he helped make it a great day to be at the races. I feel sorry for anyone who missed it.

~~~
~~~

# GOLDEN AFTERNOON

*July 4, 2001*

If anyone hears Bobby Frankel complain about anything ever again, smack him.

Frankel woke up last Sunday morning with a silver spoon in his mouth and a rainbow on his shoulder. Calling him lucky hardly does the term justice. He was blessed. He was anointed. He was nothing less than imbued with the power to change history.

But he didn't even know it until 2:30 that afternoon.

To that point, he was looking at a hard-knocking day. Lido Palace had finished second in the Suburban Handicap and Senure did the same thing in the United Nations. All Frankel could do was tighten the girths on Aptitude and Skimming for the Hollywood Gold Cup and go sit down, hoping that one of them could salvage the day.

Then it happened. Somebody pulled the switch and the luck came tumbling down. In wham-bam succession, Frankel was handed the United Nations prize upon the disqualification of With Anticipation, and then, a few minutes later, he went from a two-three disappointment in the Gold Cup to first and second when victorious Futural was taken down and placed third.

You could have sublet the grin on Frankel's face. As every racing fan knows, these things happen. Disqualifications are a part of the game. But they do not happen to the same guy on the same day in two of the biggest races of the summer season. Until now.

"In some ways, it's more of a rush than just winning a race, because of the way the emotions go up and down," Frankel said later, after Aptitude had been crowned the official winner of the Gold Cup.

For Craig Dollase and the owners of Futural, the emotions were strictly down. Their tough little chestnut had just run the race of his life to win the 10-furlong Gold Cup by a length and a half, leaving both Skimming and Captain Steve far behind.

But instead of high fives and hugs all around, it was a grim Dollase who stood out on the track, sweating in his best dark pinstriped suit and watching the big-screen replay of the offending incident in the homestretch.

"They'll take him down," said Dollase, shaking his head as the screen showed Futural put the squeeze on Skimming and Captain Steve from the outside. "What a way to lose when you've got the best horse."

It was no consolation at the time, but Dollase was in good company. Dr. Fager was DQed after winning the 1967 Jersey Derby by 6-1/2 lengths because he racked up the field right after the start. Cougar won the 1971 Woodward Stakes in a waltz but had to give it back because he veered into a well-beaten West Coast Scout where everyone could see it. And Secretariat, no less, was taken down after winning the 1972 Champagne Stakes by two lengths.

The "best horse" in the 2001 Gold Cup was circling nearby his trainer, his coat flecked with wet sand, his blue saddle towel drenched with sweat, and his tongue sticking out the side of his mouth, as if to razz anyone who would dare suggest the day did not belong to him.

It did, but only for those few thrilling moments between Futural's first-place finish and the announcement that the stewards were going to look at the stretch run. They concluded that Futural and Chris McCarron leaned into Skimming hard enough that Garrett Gomez had no choice but to rein sharply and stand in the irons, costing him all chance for a shot at second place.

Frankel celebrates his 60th birthday next week, so it's still not too late to shop. Bobby knows, though, when to back off. Asked what he wanted in the way of a gift, he let slip a small smile of noblesse oblige.

"I'm okay," he said.

No kidding.

~~~
~~~

# KING RICHARD

*October 27, 2003*

A Breeders' Cup at Santa Anita Park, with its early, made-for-TV post time, means chili and beer for breakfast. It means SWAT teams and mariachis in the paddock gardens; hazy, smoke-filled skies; nightmare traffic; and a long line at the Seabiscuit statue for photo ops at the end of the day.

It also means that Richard Mandella will have a very good time.

It didn't start out that way. When the Breeders' Cup first came to the foot of the San Gabriels in 1986, Mandella ended up with the short end of the stick after Sprint contender Phone Trick went wrong and failed to make the race. It took a while to get over that one.

By 1993, Mandella had rallied. He ran two horses in the Breeders' Cup that year and won with both, including the Turf with Kotashaan to nail down Horse of the Year. Still, there was bitter with the sweet. Phone Chatter, Mandella's Juvenile Fillies winner, came out of the race with a fractured leg and never ran again. Sardula, the filly Phone Chatter beat, went on to win the 1994 Kentucky Oaks.

Then came last Saturday, when the Breeders' Cup returned to Santa Anita for its 20th running, and the game learned a lesson it will never forget. Mandella and his crew brought seven horses to the paddock for four of the eight races, and they won all four—or 3-1/2, if you want to quibble about the dead heat in the Turf.

"No," said British trainer John Gosden, a Mandella admirer for years. "Give him the full four. Half the Turf is still a million-dollar race."

Fair enough. Four it is. Four winners for Mandella on the day of days, and nearly a third of the purse money on the table, when even the most famous representatives of the horse-racing universe were unable to manage a single win. Ask Bobby Frankel how tough it was last Saturday, and if you can't find him, try Wayne Lukas, Bob Baffert, Steve Asmussen, Todd Pletcher, or Neil Drysdale.

The Breeders' Cup World Championships are not to be confused with baseball's World Series, which is usually the Yankees' to win or lose, or the World Cup, which belongs to an elite rotation of three or four countries.

This is Thoroughbred racing, an endeavor of infinite unpredictability, egalitarian to a fault, in which nearly anyone can wake up one morning with a horse of extraordinary talent.

To dominate such a rich tapestry with four winners on racing's most significant day is almost unthinkable. Lukas came within a nose of winning four back in 1988—Personal Ensign's nose, in fact—so at least the thought had been planted. In the end, it was Johar's determination to dead-heat High Chaparral in the Turf that put Mandella alone in the record books.

He has been there before. Besides those two Breeders' Cup wins in 1993, Mandella's vita sheet includes six straight victories in million-dollar races, training both runners in a Grade 1 dead heat, and the distinction of stopping Cigar's 16-race streak cold at Del Mar in 1996. All of those accomplishments add up to a place in the Hall of Fame.

"I want everyone to know just how much work it takes from a lot of good people," Mandella said Sunday morning.

He gave ample credit to a stable staff that ranges from Pleasantly Perfect's exercise rider, Crystal Brown, who has been with Mandella so long "she used to make haircut appointments for me when I needed them," to assistant trainer Becky Witzman, who was still in high school in 1993, to his priceless grooms, some with 20 years of service.

"They do the work in those stalls every day, and believe me, it's hard work," said Mandella.

He paused. "But I'm the brains."

Brains, heart, soul—the whole ball of wax. At 52 (his birthday is November 5), Mandella comes off as a guy who can't decide if he wants to be Jay Leno or George Patton.

When NBC cameras pushed too close to Halfbridled in the walking ring before the Juvenile Fillies, Mandella backed them off with a warning. Later that day, as the temperatures mercifully fell and shadows began to cool the Santa Anita barns, Mandella stripped off his jacket and rolled like a happy Labrador in his patch of pampered grass. He'll grow more next year.

"We've been in Charlie's barn for three years now," Mandella said, referring to the weathered shedrows once occupied by Charlie Whittingham. "We've been doing a lot of digging and planting in the garden. We finally found it."

No question, good karma never hurts. Pleasantly Perfect, Halfbridled, Johar, and Action This Day eat and sleep in the same stalls once occupied by the likes of Sunday Silence, Ferdinand, Ack Ack, and Turkish Trousers. Even so, even surrounded by such noble spirits, the job tends to nurture self-doubt. Little wonder Mandella prefers to leave the pre-race interviews to trainers with more to say.

"I don't know why," Mandella said the Tuesday before the Breeders' Cup. "But I woke up this morning feeling very tense. Maybe it's because all the horses are doing so good. I'm still amazed it's happening, that they've all got to this point, and I think they all really have a chance."

That is exactly the way they ran, one after another, right down the throats of the game's toughest competitors—Halfbridled, unbeaten and now champion; Action This Day and Minister Eric, one-two in the Juvenile with the third horse five back; classically prepared Johar, dealing with the best Europe had to offer; and Pleasantly Perfect, defying illness and injury to crown Mandella's perfect day in the Classic.

It was also a good day in Idaho Falls, where Mandella's mother watched and wagered on the Breeders' Cup, at the Sandy Downs simulcast facility, 50 miles from her home in Ashton.

"I took $20 with me and bet it all on Halfbridled," said Tina Mandella. "Then I played with that $66 the rest of the day. And I really needed Johar to get that dead heat, too, because I had him in the triple with Action This Day and Pleasantly Perfect."

By the end of the afternoon, Tina Mandella was doing local radio interviews as the proudest mother in horse racing. Her only regret was that Richard's father missed the show. Eugene Mandella—adventurer, rancher, and all-around horseman—died on November 12, 2002, at age 79.

"He taught Richard a lot, but he was an old-fashioned horseman," Tina Mandella said. "He could be tough with horses when he had to be. Richard, he treats them like his children.

"I'm very proud of him. I always have been. Of course, I'm prejudiced.

But you know, watching him on the television all day, I don't believe I've ever heard him talk so much in my life."

Then again, he never had so much to talk about.

~~~

# WEAKNESS FOR THE PREAKNESS

*May 19, 2006*

There is a realm of psychoanalytic theory that pays special attention to the "middle child" born to a traditional family. According to psychology texts, the middle child is often "plagued by feelings of parental neglect, inadequacy, and inferiority." They tend to "crave demonstrations of affection, a sign of insecurity" and can have "difficulty defining a personality . . . that will give them the attention and affection they need."

Welcome to the Preakness Stakes, the middle child of the Triple Crown.

Being flanked on one side by the gaudy, "Hey look at me!" Kentucky Derby and on the other by the solemn, respectable Belmont Stakes, the Preakness often comes off as drowning in a sea of neglect, clothed in Derby hand-me-downs and staged at a tumble-down track, without even a real flower to call its own.

The Preakness is characterized as the race that Derby winners must "get through" in order to deal with the really important issue in New York, giving it all the charm of a road block, or a root canal. Should the Derby winner survive the second child—I mean, jewel—then the Preakness is soon forgotten as the aura of a potential Triple Crown winner takes command. By the same token, let the Derby winner go belly up in Baltimore and the Preakness name is suddenly mud. The ultimate party-pooper.

In defense of this lonely soul, this middle child, psychologists point out that he or she might rise to the challenge and strive "to create a clear, strong, unique identity as they are given the freedom to shape their own personalities."

This nails the Preakness to perfection. The race is unique among its Derby and Belmont siblings in one important respect. Of the three races
~~~

in the Triple Crown, the Preakness Stakes is the only one that accurately reflects the true personality of American-style horse racing.

The Derby, with its carnival NASCAR mentality and shameless cultivation of 20-horse fields, presents a set of circumstances unlike any other major American event. The best horse can lose the Kentucky Derby more often than not, given the riot at the start, the logjams, the bumping, and the unavoidable lost ground. Unless pressed into service in the Mongolian cavalry, horses are never again asked to confront the heightened dangers they faced on the first Saturday in May.

At the same time, the storied Belmont Stakes assumes that Thoroughbreds are the same today as they were a thousand years ago, when running a mile and a half at racing speed was as natural as roaming the prairie. With precious few exceptions, the horses who compete in the Belmont each year will never again be asked to run 12 furlongs in the afternoon, and then it would only be on the grass.

The Preakness, at a nifty 9-1/2 furlongs, actually looks like the rest of American middle-distance racing. There are scores of top events run each year between 9 and 10 furlongs, featuring fields of between six and 12 horses, offering an entertaining mix of frontrunners and closers, and without a clutter of no-hopers looking for miracles.

In short, if the weather holds, the best horse usually wins the Preakness, which is exactly what will happen this year when Barbaro must deal with Brother Derek and Sweetnorthernsaint—the most aggrieved parties from the Derby—along with the fresh new shooter Bernardini.

The Preakness also has one other distinction of note. Its greatest fan base can be found in the management team of the New York Racing Association.

A Preakness victory by the Derby winner makes a ka-ching noise all the way up the interstate corridor to Belmont Park, where that sound you could hear on Saturday will be the attendance projections for the Belmont Stakes going through the roof. What then happens on Belmont Day makes little difference, once that Triple Crown throng is in the house, which is why NYRA execs are big-time Barbaro fans.

"I can't argue with that," said Bill Nader, NYRA senior vice president.

"We're holding our breath. Now I know what it feels like to be an owner or a trainer. Even when they're odds-on, they still look beatable."

Nader and his crew were getting Triple Crowned before Barbaro had even cooled out in Kentucky.

"People talk like it's a layup, like Barbaro couldn't lose the Preakness," he said. "But we've been around long enough to know it just isn't that easy."

Belmont Park still prepares for its biggest day of the New York season for the Belmont Stakes, with or without the prospect of a Triple Crown.

"With no Barbaro at all, we're looking at 60,000 people," Nader noted. "With Barbaro, but no Triple Crown, somewhere closer to 70,000. With Barbaro and a Triple Crown, then we're over 100,000."

The trend is clear. Since 1997, there have been six Belmonts presented with a Triple Crown at stake. They drew live gates of 70,682 (1997), 80,162 (1998), 85,818 (1999), 103,222 (2002), 101,864 (2003, in a steady rain), and an all-time 120,139 in 2004, when Smarty Jones came to town. After he lost, the figure was still 120,139.

So hold a kind thought for the Preakness, forgotten middle child, all-American to the core, and the most important New York race of the year.

~~~

# HIDE THE CHILDREN

*June 11, 2008*

You could see it on her face, the disappointment, the exhaustion, the drool. Angelic little Sophia Rhein, 15 months old, daughter of veterinarian Kristian Rhein, clung to her father's shoulder as the crowd around her near the finish line filled the air with a deafening, full-blooded New York reaction to Big Brown's meek surrender in last Saturday's 140th running of the Belmont Stakes.

"Where is he? Where is he? He's done!"

"Oh, my God! He didn't even finish!"

"What a disgrace!"

Sophia kept her counsel, but it was easy to read her mind.
~~~

"I missed my nap for this?"

Her father, who numbers Todd Pletcher among his clients, made no apologies.

"I wanted her to witness history," he said. "Even if she doesn't remember, at least she could say she was here."

There was no chance that the crowd of 94,476, plus horseplayers everywhere, would ever speak with a single voice. (Note that the maiden, Guadalcanal, was weirdly underlaid at 25-1 compared to the 38-1 of victorious Da' Tara.) Still, even the pari-mutuel losers would have been pleased enough to have left Belmont Park that day knowing they were in on something special, a high-water mark in the treasured lore of the game.

This, despite the fact that the track's water pressure failed almost as badly as Big Brown, leaving customers high and dry. Despite the fact that they did not get the Big Brown rally towels vaguely promised by the Big Brown people earlier in the week, which, given the heat and the water pressure, would have come in handy. And despite the fact that there was no featured presence of the Hooters franchise that had attached itself to the fortunes of Kent Desormeaux, Big Brown's jockey, especially in the wake of this exchange from last week's episode of everyone's favorite reality quiz show, *Moment of Truth*.

Question: "While working at Hooters, did you ever have sex with one of your customers?"

Answer (after dramatic pause): "Yes."

Stay classy, horse racing.

In that parallel universe occupied by Hall of Fame trainer Nick Zito, such considerations were not significant. At the end of Belmont day, as darkness fell and dry lightning lit the northern sky, Zito wandered the spacious courtyard of his Belmont barn, his cellphone jangling the theme to ESPN's *Baseball Tonight*, while Da' Tara nibbled at a hay pile along with stablemate Anak Nakal, who dead-heated for third.

In the avalanche of questions and recriminations spilling forth in the wake of Big Brown's race, one single misconception screeched loudest of all—Nick Zito did not "spoil" this chance for a Triple Crown winner. Da' Tara, a Tiznow colt of modest accomplishments, did not go after a tiring

Big Brown on the lead, as Zito's victorious Birdstone went after Smarty Jones and beat him a length at the end of the 2004 Belmont. There were no apologies this time around, and none needed.

"I love the classics," Zito said. "We've been second in the Belmont, what, seven times?"

Six, actually, and two Zito wins from what is now a record 20 Belmont starters.

"The percentage isn't great," Zito conceded. "But in these big races, if you keep trying and you win one, you got it made."

Zito was asked if he had any consoling words for his fellow trainer Rick Dutrow, who promised more than once that Big Brown would win the Belmont.

"No," Zito replied. "No consoling words at all. Like I just told *Sports Illustrated*, this game will humble kings, and before honor is humility. No matter what. If you're around as long as we are, you can't guarantee anything in this sport. Right or wrong? It's impossible!"

Zito, the good Catholic boy, was quoting from the Old Testament book of Proverbs. The entire verse reads, "Before destruction a man's heart is haughty, but humility goes before honor."

Right or wrong?

There was a certain amount of "I told you so's" heaped down upon Dutrow's weary brow, although not too many from those who know first-hand how tough the game can be. And yet, for every abject failure in a high-profile event—whether it was Miss Musket in her match race, Demons Begone in his Derby, or Big Brown trying for a Triple Crown—there have been an equal number of transcendent performers who came through time after time.

"Unbelievable," said Patrice Wolfson, owner of Affirmed, as she sat stunned in her Belmont box seat after the race. "I wonder if it had some effect when Big Brown ran up on horses' heels going into the first turn."

Thirty years earlier that same first turn set the stage for the last successful Triple Crown attempt, when Steve Cauthen steered Affirmed wide on the lead and Jorge Velasquez refused to be sucked inside with Alydar. A quarter mile later, they were lapped on each other, eventually answering to the challenge of announcer Chic Anderson, "We'll test these two to the wire."

Wolfson had been ready to pass the torch, though. In her view, the Triple Crown club needed new members.

"It's time," she said the week before the race, as she prepared to attend a tribute to Affirmed at the Kentucky Horse Park, with its catchphrase "The Legend Grows."

Now Wolfson was bearing bittersweet witness to yet another 3-year-old reaching to join Affirmed and the other 10 Triple Crown winners, and falling short.

"The legend grows," she said with a sigh, "and grows and grows."

~~~

## BIRDLAND

*June 8, 2009*

Let's face it. The 2009 classic season was played for underdog drama and good-hearted laughs, along with a brief interlude of genuflection. It also will be remembered as the moment that Thoroughbred racing, like the NFL, attempted at least a suggestion of parity.

Hal Wiggins, 66 and unbeknownst to anyone outside the Midwestern corridor, crowned his quiet, steady career with Rachel Alexandra's 20-1/4-length win in the Kentucky Oaks. She was quickly sold, but Wiggins was given and deserved all the credit in the world for her victory 10 days later in the Preakness by her new trainer, Steve Asmussen.

Chip Woolley, at 45 a veteran of hard times but still swinging, guided Mine That Bird out of New Mexico with a sure hand and one good leg to win the Kentucky Derby and contend to the bitter end in both the Preakness and the Belmont.

And then Tim Ice—remember the name—capped the first year running his own stable by having Summer Bird in the right place at the right time to win the 141st Belmont Stakes last Saturday, on the trainer's 35th birthday, no less. He also got a tie and a couple CDs.
~~~

Wiggins, Woolley, and Ice—my kind of law firm—stand as absolute proof that a classic Thoroughbred can come from anywhere in spite of the top-loaded economics of the game. Best of all, they confirmed that good horsemanship runs deeply through the land, ready to be revealed when that right horse comes along, even though it comes as a surprise.

Wiggins is out of the Rachel Alexandra picture and Ice came to the Triple Crown center stage late. We'll see if the media has enough energy left to do him and Summer Bird justice as the season rolls on.

That leaves Bennie Woolley, Jr., nicknamed Chip at birth (as in "off the old block"), as the lasting image of the 2009 Triple Crown, complete with black hat, shades, horseshoe moustache . . . and crutches.

There is a tendency among journalists to idealize the fresh and the new. Woolley overcame a healthy suspicion of his overnight celebrity to become one of the most engaging Triple Crown personalities of the modern media era. The same thing hit the quick-witted Californian Bob Baffert during Cavonnier's noble campaign of 1996, as well as Philly's accommodating everyman John Servis during the Smarty Jones run of 2004.

Woolley was almost too shocked at the Derby result to enjoy the moment in full. But then, in the two weeks between the Derby and the Preakness, he hit his stride with both the media and the logistics of a Triple Crown campaign. When Rachel Alexandra beat Mine That Bird a length in Baltimore, the post-race spin was worshipful toward the filly, but also gave the Derby winner and his trainer high marks for proving the Derby was not a blind fluke.

Then came New York, and there was Woolley paying a visit to the Anna House day care facility on the Belmont backstretch, letting the little kids climb all over him like an exotic piece of playground equipment.

There was Woolley at the Belmont-eve cocktail party, where pretty girls lined up asking to try on his black hat and pose for pictures. What's a man to do?

And there was Woolley, having sent Mine That Bird out of the Belmont walking ring, fighting his way through the tunnel as fans shoved programs his way for autographs. He balanced on his crutch pads and signed every one.

When it was over, and Mine That Bird had finished third after a crowd-thrilling move around the final turn, Woolley stood in the mouth of the shedrow of Carl Domino's Barn 18 in the Belmont twilight, weary at the end of the long ride.

"Look at that, I blew a wheel," Woolley said, lifting his right crutch to display a rubber tip worn through at some point during the day.

"Are those the crutches you're gonna give to the Derby Museum?" asked Woolley's father, Bennie, Sr., the old block himself.

"Yes, they are," Woolley replied. "You know, I'm a lot taller than people think I am."

Woolley planned to take Mine That Bird, along with his all-around hand Charlie Figueroa, to Churchill Downs for decompression before heading back to New Mexico.

"We got Stephen Foster Day coming up, when we get all our Derby trophies and rings," he said. "He won't gallop at all, so Charlie can just go out there in the morning and walk him. I'll come out and check on him, and I'll try and lay up myself. Get my leg up, and get it X-rayed."

Woolley was told last March, when extensive surgery was required to put the lower leg back together after his motorcycle betrayed him, that he should take it easy and keep it elevated. Woolley shook his head.

"Fat chance of that happening," he said.

But now it was over. Time for the trainer to heal and the horse to rest. In the hazy corners of what might have been, Woolley will allow himself to wonder if it made a difference that Mine That Bird got a little wound up by the briefly disruptive behavior of another horse in Belmont's pre-race monitoring barn (the other horse was Summer Bird). He will entertain the idea that Calvin Borel could have waited a few beats longer to launch Mine That Bird's Belmont move, but he won't dwell on it. And Woolley is man enough to concede that he might have done something leading up to the race to anticipate Mine That Bird's uncharacteristically edgy behavior heading to the paddock and, according to Borel, in the race itself.

More than anything, though, Woolley went to bed Saturday night feeling like his horse had fired a winning race and lost. No trainer swallows that easily.

"What hurts is that it was the softest field he'd hooked in the three races," Woolley said, as friends and family gathered late. "But he was the only one that lit the board that ran in all three. You can't tell me that's not significant."

Nobody would dare. It was significant not only in terms of Mine That Bird's possible vulnerability as a horse who had danced them all (both Summer Bird and Belmont runner-up Dunkirk ran in the Derby but skipped the Preakness), but also in terms of history. For context, over the past 20 runnings, there have been 13 horses who finished in the money in all three Triple Crown races, namely Curlin, Afleet Alex, Smarty Jones, Funny Cide, Charismatic, Victory Gallop, Real Quiet, Silver Charm, Free House, Thunder Gulch, Go for Gin, and Mane Minister. And now Mine That Bird, the unlikeliest of all, who at that particular moment was tossing his head and wondering who he had to trample to get his dinner. A friend from home approached the trainer.

"How you doin', man?" he asked.

"Aw, it'll be all right," Woolley replied. "Eventually."

It remains to be seen if Woolley will be able to take his newfound fame and run with it. Right now, he's looking forward to running anywhere at all. By then it was almost 8:30, and the 2009 Triple Crown was easing into history. The traffic on Hempstead Turnpike, just the other side of a nearby fence, was wall-to-wall, but it was getting empty and quiet on the backstretch.

Woolley turned and walked himself to Mine That Bird's stall and leaned his crutches against the wall. Then, balancing on his good left foot, he bent over and put the finishing touches on the Derby winner's tub of hot grain.

~~~
~~~

# MUCHO MACHO MEN

*November 5, 2013*

Gary Stevens popped the top off a cold bottle of Heineken with the butt end of a Bic lighter and handed it to a visitor. He could afford to feel generous after winning the $5 million Breeders' Cup Classic aboard Mucho Macho Man just 24 hours after taking the $2 million Breeders' Cup Distaff with Beholder.

"I've had 153 text messages and seems like almost as many phone calls," Stevens said. "Stay here. Drink this. I'm gonna go take a shower."

It was late on Saturday, better known as Day 2 of Breeders' Cup, and Stevens was the only rider still in the Santa Anita jockeys' room. The day's wild buzz had been replaced by the mundane hum of the few remaining valets wrapping up their chores. Outside the traffic finally was beginning to thin and the coast was clear, but Stevens's exhortation was a welcome one. Sit still. Have a cold one. Think about the day.

An hour earlier, as twilight descended upon the main road of the Santa Anita stables, Neil Drysdale made a right turn toward the grassy patch between barns 26 and 36 and extended a hand to Charlie LoPresti.

"It was a brilliant, brilliant performance," Drysdale said in unambiguous reference to Wise Dan's second straight victory in the Breeders' Cup Mile.

"Thank you, Neil," LoPresti replied. "That means a lot coming from you."

Behind them Wise Dan grazed, oblivious to the banter.

"His race in Canada and then here today—those two runs were spectacular," Drysdale continued. "Today everything went wrong for him, and he still won. Did you see how when he came into the stretch he was kind of unbalanced or something? Then when he straightened him—boom, it was over. Well done. Truly."

LoPresti blushed. But what would Drysdale know? He's only had a first and four close seconds in the Mile to go along with five other Breeders' Cup wins.

"People don't realize how tough it's been on him this year," LoPresti said as he admired Wise Dan. "He's run on such boggy racetracks. He got his track today, but he ran hard. I don't think you'll be seeing him run quite as much next year."

That Wise Dan will be running at all should be cause for widespread celebration. The fiercely protective LoPresti and octogenarian owner Mort Fink owe nothing to no one when it comes to putting good name and welfare of their caramel-colored chestnut on the line. If Wise Dan is elected Horse of the Year again and then comes back at age 7 in 2014, he would be the first Thoroughbred since Forego in 1976 to take the field in search of three straight.

"I'm not going to think about anything until after the first of the year," LoPresti said. "I'm just going to enjoy it."

Which, after all, is the point of the exercise. To complain there is too much Breeders' Cup—and this writer has, often—ends up sounding a lot like the joke Woody Allen used to kick off *Annie Hall*, about the food in a particular Catskills resort being not only terrible but also served in "such small portions."

The Breeders' Cup portions are ridiculously large and arrive so often that a race like Beholder's breathtaking Distaff, run way back on Friday, is rendered ancient history overnight in the face of the nine BC races on Saturday. Even then, on Day 2, there was hardly time to appreciate the all-pro performance of Dank in the Filly & Mare Turf before we were dusting off Groupie Doll's old crown in the Filly & Mare Sprint and then shoving them both aside to extoll the repetitive virtues of Mizdirection in the Turf Sprint against the boys.

And how about the noble vanquished? Horses who end up second and third in Breeders' Cup races are sometimes the second and third best horses in their divisions, which ain't hay.

In the darkness of the backstretch last Saturday, a groom flicked on a light in Jeff Bonde's barn. She's a Tiger, haunches to the webbing, turned slowly and came to the front of her stall. She was the picture of a 2-year-old filly in full, at peace now hours after doing her job in the Juvenile Fillies, which was to go as fast as she could for as far as she could and still somehow manage to hold on. Her disqualification for interference in favor of Ria Antonia was only the fifth in the 258 Breeders' Cup events presented to that point, and only the second of a horse who had finished first.

"On the bright side," said Allen Aldrich, part owner of She's a Tiger, "we've got $400,000 and we've still got our mare."

He got that right. Back at the Bob Baffert barn, near the main stable gate, a pair of Breeders' Cup floral blankets were hung over a shedrow rail. One had been draped across New Year's Day after the Juvenile, the other on Secret Circle after the Sprint. Baffert and his assistant, Jim Barnes, stared at the flowers as if they were funeral wreaths.

"Only two?" Baffert said, hoping a dark wisecrack might spackle the pain.

Barnes wasn't in the mood. Game On Dude's failure in the Classic with Horse of the Year on the line was a disappointment, but there he was, eating his evening chow, content with having won the Santa Anita Handicap, Hollywood Gold Cup, and Pacific Classic in 2013. Then there was Secret Compass, the barn's little sister, who got as far as the three-eighths pole chasing She's a Tiger when her left front ankle fatally snapped, sending her to the ground and John Velazquez spinning through the air.

"That was just devastating," Barnes said. "It was hard to even put a saddle on Book Review in the next race."

"I talked to Cordero," Baffert said, referring to Velazquez's agent, Angel Cordero, Jr. "He told me Johnny said she was moving really well there. She must have hit something, for her to have..."

Baffert doesn't complete too many sentences. He gets a thought started and lets others do the rest. This one he didn't need to finish, since the empty stall on the north side of the barn that once was home to Secret Compass said it all.

"That's a danger zone right there, dropping into that turn, when they're going that fast," Baffert said. "And the good ones, they don't protect themselves. They just run."

Stevens was back from his shower. His phone was ringing again.

"I got to get this one," he said with a smile.

It was Gary's brother Scott Stevens. His older brother, that is, Scott being 52 to Gary's 50. Scott Stevens, a medical miracle in his own right, spent his Saturday riding at Turf Paradise.

"You too?" Gary said, and turned to his visitor. "Scott got disqualified today, too."

At which point the comparison ended. After winning a race earlier on the card, Scott finished a close second in an $11,000 allowance race on the grass but was disqualified for drifting out into the horse who finished third. The difference in purse money was $1,292. The price tag for Gary's DQ aboard She's a Tiger in the $2 million Juvenile Fillies was $740,000.

"I guarantee you took more chances for that eleven thousand than I did for two million," Gary said.

"I thought that big sonofagun of Wayne's was going to get you in the Classic," Scott said, summoning the image of Will Take Charge bearing down on Mucho Macho Man.

"Yeah, he ran huge," Gary said. "I ran into Lukas in the tunnel after the race. He says, 'I think I made a mistake putting you on Oxbow earlier this year because nothing would have turned out the way it did if I hadn't.' I had to admit he was about right. But it was cool. He had tears in his eyes. He was as happy for me as I was."

"Well, I was proud of you, brother," Scott said. "Enjoy the moment. I love you."

The moment began precisely a year ago, when Stevens began telling those close to him that he was going to dry out, get fit, and test his arthritic knees in a comeback that, from most angles, seemed preposterous. When he began riding again in January at Santa Anita, it had been more than seven years since he'd been a full-time jockey.

His victory aboard Oxbow in the Preakness Stakes last May was enough for any fairy tale, but Stevens insisted he was in for the long haul. His knees held up. He tied into a cluster of stakes mounts. Trainers like Lukas, Tom Proctor, and Richard Mandella disregarded the calendar and tossed Stevens the reins. Then Kathy Ritvo put him on Mucho Macho Man, and together they won America's richest race by a nose.

"On days like this, we all take chances," Stevens said. He was on his way to the parking lot now, through the shadowy paddock gardens. In the middle of the walking ring, a lingering fan was taking a cell phone photo of the Seabiscuit statue, backlit by the glow from the jockeys' room porch.

"Going to the gate for the Classic, I was thinking about Johnny, but in a positive way," Stevens said. "It's like what Jerry Bailey told the television audience. Most of the time when we fall we get up, and if we're hurt, the first thing we ask is when can we come back? They had to remove Johnny's spleen, but it sounds like everything was moving and he's going to be okay. If there is such a thing, it was a good injury on a bad day."

Stevens laughed a little at the sound of that line, but you knew what he meant. Stevens fell this year, more than once, but he kept getting up, and in a season during which superstars Ramon Dominguez, Joel Rosario, and finally Velazquez suffered serious injuries, on that warm Southern California night in early November, it seemed as if Gary Stevens was the last man standing.

Three

# ROCK OF A JOCK

*Laffit Pincay, Jr., stood at the window in the maternity wing of Arcadia Methodist Hospital and stared at the collection of newborns arranged in their bassinets. It did not take him long to figure out which one he was looking for. A grandfather just knows.*

*This particular grandfather, however, was also a professional athlete with a ferocious competitive spirit, 52 years old at the time and of no mind to call it a day. In fact, what Pincay was able to accomplish after little Madelyn entered this world on that November day in 1998 was almost as impressive as what came before.*

*To watch Pincay in action on horseback through the years was to witness one of the great sports sagas of the 20th century. Pincay was nothing less than horse racing's Roberto Clemente: a nine-inning superstar, playing hurt when he needed to, heartbroken once in a while, but always stepping up with a driving commitment to make every moment on the field count for something.*

*When Pincay became a grandfather he was still 13 months away from breaking Bill Shoemaker's record for the most winners by any jockey anywhere on the planet. The story picks up here as the moment of that record approached, accompanied by a media fanfare befitting the kind of individual that comes around only once in a lifetime.*

# ON THE BRINK

*December 4, 1999*

Laffit Pincay was awake again. Wide awake in his handsome new house, nestled on a hillside above the San Fernando Valley, with his wife lying next to him and his young son sleeping peacefully down the hall.

This was not insomnia. He did not crave a midnight snack. Neither was his mind in turmoil over the history he was about to make. He was simply, completely awake, feeling nothing different from the hundreds of other nights that his body kept to one schedule, while the rest of the world submitted to another.

Pincay wrapped himself in a light robe and padded down the thickly carpeted stairs to the family room. The soft light over the deep, L-shaped couch cast just enough glow on the opposite wall to suggest the shapes of trophies, cups, crystals, and plates covering shelves that reached to the ceiling high above. Pincay never gave them a glance as he settled into a corner of the couch, slipped on his reading glasses, and reached for his favorite pastime—a book of crossword puzzles.

What's a six-letter word for incomparable, beginning with "P" and with no end in sight?

F. Scott Fitzgerald offered the image of a dark soul always trapped in the desolation of three in the morning, day after day. But there is nothing remotely dark about the soul of Laffit Alejandro Pincay, and 3 a.m. for him is merely another notch on a clock, another hour in his ongoing defiance of both time and the consequences of age.

Now less than a month away from his 53rd birthday, Pincay stands on the brink of breaking Bill Shoemaker's all-time record of 8,833 wins. The sporting world at large has been sufficiently impressed, typecasting Pincay as the ageless guy who eats like a bird and rides like a tiger. As a celebrity he is a serene public presence who never calls attention to himself, unless on horseback. He can enlighten a listener for hours about diet, about exercise, and about the restorative benefits of meditation. He will show you his bag full of vitamins and nutritional supplements, and he'll smile while you count the bottles.

Shake hands with Pincay and his grip is soft. Horses have broken his right thumb several times, so he learned long ago never to risk the health of his fingers in a macho showdown. When the clerk of the scales calls for riders to leave the room, Pincay is always the last one through the door, blinkered to distractions, focused on the race.

Between races, when he doesn't ride, Pincay avoids the pool table, the Ping-Pong, the racetrack rummy, and the horseplay of the typical jockeys' locker room. He reads, works his crosswords, and if the reception is good, he will strap on earphones plugged into a tiny TV and treat himself to the courtroom morality of Judge Judy.

"I love Judge Judy," Pincay says with a grin. "Bobby Frankel should go up in front of her."

Such mischief is typical. For someone considered to be the finest athlete his sport has ever produced, Pincay is as approachable as the guy next door. It's just that this particular guy has a Kentucky Derby trophy, a Hall of Fame plaque, three Belmont Stakes mementos, and seven bronze figures representing each of his Breeders' Cup wins.

"No, six," Pincay notes, checking the shelf. "One time I had a party at my house and the next day one of them had disappeared. It was the one I won for Lukas—Is It True."

He also has five Eclipse Awards, more than any other jockey.

"Actually, I've got two from 1971," Pincay says. "The tail broke on the first one. I took it to a place to get it fixed. They said come back in a week. I did, and the place was closed. Closed! So I had another one made.

"Three years ago I got a call from a woman. She told me her husband just passed away, and he had a trophy of mine that he bought in an auction. She wanted to give it back to me, so she brought it to the track. It was my 1971 Eclipse Award."

Pincay also has a piece of art by Anthony Quinn, the Oscar-winning actor, hanging over his fireplace, a workout room with Stairmaster and treadmill, and a closet with two dozen pairs of ankle-high, calfskin boots, while his garage still houses the white Porsche 928 he bought with some of the prize money from Spend a Buck's $2.6 million victory in the 1985 Jersey Derby.

His pride and joy, however, is a collection of Baccarat crystal figurines—bears and bulls, cats and dogs—arrayed on glass shelves in the foyer of his home. He has been buying them for years.

"This is my favorite," he'll say, stroking a long, dappled leopard. "The dolphin, too, I really like. Look at this. Very special." And with the same hands that lifted Spend a Buck those final 50 yards in New Jersey, Pincay caresses a small hen and her tiny crystal chicks.

***

Jeanine and Laffit Pincay were married on November 29, 1992, at the Silver Bells Chapel in Las Vegas, Nevada. She was 21, he was 45. They were both wearing blue jeans.

"We drove around in a taxi until we found a chapel that didn't look so cheesy," recalled Jeanine, a native Southern Californian. "Laffit said Burt Bacharach got married at the Silver Bells, when he married Angie Dickinson. So we got our license, picked up everybody at the hotel, and went to the Silver Bells. It was very cheesy, like, 'Okay, you may kiss the bride . . . and it will be $49.95 for the video.' "

The wedding feast was at Caesars Palace, immediately followed by a brief period of gambling. Then Laffit announced, "Let's go to the arcade," and that is exactly what they did, with Pincay's daughter Lisa, and his son Laffit III. At 2 a.m. the groom was still dropping quarters.

Of course, it wasn't as if it was past Pincay's bedtime. He doesn't really have one. Jeanine quickly realized they were compatible in just about every way but their sleeping habits. She does. He doesn't, at least not with any perceivable pattern.

"I've tried everything," Jeanine said. "I got him headphones for the TV. The little reading light. Some nights he'll turn the light off at 10 and he'll be out. Some nights he just can't sleep."

But it's a small quibble. The sound of her husband stirring downstairs is sweet music compared to the clang of the telephone on a racing afternoon. There is always a chance it could be very bad news.

"It's something you don't think about 24 hours a day," Jeanine said. "But I'm always checking for messages. And when something happens to another rider, one of our friends, then it's on the tip of your brain for days."

When they met, Jeanine was not aware that Pincay's first wife, Linda, had taken her own life with a handgun in their Los Feliz home. That was January of 1985. Linda Pincay's suicidal depression apparently traced to serious health problems caused by a ruptured appendix and post-operative complications. Even before that, however, she would sometimes fast to dangerous extremes out of sympathy for her husband. Without realizing it, Jeanine fell into a similar pattern.

"When we first dated, I ate what he ate, and I lost like 30 pounds," she said. "I was skinny, skinny, skinny. Then later, when I got pregnant, I started eating like a normal human being again."

By his own measure, over the past three decades, Pincay has tried every diet under the sun. He even spent six years as a vegetarian. As a result, it is no surprise that the members of the Pincay household are keenly schooled in nutrition. Even Jean-Laffit, who turned six in October, is up to speed on proteins and carbohydrates. He knows that egg whites are the way to go, and he will sometimes eat one of dad's Power Bars instead of a Hostess Ho-Ho.

Still, there was some confusion. Years ago, Pincay discovered he could quell the craving for sweets and salts by chewing forbidden food, savoring the taste, and then spitting it out. Little Jean-Laffit thought this was pretty cool.

"The first time I saw my child chew food and spit it out, 'like Daddy,' I told him to stop," Jeanine said. "I told him Daddy did it because he had to for his job, and he didn't have to."

Now Jean-Laffit merely lies in wait for his father to prepare his tray of nightly "treats." Then he sneaks a cookie, or a handful of cereal. And swallows.

***

Laffit Pincay never really likes to talk about himself. But lately, as he has approached the record, he feels like he's been doing nothing else. Now it's a Monday morning, a non-racing day, and Pincay is at home on his Stairmaster, wearing a tan turtleneck, dark slacks, and black boots, offering a brief demonstration.

"I have a feel for when I should work out harder, and when I should work slower," he explained. "On the days I ride a lot of horses, I try to go real slow. Just enough to open the lungs and burn some calories. When I ride fewer horses, I go a little faster.

"The mistake I made when I was younger was going too fast all the time. Then when I would feel wiped out, I would think maybe I wasn't doing enough."

Pincay laughed. To him it was funny, the thought of all that physical punishment—the sweat box, the rubber suits, and the long, lonely jogs around the main track at Santa Anita and Hollywood Park. It took him, literally, until he turned 50 to fully understand his ideal caloric intake, of what it should consist, and how it should be prepared.

Consider, though, the fine line of working as a Thoroughbred jockey on just 850 calories a day. Even his exercise must be carefully rationed, because a calorie wasted on the Stairmaster might be needed later that day, inside the sixteenth pole on a tiring maiden.

"I thought that I was getting old for a while," Pincay said. "But I knew what it was. It was my diet. There were days when I was very, very low. I didn't know what to do. Some diets would work for a while, then I would go downhill.

"I had a hope that I could figure it out, though, because there were days that I felt really good, like I could go out there and win as many races as I wanted to, even though I didn't have the horses to do it. The thing was to have not so many of those low days."

The great athletes have a mental toughness that lets them move quickly from the scene of their mistakes. The rest of us linger in the past and look for sympathy.

"I hold no grudges," Pincay said. "Somebody says something bad about me, I don't like it, but I forget about it.

"Sure, I have regrets," he added. "For one thing I wish I would have kept my money in the bank and not given it to anybody."

This time he laughed hard, at himself, as he summoned the grim memory of the $300,000 bill for back taxes dropped on him by the IRS at the end of 1987. He sued his business managers and won a $1.7 million settlement.

"Would you believe that thing is still in court?" he said, now laughing a little less. "I don't dwell on it. Although at the time it really bothered me. I thought I could retire any time I wanted to. I felt like I had to start all over again. That was terrible. What you see now, I own. I don't owe a penny on anything. I own my houses. I own my cars. I have a good amount of money in my retirement plan. I have money invested. All I worry about is when I die is that I have plenty of money to leave my family."

There is no question what he has left to the game. As he shifts his focus to retirement, now that Shoemaker's record is within his grasp, Pincay will be leaving behind a set of standards difficult to copy, but certainly worth the try.

"The thing that helped me through my career is that I am very responsible," he said. "Even when I wasn't doing good, I never said, 'I don't care.' I always care about winning, about being out there in the best possible shape. This has occupied my mind constantly throughout my career as a jockey."

The question follows: After 35 years of such sacrifice and discipline, will he be able to turn it off?

"The day when I can quit worrying about those things will be a relief," he replied. "I won't have to worry about how I'm gonna be tomorrow. And even though I'm very used to it, I don't think I'll miss that feeling."

~~~

## TOP OF THE WORLD

*December 10, 1999*

It's done. He did it. And now that it's done, and the fireworks have faded, the balloons have dropped, and Laffit Pincay has driven into the sunset at the wheel of his new white Porsche with the license plate 8,834, we are the truly lucky ones who get to enjoy the rest of his career.
~~~

After all, it wasn't even supposed to last this long.

"I hope to ride until I am 40." —*Sports Illustrated*, 1976.

"I think I'll ride for about three more years." —*New York Times*, 1985.

"In two years I will know if I can keep going." —*Racing Post*, 1996.

When someone is driven by talent, imprisoned by their own unique ability, they must have many such moments. As a kid, Pincay was a champ at marbles, then a swift and sure second baseman. But there was really nothing he could ever be other than a jockey. And if it is the choice that comes easily, it is usually the rest that is very hard.

It must have been this way with Beethoven, going mad and going deaf, still hearing symphonies in his head. Or with Edgar Allan Poe, writing like a demon until he was drained. Or with Van Gogh, tormented beyond reason, tortured by the images he was compelled to create.

Pincay has suffered no less for his art. Starvation is the price he has paid. But, like a true artist, he is constantly driven by his gift. One afternoon, several years ago, he considered the contours of his incredible physique and almost laughed at the thought of his chosen profession.

"All my life as a jockey I always felt that I was in a place that I didn't belong," he said. "And I still do. What makes me go on is that I still do good. That takes some of the pain away."

There was no pain on Friday. Only bright lights and good times, triggered by the sight of Pincay barreling down the Hollywood Park stretch aboard Irish Nip to set the record. Then the flashbacks started . . .

Back to 1973, at the top of the stretch at Churchill Downs, when Pincay was low and driving his shoulders into Sham, convinced he was about to win his first Kentucky Derby. Then Secretariat broke his heart.

Back to 1977, with Pincay astride Crystal Water in the Santa Anita Handicap, deep in the lane and in a desperate fight with Eddie Maple and Faliraki. Pincay made the difference, and no one disagreed.

Back to 1983, on the first turn of the Del Mar Oaks, when Heartlight No. One nearly went down in a tangle. Pincay kept her afloat—a small miracle—then convinced her to go ahead and win the race.

Back to 1986, guiding Skywalker with a string while keeping Gary Stevens and Precisionist bottled tight on the inside down the backstretch of the Breeders' Cup Classic. Then Laffit cut his colt loose, and the race was over.

For that matter, all the way back to the evening of May 19, 1964, at Presidente Remon Racetrack in Panama City, when the 17-year-old Pincay found himself alone on the lead aboard a horse named Huelen, and on his way to victory number one. His borrowed helmet was too big. At the head of the stretch it slipped over his eyes. Pincay, riding hard, ripped it off and flung it away, riding bareheaded into history aboard his first winning mount.

"I'll never forget the feeling," he said, 25 years later. "I was so excited I couldn't get to sleep that night. All the big races I've won since, I never had that same feeling again."

"Most men, after climbing Mount Everest, enjoy the satisfaction and are fulfilled," said John Russell, the former trainer and close friend of Pincay's. "There are not enough Everests for Laffit."

"When the day comes I can't help the horses anymore, I'll know it's time," Pincay promised. "I know what I can do better than anybody else, and there's no way I'm going to keep riding if I'm going to be hurting someone's chances to win.

"I never had anybody to advise me, never asked anybody about anything," he added. "I knew that I had to work very hard to be successful. But sometimes, when I was trying to become a jockey, I was so disappointed that I wasn't going anywhere that I would quit for a few days, sometimes a week.

"Then I'd say, 'Wait a minute. I got to go back.' Because quitting is the only time you lose for sure."

~~~
~~~

# MR. ECLIPSE

*January 15, 2000*

To put things into perspective, when Laffit Pincay, Jr. earned the first of his five (soon to be six) Eclipse Awards for his performance during the season of 1971, Secretariat was a yearling, Watergate was merely a building, and you could buy a full tank of gas without applying for a home-equity loan.

Pincay's fellow champions that year included Charlie Whittingham, John Galbreath, Ack Ack, Canonero, and Riva Ridge. The date of the awards dinner was January 26, 1972, at the Waldorf Astoria in Manhattan. When he was asked what he remembered, he replied:

"I thought Cordero won that year."

Okay, so forgive the guy for the minor slip. After all, Pincay also took home the trophy at the Eclipse Awards dinner in New York in January of 1974, in San Francisco in January of 1975, back in New York in February of 1980, and in Miami in February of 1986.

"That first one in New York, my wife forgot to pack my overcoat," Pincay said. "Man, was it cold."

It should be a relatively balmy night this Monday in Los Angeles, just over the hill from his San Fernando Valley home, when Pincay accepts Eclipse number six. This one is special, and as far as Pincay is concerned, it means as much, if not more, than the rest, since it honors his achievement of breaking Bill Shoemaker's record for lifetime victories.

Pincay set the record on December 10 amidst a media focus not seen for a single personality in California racing since Shoemaker retired in 1990. In the subsequent month, Pincay's life has returned to normal—or at least as normal as it can be for a 53-year-old man who competes against athletes half his age and eats his meals by the ounce. Pincay even treated himself to a three-day break last week—courtesy of the Santa Anita stewards—and spent his suspension hanging around the house, shopping the malls, and stoking the fires of his energy.

In the wake of his record-setting spree, during which Pincay also won the Hollywood Park riding title, the rider has been swamped with pleas to use his name to raise money, hype products for chump change, and otherwise make people look good by having him around. He is not anxious to dive headlong into such waters.

"For one thing, I don't like to give speeches," he said in the Santa Anita jockeys' room Thursday as he chewed (without swallowing) a snack of seasoned rice. "It's very hard for me—something I worry a lot about when I have to do it. I feel a lot of pressure."

Sorry if that makes no sense at all. Pincay's pulse barely stirs when faced with a wall of horses and nowhere to go at the head of the stretch. But the idea of a banquet room packed with people hanging on his every word? Now that's scary.

What Pincay doesn't mind, though, is acknowledging his fans. He will have the chance at Santa Anita on Saturday when the track presents "Laffit Pincay Day," a belated but very appropriate celebration of the record he set at Hollywood Park. There will be speeches. The fans will get goodies. And whatever Pincay decides to say will be right on the money.

In the meantime, Pincay said he has had a few recent nibbles to do commercials. If anything comes off, this should be headline news, since jockeys break through with mainstream product endorsements about as often as superstars of the Scottish X-Games.

"I'm gonna go for it," Pincay said. "I've never done it before, so maybe I can take advantage of breaking the record. It's hard, though, because those things take a lot of time, and I still enjoy riding horses."

With a career in racing that bridges the sports boom of the last three decades, and the attendant endorsement riches flowing to athletes, Pincay has found himself on the outside looking in. He has never been surprised.

"You have to look at it this way," he said. "Kids don't think about being a jockey unless they are around the racetrack. Most kids want to be football players, basketball players, tennis players, because they see it every day on TV. Horse racing just isn't as popular."

Among the offers Pincay is considering is a commercial deal with George Foreman. The proposed package includes an exercise video (although a pie-eating contest would be more fun to watch), and other endorsements.

What we really need, though, is the movie of his life. And even though it isn't over yet, Pincay smiled at the thought of casting the starring role. His first choice was the best choice.

"That guy, the one in the action movies," he said.

Um, Bruce Willis? Arnold Schwarzenegger? Jean-Claude Van Damme?

"No, no," Pincay replied. "Jackie Chan."

Perfect. And the guy knows how to take a fall.

~~~

## BIRTHDAY BOY

*December 29, 2000*

Pity the poor Christmas-week babies. Born in the shadow of our culture's most extravagant holiday, they are lifelong afterthoughts. Their gifts, if they come at all, are wrapped in used reindeer paper. They get hand-me-down fruitcake. Fine wines of Idaho. Ties and trinkets bought for half-price or less.

And that's just fine with Laffit Pincay. If you ask him, he will tell you that his birthday is no big deal. He holds no grudges if folks let December 29 slip by without fanfare.

"I just take it easy," Pincay said Thursday morning in the Santa Anita jocks' room. "Sometimes we go to dinner. Sometimes we have a little something at the house. But this year I'm just going to be quiet. I don't want to do anything."

Fine. Be that way. Reluctant celebrities have a certain charm, and Pincay has never pushed his fame in anyone's face. But excuse this reporter if he refuses to ignore the anniversary of the birth of a national treasure. Laffit Alejandro Pincay, Jr. is 54-years-old, and if he thinks he can let December 29 slide by without special recognition from his friends and admirers in the racing world, he is badly mistaken.

There are other well-known people who share Pincay's birthday, including Ted Danson of *Cheers*, Ray Nitschke of the Packers, and Rose Lee Maphis of *Hee Haw*, to name but a few.
~~~

Birthday-boy Jon Voight won his Best Actor Oscar for *Coming Home* a month after Pincay won the 1979 Santa Anita Handicap aboard Affirmed. Birthday-girl Mary Tyler Moore has four Emmys, two fewer than Pincay has Eclipse Awards. And on the very same day and year Pincay was born in Panama, Mr. and Mrs. Faithfull of Hampstead, London, were welcoming their daughter and future super-groupie Marianne into the world.

Pincay also shares a birthday, almost, with fellow Hall of Fame jockey Jorge Velasquez. They were born within 12 hours and 25 miles of each other—Pincay in Panama City and Velasquez in the country town of Chepo.

"Jorge was born the night before, on December 28, and I was born the next morning," Pincay said. "I always tell him that's why his skin is dark and mine is light.

"I used to see him in the barns when I started working at the track," Pincay went on. "He was learning in another stable. I would see him when he started galloping horses, then riding. He started doing really good. About a year later I started riding and competing against him."

Their professional lives continued in virtual parallel after coming to the United States. Velasquez won national championships in 1967 and 1969. Pincay began a run of five straight titles in 1970. Velasquez won a Kentucky Derby in 1981. Pincay won his in 1984. By 1975, Pincay had done enough to be elected to the Hall of Fame. In 1990, Velasquez joined him there.

Now their careers have diverged. Velasquez retired in 1997 with 6,795 victories. He was a part-time racing official, but that didn't take. He has found more satisfaction in the last year as a jockey agent, handling the books of two riders at the current Aqueduct meet.

In the meantime, Pincay continues to ride with no end in sight. He admits, however, that he has considered a second career as an agent.

"I thought about bringing up a young kid and teaching him, and probably I could do pretty good with him," Pincay said.

"But now, I don't know if I want to do that. You have to get up early every morning and be there every day. You need a rider who is easy to work for, and one who is willing to work. So it's not an easy job at all if you do it right."

Nobody works harder than Pincay. At the age of 54, he continues to approach his craft with the discipline of a Dominican monk. Last into the paddock, methodical on the ground, he has stripped things to the essentials, saving his energy for the intensity of the race. Anyone who watched him win another one on Tuesday, when he beat Chris McCarron in a close one to wrap up Santa Anita's opening day, will swear that time has stopped. Won't this man ever show his age?

"I never paid much attention to birthdays, even when I was a kid," Pincay said. "My mother would sometimes have a party for me. But then I had to dress up, and I didn't like any of that."

He still doesn't. That is why Laffit Pincay intended to celebrate his birthday by riding at Santa Anita, and nothing more. His wife, Jeanine, planned to be in the stands.

"I asked if he wanted a dinner party and he said no," Jeanine said. "All he asked for was that I cook him his favorite fish soup."

Guess that means there won't be candles, either.

~~~

## THE LONG GOODBYE

*July 13, 2003*

The last time Laffit Pincay was seen wearing silks, on March 1 of this year, he was walking into the first aid station at Santa Anita Park holding his neck. He said it hurt.

Initial reports relayed around the track that day indicated Pincay would be okay. And he was, in the cosmic sense. Braced for dreadful news, Laffit fans were relieved to hear that their Rock of Gibraltar had risen from a heap on the dirt crossing of the downhill turf course to leave the field under his own steam. Give him a few days off and he would be fine.

Only he wasn't. In fact, a vertebra in his neck had suffered multiple fractures. Another vertebra in his back was fractured as well. His recovery has turned out to be long and uncomfortable, and sometimes painful.

Finally, though, he is free of all neck supports. As of last Wednesday, his
~~~

most recent visit to a doctor, he was given the green light to begin a more vigorous routine of exercise.

"He thinks that in two or three months, the injury might be okay," Pincay said Friday morning. "I usually heal very quick. But the neck I guess is different. It was just a very severe injury."

Never mind Pincay's neck. The racing game itself will take an eternity to recover from the loss of its most enduring star. The jockeys' room without Pincay has been a strange place, as if a support beam was suddenly removed. Other riders have taken up the slack of Pincay's prodigious work load—among Southern Californians, only Pat Valenzuela had more mounts than Pincay's 1,189 in 2002—and yet fans have been left longing for the straightforward purity of the classic Pincay ride.

It was never more apparent than in the 2002 Hollywood Gold Cup, in which Pincay willed the ambitious miler Sky Jack to a narrow victory over Momentum at the end of a mile and one-quarter. Doug O'Neill, Sky Jack's trainer, still walks around in awe of what happened that day, courtesy of a jockey 21 years his senior.

It is perfectly fitting that the tribute to Laffit Pincay is being held on Sunday afternoon, on the day of the 64th running of the Hollywood Gold Cup. Pincay won nine Gold Cups, including the 1979 running with Affirmed and the 2001 renewal with Aptitude, which fell in his lap after the disqualification of his pal Chris McCarron and Futural.

Pincay won his first Gold Cup in 1970 with Pleasure Seeker, doing a feathery 114 pounds in the process. His reaction today: "I did?"

Ancient Title, Crystal Water, and Affirmed followed in the 1970s, then came Perrault in 1982, Greinton in 1985, and Super Diamond in 1986. Pincay retains vivid memories of them all. Super Diamond, however, lingers with a twinge.

Pincay often played hurt while he rode. All jockeys do, primarily because they do not get paid if they do not ride. It is also a fact that the tolerance for pain goes up in proportion to the amount of the purse. The 1986 Gold Cup tested Pincay to the extreme.

"About two weeks before the Gold Cup I tore a lot of cartilage in my left ankle," Pincay said. "I was riding in a lot of pain, and there were even a couple of days I had to take off because I just couldn't stand the pain. I was afraid that the whole ankle was going to rip open."

Pincay consulted with Dr. Robert Kerlan, the famed orthopedic surgeon with the all-star sports clientele. The message was mixed.

"He told me that as long as I could take the pain, I could ride," Pincay recalled. "At least I knew then it wasn't going to be injured any worse."

Kerlan injected the ankle on the morning of the Gold Cup, which brought some relief. Still, Pincay had to cut his boot to get it over the angry joint. Eddie Gregson, Super Diamond's trainer, took one look at his jockey and winced.

"The way he limped into the paddock didn't give the owner a great feeling of confidence," Gregson said.

Super Diamond won by a length and one-half, with favored Precisionist third. Pincay, grateful he had survived the ordeal, decided against his customary victory wave of the whip.

"I was too tired," he said. "I was afraid I would fall off."

Now that Pincay is on the ground for keeps, unable to jump on a fast horse and ride away, he will become a sitting duck for the affections and everlasting gratitude of his fans, friends, and family. It is a shame that he was not able to retire on his own terms. But, given the worst-case scenario of neck trauma, it is a blessing that he still stands tall. Sunday's tribute was going to happen sooner or later, so he might as well relax and enjoy the fuss.

"It's gonna be hard," Pincay said. "I have a lot of pressure on me. I have to speak. And it's hard to keep it short when I have so many people to thank."

Let him take all the time he wants, because the game will never see the likes of him again.

Four

# THE ONE AND ONLY...

*Ron Crockett, who made his fortune in aircraft maintenance, preserved the racing industry in the Pacific Northwest by sheer force of will and considerable personal expense. Maggi Moss, a trial lawyer by trade and horse owner by joyous choice, has dedicated untold time and energy to the care of Thoroughbreds who have retired from the track. Jenine Sahadi, the first woman to train a horse to win a Breeders' Cup race, is the driving force behind a foundation that provides college scholarships to the children of backstretch workers. Frank Lovato, Jr., who won an Eclipse Award as an apprentice rider, runs an organization called Jockey World and a summer Jockey Camp for youngsters who may someday pursue some sort of life in the game.*

*And so on. Every corner of the Thoroughbred racing community is packed with fascinating, accomplished, unusual people who have lifted the sport and made a difference. From this vast writer's paradise I have selected the following profiles as representative of the high-calorie banquet from which I have dined.*

*Inevitably, though, the feast moves on. Horse racing lost Charlie Whittingham in 1999, Jimmy Jones in 2001, Lefty Nickerson in 2004, Joe Hirsch in 2009. Allen Jerkens, however, has remained active as America's most respected Thoroughbred trainer, still seeking those elusive grails. As for John Nerud, the conscience of the sport, he turned 101 in February of 2014. I can't wait to hand him this book.*

# CHARLIE WHITTINGHAM

*November 21, 1998*

The nurse leaned in and treated her patient like a frail old man. The chart said he was 85, so of course he must be deaf.

"HOW ARE YOU TODAY MR. WHITTINGHAM?" she yelled.

How was she to know that this guy could hear a mouse break wind in a thunderstorm. Mr. Whittingham smiled and locked onto the nurse with his one good eye.

"I'm right here," he softly replied.

Now Charlie Whittingham was two days out of the hospital, back home in his Sierra Madre townhouse filled with the memories of his 70 years in the racing game. He was feeling pretty good for a guy who had just gone 10 rounds with a nasty bout of viral pneumonia.

He had a right, though, to feel every one of those 85 years. For a while there he was a very sick Marine. Malaria couldn't kill him during World War II. Prostate cancer took its best shot and missed. A couple years ago he went in for routine cataract surgery and picked up a dangerous staph infection that could have turned out the lights for good. He gave up the eye and kept the rest.

Whittingham has survived border town bar battles in old Tijuana, a trip to Buenos Aires with Horatio Luro and a boatload of accommodating school teachers, close encounters with Japanese hostiles on Guadalcanal, and a variety of damage inflicted by horses of questionable intellect and class. But the pneumonia nearly got his number.

Whittingham was in a Pasadena hospital for 12 days, most of it in intensive care. His wife, Peggy, and daughter, Charlene, were on the scene nearly round the clock, while Mike Whittingham, his son and assistant trainer, tended to the business back at the track. This was the real thing, not some bump in the road. A dark alarm went out to a racing world still mourning the loss of Woody Stephens, Brian Mayberry, Willard Proctor, and Clarence Picou.

Whittingham was weak in body, but from time to time the old spirit flared. Just ask the nursing staff.

"I don't think they'll ever forget he was there," said Peggy Whittingham, Charlie's wife of 53 years.

"How long?" Charlie was being a scamp. "Fifty-three years? I thought you had more sense than that."

"One of the nurses was doing a routine examination and touched his head, right here," Peggy said, lightly stroking her husband's bald dome where most foreheads usually end. "She said she had never felt a harder head in all her experience as a nurse."

Gee. What a surprise.

"Was he sent home or kicked out?" asked a friend when informed of Whittingham's discharge from the hospital. Once his blood cleared of all sign of infection, Charlie was shown the door. Now he needs meat on his bones so he can get back to the barn, and plenty of company to feed his undying love of the sport.

"Since he's been home he's eating better," said Tim Yakteen, Whittingham's former assistant and unofficial son. "He's polishing off everything but the glaze on the plates. And the more people who can come to visit will definitely stimulate him."

While he was in the hospital, the gang from Clockers' Corner at Santa Anita paid a call and put on a backstretch lounge show, complete with ragging, ripe gossip, and unfettered disrespect for each other's heritage. Mike Chambers, Bobby Mitchell, and Sean McCarthy were among them—trainers, old-timers, Whittingham acolytes. They figured that if Charlie couldn't go to the racetrack, they would bring the racetrack to Charlie.

Whittingham got a surprise visit at home this week from Ferdinand, the best barn dog in America. The Australian shepherd bounded into the room and licked a layer of skin off Charlie's face before anyone could get in the way. As therapy goes, Ferdinand probably felt better than his master.

"We're allowed to have two dogs in this complex, but they can't weigh more than 20 pounds," Peggy Whittingham said. "I'm thinking of asking for permission to have one 40-pound dog, or maybe Ferdy can come just halfway in the room."

It has been more than two weeks since Whittingham was knocked for a loop. He felt good enough Thursday to visit his Santa Anita barn in the afternoon and stick around to watch the simulcast of the feature from Hollywood Park. Whittingham was running a horse in the race, named Young at Heart, who managed to beat Reraise at Del Mar last summer.

It is easier to contemplate a world without chocolate than to imagine horse racing without Charlie Whittingham. "No good-byes yet," he said, and he hopes to be back at the track full-time within the next few weeks. That should be enough to satisfy anyone's idea of Thanksgiving.

~~~

# ALLEN JERKENS

*August 30, 2001*

The audience made a sound that could best be described as a cross between a gasp of wonder and an "ahhh" of devout recognition. There before them, striding to the podium, was a tall, big-chested man wearing gray slacks and a blue blazer. He was being introduced as Allen Jerkens, but that was impossible, because the last time most of them heard the name, Allen Jerkens was flat on his back in a hospital in Florida.

And even if it was the real Allen Jerkens, there was no way he would be saying much, especially in front of the large crowd gathered in the Fasig-Tipton sales pavilion for the 2001 Thoroughbred Racing Hall of Fame induction ceremonies. The real Allen Jerkens gave speeches like the one he delivered when he received an Eclipse Award for outstanding trainer of 1973. That one consisted of the words "thank" and "you."

The hush gave way to great applause, which died down just in time to catch Jerkens presenting Richard Mandella as the newest trainer admitted to the Hall of Fame. Jerkens kept it very short and properly sweet, basically doing a twist on the old Steve Allen shtick of "a man who needs no introduction–so here he is." Then Jerkens turned, shook Mandella's hand, and beat a hasty retreat.

Down in the audience, Liz Jerkens had to laugh. "That's it? He's been practicing a speech for days, pacing around at night, worrying about what
~~~

to say," she said of her 72-year-old husband. "You wouldn't believe how nervous he was."

Jerkens should have known better. His mere presence made the moment worthwhile. Mandella had been telling people for weeks that Jerkens would be standing beside him on Hall of Fame day, acting like a kid who gets the Pope to appear at his confirmation. This is a fairly typical reaction from a younger generation of trainer, growing up on bits and pieces of the Jerkens legend. But his peers among senior trainers feel the same way. And if "Sunny" Jim Fitzsimmons or Eddie Neloy or Buster Millerick could come back from the grave, they'd agree. That Jerkens kid could really train.

How is it possible? How did it happen? How did such a reputation evolve? Jerkens has never won a Triple Crown race, never won a Breeders' Cup race, and never won a national championship. He has spent his career working the New York–Florida circuit, rarely straying far from the East.

Yet the name of Allen Jerkens remains magic far and wide, treated with reverence, awe, and consummate respect, a half-century after he saddled his first winner on the Fourth of July, 1950.

***

On a recent morning at his Saratoga barn, Jerkens had just climbed off his pony, named Circus, who used to belong to Margie Cordero. She loaned him to Jerkens last year when his old pony came up lame. Then, after Margie Cordero was killed last winter by a hit-and-run driver, her husband, Angel, gave Jerkens the horse for keeps.

"They never tell me anything!" Jerkens was railing. "When did they move the winner's circle? They must have moved the winner's circle, because I sure as hell can't find it!"

Jerkens was going through a slump—at least by his own definition—and the world had once again ganged up against him. Someone suggested that things would never get so bad that he would be kicked out of the Hall of Fame. Jerkens found no comfort in the knowledge.

"Yeah? They'll probably just turn my plaque around," he snapped.

Fat chance. You don't mess with an institution, even one like Jerkens, who has been known to weep like a mother at losses, then turn those same tears to joy when he wins.

"I don't know what I've got to do to win one of these things!" Jerkens said once, cursing the fates, after his grand filly Sky Beauty finished up the track in the 1994 Breeders' Cup Distaff. "What am I doing wrong?!"

Not much, especially when viewed through the prism of his record from the very start. Old-timers still marvel at the way Jerkens turned a mid-1950s sprinter named Admiral Vee from a $7,500 castoff into a major winner at two miles, at how he beat Kelso three times with Beau Purple in 1962 and '63, and at how he upset Buckpasser with Handsome Boy in the 1967 Brooklyn.

Ancient history, you say? Okay, then it was the same Allen Jerkens who was every bit as pertinent in the 1990s with Sky Beauty, Devil His Due, Kelly Kip, Missy's Mirage, Virginia Rapids, and November Snow. It was the same Jerkens who won the two-mile Display Handicap in 1955 with War Command and then, 43 years later, the 1998 Jockey Club Gold Cup with Wagon Limit.

The years have not mattered to Jerkens. His skills with a racehorse have survived any changes the game could throw his way. There was an Allen Jerkens who led the New York trainers' list in 1957, and then there was an Allen Jerkens who led the standings at the end of the Aqueduct spring meet in 1998. Same fellow.

In fact, there are very few horsemen who have maintained such a level of excellence over such a long period of time. In 1957, Jerkens ranked 13th on the national list of trainers in terms of purse money. In every decade since then, he has maintained a presence among the top 10 names.

In 1966, Jerkens finished third behind Eddie Neloy and Hirsch Jacobs. In 1969 he was third to Elliott Burch and Charlie Whittingham. In 1973, the year of his Eclipse Award, Jerkens ranked third to Whittingham and John Campo. And so on . . . 10th in 1979, eighth in 1983, sixth in 1993, and ninth in 1995. By that time he had outlived—and out-trained—an entire generation.

"He's the most remarkable, gifted trainer I ever saw," said V. J. "Lefty" Nickerson.

"He lived and breathed horses," said Nickerson, who trained alongside Jerkens at the old Aqueduct racetrack in the 1950s and early 1960s. "Somehow he knows what they're thinking. As for people, he might not always have time for them. He was always sort of lost in thought. Except at the table. He was a great dinner companion."

Most of the time.

"One night we went to Lundy's in Sheepshead Bay," recalled Ron McAnally, a fellow Hall of Famer. "It was me, Lefty, and Allen, and in the middle of dinner, Allen gets up and leaves without saying a word. Left a big plate of food. We figured he went to the men's room, but he'd gone back to the barn because he was worried about some horse. He had to feed it milkweed or something, stuff he was growing right there at the barn."

Hand-feeding frail fillies their evening meal. Carrying burlap rags to shoo flies from his ponies. Screaming at grooms who pull a mane after a horse has been entered in a race.

"Why do you want to go picking on that horse for! What did he ever do to you?"

Herbs, grasses, constant observation, and a sympathy for the nature of the horse: the recipe for the Jerkens mystique has been debated for years. With so many things that can go wrong around a Thoroughbred, there is no detail too small, and it was usually Jerkens who noticed those details.

"He's from the old school, like Charlie Whittingham," noted Alex Hassinger, a Whittingham disciple who has trained two champions. "But not even Charlie was as hands-on as Jerkens. He's a guy who still sets his own feed every night."

Jerkens himself describes his style as "thorough" and cites the example of a stakes raid made long ago across the New York state line to the little track Green Mountain.

"I think it was the only stakes they ever ran in Vermont," he said. "I had Ron Turcotte to ride, Bill Boland to saddle him, the groom, a nightwatchman, the pony boy, and the pony. The purse was $15,000."

Notice, there was no exercise rider. None needed. Jerkens would often give a horse a pre-race, riderless "blow out," accompanied by a pony. On the morning of the race, Jerkens called for an update.

"Don't know what they gave the horse," Boland reported, "but the pony went in :13." Later that day, the horse won by 15 lengths.

***

"Maybe I should hire a landscaper," Jerkens said, staring off in the direction of the immaculately trimmed Saratoga barns of Mark Hennig and Dallas Stewart. "But I really don't know what growing flowers has to do with training a horse."

Jerkens cites his father, Joseph Jerkens, as a primary influence in the development of his horsemanship. Joseph Jerkens was a former Austrian cavalry officer who immigrated to New York in the early 20th century and set up shop in the racing business, earning a reputation as a man who could get a lot out of horses who were thought to be at the end of the line.

Jerkens also reads books, whether the subject is 19th century racing and training, or the more contemporary works by Hall of Famer Preston Burch and trainer-turned-racing official Keene Daingerfield.

"Most of the time, it's common sense," Jerkens said. "You might read a lot and not learn anything you don't already know. Then you'll come across some little thing some guy did back in the 1800s. It will make sense, and you'll try it."

Retired Hall of Famer Mack Miller is 79 and trained against Jerkens for the better part of four decades. While Jerkens handled the runners of Hobeau Farm for Jack Dreyfus, Miller worked privately for Charles Englehard and then for Paul Mellon.

"I think Carey Winfrey helped Allen a lot in his younger days," Miller said, referring to the father of Native Dancer's trainer, Bill Winfrey. Both Winfreys are in the Hall of Fame.

"Certainly, I saw a lot of Winfrey's influence in Allen's horses," Miller went on. "Winfrey had a horse called Squared Away. They stayed in New York all winter, just jogging around the shed. And every spring he came out for the Paumonok Handicap, all shed out with a beautiful coat of hair, just like a horse who'd been in Florida. Allen's horses came out like that.

"He's been one of the truly great horsemen of our time," Miller added.

"And you know, he might not be through. The sonofagun is still young."

***

"I was fired in 1961, and I got lucky," Jerkens said. "Not long after that I was introduced to Jack Dreyfus."

Just like that, the perfect owner-trainer relationship had been created. The Wall Street investor and the cavalryman's son forged a bond that has lasted to this day. Besides Beau Purple, Onion, and Prove Out, they have collaborated with Step Nicely (who beat Forego), Group Plan (who beat Wajima), and Sensitive Prince (who nearly upset Affirmed).

Asked to describe Jerkens, the 87-year-old Dreyfus was glad to oblige.

"I can do it in a few words," he said. "He's no good."

Asked to elaborate, Dreyfus said, "He's no good at all," and by then the joke was clear. The two men enjoy a rugged simpatico that has transcended all conceivable ups and downs of the racing game. They are not simply patron and artist. They are friends.

"Jack saw through Allen to what he really was," Liz Jerkens said. "He stuck with him, just like Allen was always loyal to Jack. They're just alike."

Dreyfus agrees.

"For starters, we're both nuts," he said. "I think I'm the only owner who has had to cool out the trainer after losing a race, rather than the other way around."

There wasn't much to grouse about in 1973, when the Dreyfus runners spoiled every proper party. First Onion beat Secretariat in the Whitney. Then Prove Out beat Secretariat in the Woodward. Then Prove Out beat Riva Ridge in the Jockey Club Gold Cup.

"That was a great day," Jerkens says now about the Whitney. "It was the only time they saddled on the turf course. Onion looked as good as Secretariat that day."

Dreyfus acknowledges the Jerkens heroics of 1973. But he cherishes most their first good horse together, Beau Purple, who came along in their first year as a team.

"I didn't know enough back then to see that Allen was different," Dreyfus said. "Of course, I didn't know I was different, either."

"The first time I met Allen, I was the emcee of the morning workout program at Belmont Park," Liz Jerkens said.

"There were a group of schoolkids at the track one morning, and Allen was on his white pony. I went up and asked if the children could pet his horse. He said, 'Sure. Would you like to go for a ride?' " They have been married since 1987, the second time around for both.

Last winter in Miami, where Allen and Liz had set up shop for another Gulfstream Park meet, he was stricken with a terrifying shutdown of his pancreatic functions that nearly sent him into a coma. For days he was in grave condition. For weeks any complete recovery was a longshot. Even Jerkens had his doubts.

"They wanted me to try some rehab, to get some strength back, but the first time I tried to walk I couldn't do it," he said. "I didn't think I'd ever walk again."

Liz Jerkens was amazed at the parade of friends that made the pilgrimage to the hospital. They needed to pay homage to the man they all call "Chief."

"The waiting room always seemed to be full," she said. "Even after visiting hours ended, one of our men wouldn't leave until he was able to see Allen for himself."

Jerkens made it back, slowly at first, and with a few lifestyle changes.

"No more salt," Jerkens said. "No more drinks. Non-alcoholic beer, and it's not bad, I guess."

It might be a while, too, before Jerkens gets back to running his famous touch football games, when he would linger at the backstretch rail, shirtless, wearing shorts and dark shoes, and call out to jockeys as they warmed up for the last race, "You playing tonight?" as he tossed a football hand to hand.

But for pleasure, in those rare moments he is not thinking about his horses, Jerkens can still enjoy his beloved movies and his collection of *The Honeymooners* tapes. It should come as no surprise that when asked to name his favorite film, Jerkens answered without a second thought.

"It's *Casablanca*," he said. "I love that movie."

That figures. Jerkens and Bogart, two of a kind. In another life, Jerkens would embody the enigmatic Rick Blaine of Rick's Café Americain. He would play Rick just like Bogart played him, as the world-weary idealist, the tortured romantic, the reluctant hero. And when he walked off in the end, off to the start of a beautiful friendship, it would probably be with a racehorse. Or with Liz. What was it that Rick Blaine said about his pal, Louis Renault?

"He's the same as any other man, only moreso."

He might as well have been talking about Allen Jerkens.

~~~

# MICHAEL DICKINSON

*November 22, 2003*

Alert the peasants. Light the torches, and get the children out of the woods. The Mad Genius has left his castle in Maryland, and he is wandering about the land, with sightings as far afield as the stables of Hollywood Park.

Stay on guard. The Mad Genius is a master of disguise. He may appear as a tall, pleasant gent with a boyish shock of salt-and-pepper hair and a charming, polite demeanor. He might engage the unsuspecting bystander in bright, witty banter, replete with sly cultural references and a self-deprecating sense of humor. But don't be fooled. He's mad, do you hear? Mad!

Nicknames are tough to live down, especially when they are thickly applied by a doting media. Thoroughbred trainer Michael Dickinson gets saddled with Mad Genius—or "EmGee" as he's known on the street—because he wins races in ways not readily explained by conventional means. As nicknames go, it's better than Stinky.

To acquire mad genius status, Dickinson has borrowed generously from such role models as Charlie Whittingham, Don Quixote, and Sherlock Holmes. It was Holmes who said, at one point in *A Study in Scarlet*, that "One's ideas must be as broad as Nature if they are to interpret Nature." He could have been quoting Dickinson.

This is the same Michael Dickinson who at various times has tilted at
~~~

such formidable windmills as the Hong Kong Jockey Club, the Breeders' Cup, and the West Virginia Racing Commission. He has been known to don a pair of lady's heels and walk a turf course, testing for penetration. He will diagram a race for a jockey, furlong by furlong, or fax them a pre-race evaluation of their chances, with columns listing positives and negatives.

He is also deadly frank when it comes to his chances. Sometimes, all he can muster under the plus column is something like: "He's a Thoroughbred, and he's sound."

Like Holmes, Dickinson mixes a distracted, British eccentricity with a feverish work ethic that allows precious little time for trivialities. There is no such thing as a casual conversation with Michael Dickinson. His obsession is divine, however, for he pours his heart and soul into his Tapeta Farm training center, on the northern shore of the Chesapeake Bay, where Dickinson has provided himself with the luxury of a controlled environment. At 200-acre Tapeta, it is Michael Dickinson who decides when to train, how hard to train, and over which of several surfaces to do that training.

"There are two things we can't do, though," Dickinson said. "We can't ever make a slow horse into a faster one. And we can't eliminate injuries, although I think we get less than other people. In fact I know we do, because we can make it with horses that wouldn't make it any other way."

Dickinson earned his nickname as a big-race miracle worker with the likes of Da Hoss, Cetawayo, and Amerique, horses who disappeared into some kind of equine witness relocation program, only to emerge years later at the top of their game.

The Mad Genius was at it again last weekend, winning the De Francis Memorial at Laurel with the rarely sighted A Huevo, whose image had adorned milk cartons up and down the Eastern seaboard. Just for kicks, Dickinson also won the Laurel Futurity with Tapit, a more conventionally campaigned 2-year-old who was making his second start.

But hold on. Dickinson's 2003 stats through last Sunday showed a record of 35 wins from 145 starts. Another 45 starters hit the board, but can a Mad Genius be satisfied losing 110 races?

"The first six months it was dreadful," Dickinson said. "It was a combination of bad weather, bad luck, and bad training. You've always got to look in the mirror."

Dickinson is on a roll these days, and he is at Hollywood Park this week with his grass horse Bowman Mill, a 5-year-old son of Kris S. who will run on Saturday in the $250,000 Hollywood Turf Cup. In 10 races for Dr. John Chandler, Bowman Mill has never run a bad one, while winning four and finishing second three times over seven different grass courses. He is Cetawayo's younger brother.

This is Bowman Mill's second visit to Southern California. He was at Hollywood Park two years ago, during a wet and dreary November, intent on running in the Hollywood Derby. Dickinson, however, was not completely satisfied with the condition of the Hollywood turf. It didn't take a genius—mad or otherwise—to figure out that the going was difficult. After walking the course and consulting with Chandler, the trainer scratched his horse, turning his back on a $500,000 purse. Now they are back, counting on firm ground, but up against it when compared to the credentials of The Tin Man and the filly Megahertz.

"We'll be 20-to-1," Dickinson said. "We've got a lot left to prove. We won in soft going in Canada, but that is a long way from a Grade I race in California."

Still, strange and wonderful things can happen when a horse is prepared by someone called the Mad Genius.

"Well, they're only half right," Dickinson said. "And you and I know which half."

~~~
~~~

# ALLEN PAULSON

*July 28, 2000*

At the conclusion of the memorial service held for Allen Paulson at the Church of the Nativity in Rancho Santa Fe on Tuesday afternoon, Madeleine Paulson sent a single white dove skyward in tribute to her late husband, closely followed by 99 of its friends, released from white wicker baskets at the edge of the courtyard crowd.

It was an inspiring sight, as the doves swooped into the clear, forming impromptu squadrons and raining down soft white feathers. One of them apparently had more to offer, however, and Paddy Gallagher got in the way, providing a moment of pure racetrack serendipity on an otherwise melancholy day.

"First Allen takes Geri away from me, then one of his birds gets me," Gallagher said, grinning from Irish ear to ear.

Of all the many Paulson trainers in attendance, all of them beneficiaries of the Paulson Thoroughbred empire, the wry Gallagher was the perfect target for such an airborne souvenir. It could have been Bill Mott or Ron McAnally, Gary Jones or Patrick Biancone, Simon Bray, Neil Drysdale, or even Alex Hassinger.

There were celebrity targets as well. With a slightly different trajectory, the bird could have nailed a corporate giant, like Lee Iacocca or Marty Wygod, Bob Lewis or R. D. Hubbard, John Mabee or Dick Duchossois, Carl Icahn or Gary Biszantz.

The head dove-wrangler, mortified by the splash on Gallagher's jacket, apologized profusely and scrubbed it with a cloth, promising the bemused trainer a lifetime of dry-cleaning. Gallagher tried to get the point across that such an accident was considered very good luck around the racetrack, and tantamount to a heavenly blessing if the receiver is leading a horse over for a stakes race.

"I told Paddy he should supplement something for the Pacific Classic," said Gary Jones, who was standing next to Gallagher when the shot was fired. "He couldn't lose."

Allen Paulson, who died the night of July 19 after taking cancer deep into the 15th round, was not a big believer in superstition and luck, racetrack or otherwise.

"One thing I will always remember Allen saying was that he never met a lazy, lucky guy," recalled Clay Lacy, Paulson's friend and fellow pilot, during one of several eulogies.

The combination of Paulson's hard work and America's romance with aviation landed the Iowa farmboy in rarefied circles. Down here on the ground, where a balanced checkbook or loose change in the couch give rise to great celebration, the rest of us get a little dizzy trying to grasp the scope of Paulson's dealings and the people with whom he traded.

Iacocca, who purchased Gulfstream Aerospace from Paulson when he was head of Chrysler, told the tale of a coy Paulson diversion during negotiations that drove the pricetag from $625 million to $636 million. As a result, Paulson had more cash to spend on racehorses, and Iacocca had an $11 million anecdote to share with his friends.

Dick Enberg, the respected TV broadcaster and Paulson's neighbor, tried to sum up his friend in a few choice words.

"It may sound politically incorrect these days, but Allen was a man's man," Enberg said.

True enough. And one of Paulson's rules of being a man's man was being a gentle man, in every sense of the word. How else do we explain his devotion to Frosty, Lucky, and Angel? Paulson's improbable trio of standard French poodles went with him literally everywhere—on the Gulfstream, in the helicopter, fighting for the prime spot next to their master in the golf cart.

The three dogs were holding court at the Del Mar Country Club, freshly shampooed and barbered and looking slightly lost, as friends and family gathered after the memorial service. The place was decorated with the trappings of Paulson's many achievements. The emphasis was on fast horses and fast planes, and how the Paulson legacy would be carried on by his wife, and the horses they bred together.

Then, without warning, two dots appeared in the sky to the north, heading right for the crowd. More dots appeared, and as they grew larger, they became fighter planes, Lear jets and Gulfstreams. At some point a throbbing Sikoursky helicopter joined the fun, hovering over the first tee and threatening to land, while high above them a majestic bomber sailed past at its own special elevation.

The jets buzzed low over the 18th green and past the clubhouse, filling the air with their engine screams. People rushed onto the patio terraces for a better view. Then the jets disappeared over the hills to the south, banking east for a wide, distant turn, and it was suddenly still. Three hundred people, faces upturned, and all conversation had ceased. It was a moment of silence in the finest sense, the perfect farewell for a quiet man.

Then the jets returned, lower and louder than before. To his credit, Gallagher never flinched.

~~~

## LEFTY NICKERSON

*December 26, 2000*

It was about 5:30 on the backstretch at Santa Anita last Thursday morning when the phone in Richard Mandella's stable office started to ring. The sound was unlikely at such an hour.

But then, Christmas was approaching, so maybe it was some early riser with a holiday message of good will for the trainer and his crew. There was also the first day of the Santa Anita Park meeting right around the corner, and Mandella was poised with 2000 Haskell winner Dixie Union for the opening-day Malibu Stakes. Perhaps the caller wanted to deliver a wish for good luck and success.

"You start winning any races yet?"

It was Lefty, calling from New York.

"Yeah," Mandella replied, indignation in his voice. "As a matter of fact I won a couple races last week."

"What kind of races?" Lefty needed more.

"Maidens," Mandella answered.

"You'll have to do better than that," Lefty shot back. "I'm expecting a pretty good Christmas bonus this year."
~~~

Victor J. Nickerson, the man known far and wide as Lefty, was in good form. His sardonic sense of humor was hitting on all cylinders, and Mandella was glad to hear it.

"He can feel a little sorry for himself sometimes," Mandella said. "But he's been good lately. Really giving it to me."

If anyone has a right to a taste of self-pity, it's Nickerson. After a training career of nearly 40 years—highlighted by horses like John Henry, Big Spruce, Magazine, High Tribute, Globe, and Reinvested—Nickerson suffered a stroke in February of 1996 that nearly claimed his life and left him partially paralyzed.

To his everlasting credit, Nickerson has battled back from the initial depression brought on by his sudden illness. He has worked hard to regain some of the use of one arm and one leg. And, thank goodness, he learned how to talk again. He can't outrun you and he'd probably lose a pillow fight, but his brilliant mind and bone-dry wit are both still firmly in place.

"I'm feeling a little bit better," Nickerson said last Saturday morning from Smithtown, in Suffolk County on Long Island, where he has lived with his daughter since being released from those first, terrible weeks of hospitalization.

"My left side is still paralyzed, but I'm working hard on that," he said. "It's rough, I'll tell you that. But my spirits have been good. You're never down for the count as long as you can breathe."

And as long as you can laugh in the face of adversity. Or at least spit in its eye. A couple of years ago, an acquaintance of Nickerson's was surprised to see his old friend in a wheelchair at the races in New York.

"What happened to you?" the man wanted to know. Nickerson's reply was deadpan perfect.

"Mad cow disease."

Sitting upright remains a painful chore for Nickerson, limiting his ability to travel much farther than his spacious backyard on warm days, or short car hops when necessary. When he is not putting himself through an exercise routine, Nickerson can be found in his comfortable chair, getting his fill of the world through television.

It was with a certain amount of trepidation, however, that Nickerson's caller inquired as to what kind of TV shows were keeping him entertained these days. This is the same guy who once ditched The Jockey Club Ball because he said he couldn't miss *Mork & Mindy*.

"I like sumo wrestling," Nickerson said. "I especially like the girl wrestlers. I'd hate to feed them, though."

Nickerson spent most of his career in New York, yet there is a deep streak of California in his bones. He traveled the Western racing circuit in his youth, hauling horses to places like Ryana Ranch in what is now the suburban sprawl of the San Fernando Valley. In 1988, Nickerson moved his stable to California, where he eventually was reunited with one of his earliest clients, Marty Wygod.

When he was stricken, Nickerson was just beginning a second career training the young horses at Wygod's River Edge Ranch in the Santa Ynez Valley. Wygod's considerable success since then—with runners like Exotic Wood, Tranquility Lake, Twice the Vice, Smooth Player, and Benchmark—could have been Nickerson's to share. But the patron has not forgotten his trainer and close friend. As far as Wygod is concerned, Nickerson always will be on the payroll.

As for Mandella, he could slip Nickerson a bonus every Christmas from now until eternity and never repay his debt. Mandella's two years as Nickerson's assistant in the early 1970s remain the most important of a career that is now heading for the Hall of Fame.

"Nobody taught me more than Lefty," Mandella will tell you. "And not just about training horses, cither. I learned a lot about life from him, too."

A few years ago, Nickerson got wind of such kind words from Mandella's lips. His reaction?

"Gratitude is nice," Lefty said. "But when is he going to send money?"

~~~
~~~

THE ONE AND ONLY...

# JIMMY JONES

*June 13, 2001*

Jimmy Jones lifted his head from his hospital bed pillow and reached out with a speckled left hand. His handshake was firm. He held it a long time. He peppered his guest with greetings.

"Good to see you. Come sit down. When did you get in? How long can you stay?"

His voice was gravelly, but strong enough so that every word was heard, and it rang like sweet music to the ears of anyone who believed the stories circulating a few weeks earlier that had the 94-year-old Hall of Famer knocking on death's door. If he was, no one bothered to answer.

"I'm feeling better," Jones said. "Have a seat. Did you eat yet? Don't know what they've got around here. Wish I could take you up to the house."

For a man due to turn 95 next November, Jones was doing pretty well until he got back to Parnell in April from his traditional winter in Miami. Since then, he has been battling symptoms of pneumonia and circulatory problems in his legs, while suffering what his doctors suspect have been a series of mild strokes that have taken a toll on his normally high energy level. He has been hospitalized for nearly a month.

"There was a time there a few weeks back I thought we might lose him," said Hale Sanders, a close friend of Jones since childhood. "But he's tough. He's been getting a little stronger every day."

"Well, I don't know," Jones said. "My heart valve keeps making a funny noise."

"The time to worry is when it stops making that noise," Sanders replied.

It was okay to laugh, now that Jones was showing signs of improvement. Still, he has a daily battle on his hands.

"Never been in a hospital this long before," Jones said. "Had Legionnaires' disease and beat it. Had that heart valve put in about 20 years ago. I guess I'll stay right here until they tell me I can go."

Even flat on his back, dressed in hospital garb and sporting a plastic bracelet that reads "Horace Jones," this was still the real Jimmy Jones,

Thoroughbred racing's ambassador-at-large, glad-handing politico, and gracious host, not to mention the trainer of Citation, Iron Liege, Tim Tam, Miz Clementine, Two Lea, and a Hall of Fame full of Calumet Farm champions.

Horace Allyn Jones, nicknamed Jim Crow as a boy, always has been a chatty gadfly who has borne witness to nearly a century's worth of racing history. He has also made his share of it along the way.

Even while laboring in the shadow of his famous father, Ben A. Jones, Jimmy managed to carve out a proud reputation of his own. To those who knew them, the two men were as different as night and day. Ben was a big man, a thick six-footer with a hard, flat face and a manner that brooked no nonsense. Jimmy was short and on the round side, with a beaming countenance that always seemed more comfortable when fitted with a smile.

Still, there may have been those in the public who grew confused over which was which, B. A. or H. A., when noting the trainer of some Calumet Farm monster. Their names appeared interchangeably on such runners as Real Delight, Wistful, Coaltown, and Bewitch, depending upon where they were trained. After a while it didn't really matter. The son learned from the father, and the father relied on the son. They were known as simply the Jones Boys, a handle that became synonymous with unprecedented success at the highest national levels. Two Triple Crown winners, eight Kentucky Derby winners, and four different runners hailed as Horse of the Year in a span of eight seasons. No one has ever done it better.

Since June 13, 1961, there has been only one Jones boy. Ben Jones died that day in Lexington, Kentucky, after a long battle with the effects of diabetes. He was 78. His body was returned to his hometown of Parnell, a small farming community in the northwest corner of Missouri that was built by his father, the original Horace Jones. After a ceremony at Parnell Methodist Church, Ben Jones was buried on a knoll in Rose Hill Cemetery alongside his wife, Etta, who had died two years earlier. The minister and his wife sang "Shall We Gather at the River." Among the casket bearers for Ben Jones were his cousins Frank Jones and Austin Felton, and his good friends Ted and Paul Sanders.

Forty years later, almost to the day, Paul's son Hale sat at the hospital bedside of Jimmy Jones and reminisced about old times, when Ben Jones was the main man in Parnell and Ted Sanders was a smooth operator in Kansas City politics. "Tell 'em about the goats," Hale said. "Up at the track in Omaha."

"Oh, those goats," Jones moaned. "They belonged to Frank McClain, a big man, hands as big as your head. Would fight all the time."

"Wore a 15-gallon Stetson, he was so big," said Hale, who just happens to be married to McClain's granddaughter.

"I had a new Ford," Jones went on. "I was fond of that car. Parked it outside the barn at Omaha that I shared with Frank. I walked out and every goat in the world was dancing around on my car. Frank's goats. Sharp little feet just tearing it to pieces. Frank never did a thing about it. Wasn't the type of fellow to apologize."

Sanders laughed. Jones smiled, and for a moment they were both 70 years younger, back to the days before Calumet Farm, when Ben and Jimmy Jones hauled their Missouri-bred racehorses from a train siding in Parnell, all over the West, from Tijuana and Juarez in Mexico, to the prairie provinces of Canada.

"Remember Rattlesnake Hill?" Jones was digging deep now, to a notorious border landmark south of San Diego. "My father bet a guy named Red Meat five dollars he could bring back a rattlesnake. Dad went off and came back a little while later trailing a rattler by the head. Hell yes, it was alive. That was the bet.

"Three weeks," Jones went on. "That's how long it took to get to Tijuana. We kept the horses in the cars. They did better that way. Just cleaned 'em and fed 'em. Made a sweat box for us boys to sleep in. Pushed tack up against the horses and stacked bicycles on top. Worked fine for us. We didn't know any better."

What they knew how to do was win races, at first for their own Jones Stock Farm and then for Herb Woolf of Kansas City. By the time the Joneses were hired by the Calumet Farm of Warren and Lucille Wright in 1939, they had already won the 1938 Kentucky Derby for Woolf with a bad-footed colt named Lawrin. Among the colts in their first batch of

Calumet Farm 2-year-olds was the lugging-out head case Whirlaway, winner of the 1941 Triple Crown.

Ben Jones did pretty much one thing his whole life. He was a horse trainer. Jimmy, on the other hand, found the world to be a larger, more interesting place. He attended Northwest Missouri Teachers College for two years in the 1920s. He dabbled briefly with the idea of a veterinary career. He served as mayor of Parnell for a term during the depths of the Depression. And, at the age of 36, he enlisted in the Coast Guard during World War II.

By the time Jones left the service, he was ready to plow heart and soul into the fortunes of Calumet. In 1947, Ben assumed the title of Calumet general manager, and Jimmy ran the racing stable. That season, Jimmy Jones more than doubled the previous record for earnings by a trainer on the strength of a stable that included 2-year-old champions Citation and Bewitch and Horse of the Year Armed. His total topped $1.3 million. The old record was $601,660, held by Ben Jones.

Jimmy Jones retired from the Calumet Farm job in 1964. He'd had enough of the grind, and he had a pretty good offer from Monmouth Park to sit behind a desk as the director of the racing department. He lasted at Monmouth until the end of 1976, and for the last 25 years Jones has spent his second retirement in ready availability for just about any racing cause or event.

Now he is in St. Francis Hospital in Maryville, Missouri, a town of about 10,000 located a couple hours north of Kansas City and 20 miles southwest of tiny Parnell. Whether or not Jones ever leaves St. Francis is up to his legs. Without them, he will never be able to negotiate all the twists and turns of his stately brick home in Parnell, built in 1904 by his grandfather.

"He loves that old house, and every tree on the grounds," said Hale Sanders.

Sometimes, when Jones has spent too long in the company of hospital visitors who summon up stories of the past, he will grow weary and imagine that he is back home in Parnell, sitting in his easy chair in the corner of his favorite room, surrounded by the memories of a lifetime in a racing wonderland. It is easy to understand why.

# JOE HIRSCH

*October 31, 2003*

The item in today's paper is brief and to the point. Joe Hirsch, journalist by trade, will write his final column for *Daily Racing Form* later this month. November was already turning cold and damp. Now this.

The news will be greeted far and wide with a sigh of the inevitable. Some things simply are not made to last. Laffit Pincay was supposed to ride forever. Bill Shoemaker should never say good-bye. Joe Hirsch, racing's clarion voice, could never call it a day.

But he will.

"I'm packing it in," Hirsch said this week from his home in Manhattan. "I have to do it. I can't do any more work."

Joe Hirsch is 74. He has been working since 1948, the year he emerged from New York University with a degree in journalism he put to use briefly for the *New York Times* and then for the *Morning Telegraph*, sister publication of *Daily Racing Form*. After four years in the service, Hirsch picked up where he left off. The Army's loss was racing's gain.

"Anyone can make history," wrote Oscar Wilde. "Only a great man can write it." He wasn't necessarily referring to Joe Hirsch—the two men never actually met—but the sentiment certainly applies.

More than a journalist, Hirsch has borne witness to an age and left its tales etched in stone. His tireless chronicling has captured both the shifting winds of a restless industry and the bedrock values that give Thoroughbred racing its permanent place in the heart.

Hirsch filed his first major pieces for *Daily Racing Form* in 1954, nearly half a century ago. If that seems like only yesterday, Hirsch must suffer a large part of the blame. The characters who populated his stories in the 1950s seem every bit alive today as they were back then, when horse racing fancied itself a rich man's pastime populated by cowboys, hardboots, and card sharps.

"Racing just has so many great people," Hirsch told the equine magazine *Spur* in 1981. "They're simply more mature than the people in other sports, and they always have a story. In baseball, for example, you have so many teams and so many players and a lot of them are spoiled and don't like to talk. But racing involves a leveling process. It's probably the only sport where if you're in it a long time, you have to lose more than you win. And that's a very humbling experience for people who can't stand to lose, so you'll find those people getting out of it very quickly. Very few people who stay around any length of time aren't nice."

Joe Hirsch treats all people as if they might be nice, or at least as though they showed some potential. And while it cannot be said that Hirsch invented the benefit of the doubt, he puts it to very good use. How else could he have functioned, for 36 seasons, dutifully recording some of mankind's most fantastic dreams in his annual version of the Yellow Brick Road? He called it "Derby Doings."

"The Kentucky Derby is indeed bigger than life," Hirsch wrote in his introduction to the handsome *Kentucky Derby: the Chance of a Lifetime*, a vibrant telling of the Derby legend. "I have yet to find an individual who was not affected by the experience."

Straight-faced, drawing upon a moral discipline that has served him so well, Hirsch would put forth the stories of hopeless Derby longshots and their semi-delusional owners and trainers, giving them equal rights to a brief place in the sun alongside the brahmins of the game. It was up to the readers to call them names and rue the way they cluttered the field. Hirsch, for his part, never wasted time sitting in judgment.

"There's always something in racing. Always something new," Hirsch said this week. "Racing has a resiliency . . . that's why I love it so much."

The same can be said of the man who delivered the line. Resilient, consistent, thoroughly professional, and passionately fair, Joe Hirsch has set standards his fellow writers can only hope to approximate. As the iconic figure among racing journalists, he is intimidating quite by accident. Nothing could be further from his intent. Joe Hirsch has awakened each morning for the past 50 years wondering how he would share his gift of horse racing on this particular day.

"It's really easy to find people who Joe Hirsch has helped," columnist Skip Bayless told *Spur* long ago. "A better story would be to find somebody he hasn't helped."

Or inspired. Or comforted. Or blessed with a simple word of encouragement. It never took much from Joe—just a simple nod, or his hand on your arm. A few years ago, in the midst of another chaotic Derby scene, Hirsch slipped quietly into the chair next to a daydreaming colleague and placed a small velvet box on the table.

"I thought you might be able to put these to use," he said.

Inside the box, nestled in a groove, rested a pair of plain gold cufflinks. They were square in shape and bore traces of regular wear. In the center of each was the block-lettered monogram "JH."

Stunned, the dumbstruck recipient looked up to choke out a thank-you, but Joe was gone, back to his desk.

Back to work.

~~~

# JOHN NERUD

*June 1, 2005*

John Nerud stood on the back patio of his classically simple Long Island home, its two roomy stories sitting serenely upon ten well-minded acres in the gentle hills above the village of Glen Cove. Nerud's thick shock of white hair collected a spritz of the light morning mist as his gaze moved from the distant field that doubled as a practice golf hole, past the tall stand of windbreak trees, to the expansive lawn beyond the deck, where his son was married and the Nerud clan would gather. The only thing missing was the horses.

"Horses?" Nerud exclaimed. "Nope, no horses. If I had horses here I'd have to take care of them, wouldn't I? But I do wake up every morning and wonder, how the hell did I put all this together?"

The answer, at least in part, was displayed inside on the walls of the bright, airy rooms. Photographs and paintings of horses hung everywhere, leaving no doubts about their speed, their class, or the identity of the man who helped them realize their fullest potential. And while their exploits took place far and wide, at racetracks all over North America,
~~~

it was clear from the small print that John Nerud made his greatest and everlasting mark on the Thoroughbred world embraced by the racing emporiums of New York.

New York is where Nerud won his classic, the 1957 Belmont Stakes with Gallant Man. New York is where Nerud's finest horse, the incomparable Dr. Fager, burned brightest. And New York is where Nerud has been enshrined in Thoroughbred Racing's Hall of Fame for the past 35 years. Not bad for a farm boy from a dusty corner of western Nebraska.

Nerud's ascent to the big time began more than half a century ago, marked by a courteous word from the trainer to his good friend Louis Smith, the impresario of New Hampshire's Rockingham Park. Nerud had been a regular on the New England circuit since his pre-war days as a jockey agent, then his post-war emergence as a trainer of increasing visibility. His reputation in Chicago and Florida was growing as well, and by the end of 1955, he was becoming known as a man who could win races with any kind of horse. The time, figured Nerud, was ripe for the biggest jump of all, since New York was where the serious money lived.

"I won't be back next year," Nerud told Smith. "I'm gonna try and get me some of the Big Apple."

And what a bite it was. Nerud's everlasting mark on the last half of horse racing's 20th century was accomplished from his headquarters at Belmont Park, from which issued the talented runners of such patrons as Ralph Lowe (Texas oil), Joe Roebling (New York construction), and William McKnight (Minnesota Mining & Manufacturing). No celebration of Belmont's 100th birthday would be complete without a nod toward Nerud's influence over the Belmont scene, which commenced roughly with Gallant Man's Belmont and continues to this day, in his so-called retirement, as adviser to the breeding operation of Sugar Maple Farm, one of New York State's leading establishments.

A visit with Nerud always begins and ends with Dr. Fager. In between, however, lies a saga of bedrock Americana. One of nine children, Nerud was raised dirt-poor by modern standards, but was richly endowed with ambition, and rarely let circumstance get in the way. From his earliest, scuffling days as a cagey horse trader and all-around hand, he eventually escaped the Great Plains of the Depression to dine with industry's giants and drive to work in a chauffeured Lincoln Continental.

"If you were smart, you never tried to be something you're not," Nerud likes to say. "I'm just an old groom, an old country boy come from the ranch. I can't be anything different and be myself. If you're big, somebody will recognize it. As far as I'm concerned, I'm 92 and I still remember my name."

His name, and then some. Just ask him a question and listen to Nerud roll. Always outspoken, frank to a fault, possessed of a memory that refuses to fade, Nerud has been described through the years by some of racing's most respected journalists as "that fresh little cowboy" (Jack Mann in the *Washington Star*), a "feisty little maverick" (Red Smith of the *New York Times*), and "a cattle baron whose haberdashery has an éclat as yet undreamed on Carnaby Street" (Charles Hatton, the dean of *Daily Racing Form*).

According to family history, Nerud's paternal grandfather migrated from Prague to Germany, then sailed for New York City in 1862 upon the ascension of the warlike German foreign minister Otto von Bismarck.

"He was learning to be an ironsmith, which is a blacksmith, but Bismarck ordered every student to serve time in the army," Nerud said, sitting behind the utilitarian desk of his no-frills office. "How he got from New York to Nebraska I don't know, but there were a lot of Czechs and Poles farming out there at that time.

"He was there with a small ranch at the last real Indian uprising," Nerud went on. "Everybody ran but him. Neighbors would come by with their wagons—in the summer the wooden wheels shrank because of the heat, and the rims would get loose—and he knew how to tighten them. They'd say, 'You can have anything you want, just tighten our rims so we can get out of here.'

"He'd dig a hole by the house, and when the Indians come, he'd put his wife and two kids in the hole and cover them with tumbleweeds. Then he'd go meet the Indians—warriors in full paint—and they wanted fresh horses. So they took his best horses, left the old ones, and never shot him. That took a lot of guts."

Nerud was a teenager by the time of the 1929 stock-market crash that triggered America's deepest economic crisis. For a farm kid, a tough life only got tougher.

"They wouldn't believe you, how bad it was," Nerud said. "They couldn't believe you. There was such terrible, terrible destitution."

By his late teens, Nerud was training horses at far-flung fairs in Nebraska, Montana, Wyoming, and the Dakotas, rarely running for more than eating money. But even then, the young horseman knew how to court a patron of influence. His primary owner was Sid Williams, sheriff of neighboring Sioux County.

From there the adventurous Nerud made his way to New Orleans, went bust, tried Mexico and Cuba, then headed back to Florida, always following the scent of racehorses. He eventually wound up in Saratoga Springs—it was 1937—flat broke and sleeping in Congress Park. The same Congress Park just down the Union Avenue from the modern-day Racing Hall of Fame.

That lasted only as long as it took for Nerud to learn that they paid a man a dollar a head to lead a horse from the local railway yard to the Saratoga sales barn. He rubbed jumpers for the Jock Whitney stable and groomed runners for a series of owners and trainers before someone suggested he take a jockey's book as agent. One of his first clients was the young, future Hall of Famer Ted Atkinson.

He also met a Boston girl named Charlotte Fitzgerald—Atkinson married her best friend, Martha Shank— but before they could even knock the dust off the dowry, the Japanese attacked Pearl Harbor and, in Nerud's words, "I went to work for my uncle."

Nerud spent his three-year tour with the Navy on transport ships hauling troops, munitions, and equipment around the Pacific Theater, as the American forces hopped from one bloody island encounter to the next.

"People can't believe the depravity those soldiers went through on those islands," Nerud recalled. "After moving troops from island to island, every nine months or so we'd load up with wounded and come back.

"We never got into real bad fighting, but we never had an escort, either," Nerud went on. "We were assigned to a Dutch ship, could run maybe 18 or 19 knots, and we had a captain that was a magician. Greatest man I ever saw sail a ship.

"One night we're steaming full ahead," Nerud said. "I was on the bridge, because I was a signalman. Captain come up and I could tell he was nervous. 'Han,' he said—which is what he called me because my initials were J-A-N—'Han, I think there's an island in front of us. Forty degrees to port.' 'What does the map say?' I asked. 'Map no good,' he says. 'Made by Einsteins in San Francisco.' In about an hour the sun come up and here's the island. He had instinct."

War stays with a man for life. But Nerud, never shy, left an unmistakable wake as a sailor who spoke his mind.

"We were loading another boat in San Francisco," Nerud recalled, "and Roosevelt comes on and says, 'Someone has accused me of loading ammunition with troops. I promise your mothers that I would never load ammunition on the same ship as troops.'

"Well, there we are, loading equipment, ammunition, and soldiers. I said, 'Listen to that old lying sonofabitch.' So here comes the ensign. 'You can't call the commander in chief a lying sonofabitch. I might have to put you in the brig.' I said, 'Now that would be a disaster. I wouldn't have to go back to the South Pacific, would I?' "

Mustered out and reunited with Charlotte, Nerud dove right back into horse racing. He made his first headlines between 1948 and 1950 while training the Woolford Farm runners of Herbert Woolf, the owner who put Ben A. Jones on the map with Kentucky Derby winner Lawrin. The stable campaigned in Florida, Chicago, and New England, and was led by Delegate, who earned a share of the national sprint championship in 1949.

"They trained hard then, and horses were lean as a hound," Nerud said. "We bred them sound and flinty, but the horses didn't run as fast, or exert themselves as much as they do today. But they ran. They took the pressure and they ran.

"When I took over Woolford Farm, Ben Jones came down and said, 'Son, you ain't got enough sense to train these horses, so I'm going to tell you what to do.' "—here it should be noted that Nerud is doing a dead-on nasally Ben Jones impression—" 'You feed 'em good, keep 'em fat, and work 'em a half a mile. They're gonna win in spite of you.'

"He was right, and I never changed," Nerud went on. "Later on, when I came to New York with a public stable, I watched John Gaver work Tom Fool a mile and a quarter faster than he won the race. All the old-line trainers did it that way. There I was working my horses half a mile—and starting to beat 'em! That's when they started calling me 'that half a mile sonofabitch.' "

The iconoclast was in his element, winning races and running his Belmont stable with nothing like the somber decorum of The Jockey Club trainers around him. Chances are, you could hear a Nerud set coming from half a pole away.

"I let my people talk, have some fun," Nerud said. "You had to let them have a good time. People don't realize the horse has to be happy. They like a little B.S. too. And I didn't mind hiring drunks, if they can control themselves in the morning. But did you ever see one of my horses that wasn't on a loose rein, or somebody snatching on a horse? No, you didn't."

It is safe to say that John Nerud never made a move without a plan, which is why his story of success can be traced to an almost unbroken daisy-chain of good horses, patrons, and smart deals.

His work with the solid handicap horse Switch On in 1955 and early 1956 attracted the attention of Ralph Lowe, who sent Nerud a draft of runners that included an underachieving maiden 2-year-old that had been purchased from the Aga Khan. His name was Gallant Man.

Gentle as a puppy but precociously fast, Gallant Man soon revealed to Nerud that he was a distance horse in disguise. Nerud began to train the colt with the 1957 classics in mind.

"The Kentucky Derby is the biggest race we have, and there's no use saying it ain't," Nerud said. "I thought Gallant Man could win it."

He was, in fact, on his way to winning the Derby when his rider, Bill Shoemaker, mistook the sixteenth pole at Churchill Downs for the winning post. Shoemaker stopped riding Gallant Man just long enough to give Bill Hartack and Iron Liege the break they needed to win by a nose. Shoemaker's uncharacteristic miscue became the racing story of the year.

"He was the greatest rider who ever lived," Nerud said. "He did things on horses nobody else could do. I still don't know what happened. All I asked was for him to admit he pulled up the horse, and he did. I rode him right back on the horse and he won the Belmont. You can't hold grudges, because it will kill you."

The 1957 exploits of Gallant Man—which also featured wins in the Travers and the Peter Pan in New York—prompted industrialist William McKnight to contact Nerud about training some horses. They came to terms, but before long Nerud began to think big. The trainer proposed an operating strategy that would put McKnight on firm ground in both breeding and racing. Nerud even vowed to invest his own money. McKnight agreed, and Nerud rolled the dice, buying a Florida farm and spending $650,000 on the potential stallion Intentionally, a son of Intent with proven distance limitations.

Nerud proved those limitations wrong by winning the nine-furlong Seminole Handicap of 1962 at Hialeah with Intentionally, beating 1961 Derby winner Carry Back by eight lengths in the bargain. Intentionally was immediately retired to stud in Ocala, where Nerud was building McKnight's bloodstock empire on ground once owned by Bonnie Heath, the man behind Derby winner Needles. Besides Intentionally, there would be the 14-year-old stallion Rough'n Tumble and a collection of mares known more for their racing credentials than their pedigrees. One of them was named Aspidistra.

"I took solid racemares—they didn't have to be stakes winners—and bred them to a horse worth three times what they were worth," Nerud said. "The people in Kentucky went crazy, seeing me do that. They said, 'John, you'll never get out on that foal.' But I wasn't looking to get out. I was looking for a racehorse. And I was giving the mare a chance.

"Today we're not breeding with any intelligence," Nerud continued. "We're breeding with only one thing in mind—the sales ring sign at Fasig-Tipton and Keeneland. The only thing we look at is the flash on the board—$200,000, $300,000.

"When I came around, the breeding was controlled by the families of The Jockey Club. They culled with a sharp knife, and they only bred to the tops. They never sent a horse to stud unless they thought he was some sort of a champion. When 'Sunny' Jim Fitzsimmons would run a Phipps family mare in a claiming race, everyone would think, 'There's a helluva broodmare prospect.' She wasn't. Old man Fitz recognized a broodmare, and so did I."

By now the record is crystal clear. A legion of quality animals can be traced to the John Nerud master plan, including such major stakes winners and champions as Ta Wee, Dr. Patches, Cozzene, Fappiano, Codex, Ruffled Feathers, Western Warrior, Who's for Dinner, and Clabber Girl. The list must also feature Unbridled, the 1990 Kentucky Derby winner who was a son of Fappiano and a great-grandson of Intentionally, bred by McKnight's Tartan Farm and raced by Frances Genter.

The jewel in the crown of the Nerud legacy is Dr. Fager, the most comprehensive champion in the history of the sport. He was an animal of pure Nerud breeding, a son of the Tartan Farm sire Rough'n Tumble and the salvaged mare Aspidistra. In 1968, as a 4-year-old colt, Dr. Fager was acclaimed North America's best sprinter, best handicap horse, best grass horse, and Horse of the Year. He carried weight, torched track records, and established a one-mile standard for the dirt that still stands after 37 years. And he did it carrying an unthinkable 134 pounds.

Nerud speaks of Dr. Fager as he would a brother, a son, or the deepest lifelong friend.

"Dr. Fager was the fastest horse I ever saw," Nerud said. "He just kept that long stride going, and just kept laying on you, and could go the first three-quarters in seven. He didn't want to be hit or abused. He just wanted to be left alone to do his own thing. And he'd do the best he could."

Dr. Fager lost only three of his 22 races: once on a knee that was beginning to bother him at the end of his 2-year-old season, and twice when the opposition used pace-making "rabbits" to hound him out of the gate before retreating to the back of the field. He was also disqualified from a lopsided victory in the 1967 Jersey Derby for a gross jockey error right after the start.

"There never was a horse in the world who could run with him and win," Nerud said. "They didn't enter those rabbits with the intention of winning, but you just couldn't take him off them. That was just him."

In April of 1967, Dr. Fager came off a six-month break to beat Derby favorite Damascus in the Gotham Stakes at Aqueduct. Coming off a bout of colic, he beat Damascus again in the 1968 Suburban Handicap at Aqueduct while carrying 132 pounds. In the 1968 United Nations Handicap at Atlantic City, Dr. Fager slipped and skidded through his only grass race to beat Advocator by a neck. And then there was the 1968 Californian at Hollywood Park, which seemed worth the travel trouble, since the purse was ripe and the weight assignment was a merciful 126 pounds. Or so Nerud was told.

"John, I've got some bad news," said Bob Benoit, Hollywood Park's top publicist, when Dr. Fager arrived two days before the race. "They calculated wrong in the racing office. Your horse carries 130."

Nerud took a deep breath and bit his tongue.

"That's okay, Bob, we came to run," Nerud replied. "Besides, I'm just as much to blame for not checking the weight myself."

In the Californian, before a grateful West Coast crowd, Dr. Fager beat champion mare Gamely by three lengths.

"You could see that day, going down the backstretch, the other horses were taking a stride and a half to his one," Nerud recalled. "It hardly seemed fair."

There is more to the Dr. Fager tale, however, than just a man and the brilliant horse he trained. They were also linked by Nerud's own mortality.

On an early morning at Belmont Park, in October of 1965, Nerud fell from his pony, Nebraska, during one of those tangled moments when someone's loose horse disrupts the normal decorum of training hours. Nerud struck his head hard on the ground, but true to the tough guy code, he soon went on about his business.

Within weeks, however, Charlotte Nerud became increasingly worried over her husband's health. He was becoming lethargic, inattentive, and withdrawn—in short, all the things the real John Nerud definitely was not. When the symptoms became worse, Charlotte took action, contacted friends back home in Boston to get the name of a specialist, and loaded John on a plane from New York.

In short order, Nerud was hospitalized and under the knife to relieve the pressure of a subdural hematoma—a blood clot on his brain. In reporting on the procedure, this is what the surgeon found:

"The skull was penetrated and the opening expanded widely enough to gain a good exposure of the dura, tense and overly dark, distended by the pressure of blood accumulated between it and the brain beneath. A small incision in the dural surface yielded the expected rush of chocolaty fluid spurting over the drape-covered scalp. After a second skull opening, the full extent of the liquefied hematoma could be seen and aspirated, exposing the right side of the brain indented, depressed deeply within the cranial cavity, and obscured in places by patches of more solid clot with its currant-jelly appearance."

The surgeon went on to affix a small drain that continued to remove the fluid and relieve pressure on Nerud's brain. The procedure was described as "brisk and simple—as familiar and routine to neurosurgeons as any operation could be." It also saved Nerud's life.

Weeks later, as he was being discharged from the hospital, Nerud promised the surgeon that, in gratitude, he would name a horse in his honor. The surgeon knew very little about the world of horse racing, but he appreciated the gesture and bade his patient farewell.

"I've still got five holes in my skull where they did the surgery," Nerud said. "Got one hole when I talk you can feel my brain vibrate."

The man who drilled those holes heard that and smiled.

"Well, actually there was only two pretty good-sized holes, but if we hadn't gotten to John at that point, he would not have made it through the night without slipping into a coma," Dr. Charles A. Fager recalled, from his Boston-area home. "If that had happened, there could have been permanent damage, or worse. Fortunately, we got it soon enough."

Nerud made good on his promise, and one year later, Charles Fager read the news about the 2-year-old colt Dr. Fager winning the important Cowdin Stakes in New York.

"The medical profession in those days was quite different from what it is today," said Dr. Fager, now 81. "In those days you just didn't advertise. Once the horse gained a measure of fame, I had many offers to come see him race, but I turned them down. I tried to keep it as quiet as I could."

His family, on the other hand, was having a ball. Fager's children collected newspaper clippings by the bushel as their father's famous namesake raced through his remarkable career. Fager himself enjoyed a sterling reputation, with a Supreme Court justice, a Boston mayor, and baseball great Ted Williams among his high-profile patients.

None of them, however, named a champion racehorse after their neurosurgeon. Fager remained a friend of the Nerud family and eventually watched Dr. Fager run on several occasions. In retirement, Charles Fager gave the story everlasting life in a memoir he called *A Hole in the Wind—the Story of a Man and His Horse*, published in 2004.

"John has thanked me many times through the years," Fager noted. "He's made contributions to an endowment that bears my name, established for research. One thing I'll never forget, though, was what John said when my son Jeff wanted to go to work for him at Belmont. It bothered me that he would be exposed to a mix of people who might be taking drugs, doing a lot of gambling. John said simply, 'It ain't gonna hurt him none, doc.' So Jeff worked at the track, and he's is now executive producer of *60 Minutes*."

Dr. Fager, the horse, retired at the end of 1968, while Nerud kept at the training grind for another 10 years. At the end of 1978, he turned over the day-to-day reins of the stable to his son Jan Nerud, and focused his attention on the breeding end of the operation. Before long, he became involved in a project that became known as the Breeders' Cup, serving as a founding member of the board of directors.

"It was all about marketing," Nerud said. "That's why I wanted to head the marketing committee. The Breeders' Cup, you see, was never meant to be just a bunch of good races. It had to be a real event if it was going to be a success."

The debut of the Breeders' Cup in 1984 was a success, thanks in large part to the marketing of the event as a World Series or Super Bowl of Thoroughbred racing. As a midwife to the process, Nerud was rightfully proud. Of course, that didn't stop him from playing the game.

"I insisted they have a mile race in the program," Nerud said. "It only made sense. All the greatest stallions have shown themselves superior at a mile, if nothing else. If it was going to be called the Breeders' Cup, you had to have a race at a mile. Of course, they said I wanted the mile just so I could win it."

And he did. In 1985, the Breeders' Cup made its first appearance in New York when it came to Aqueduct. The $1 million Breeders' Cup Mile attracted an all-star field, stocked with champions from Europe and accomplished Americans. In the end, though, the race belonged to Cozzene, a 5-year-old streak of gray who carried the blood of a treasured Tartan Farm family, along with the red and white colors of his owner, a Nebraska farm boy named John A. Nerud.

Five

# RIDE ON

*Sometimes you've got to wonder why they do it. Why these men and women, most of them with families, commit to the job of being a professional Thoroughbred jockey. Why they risk life and limb for no guaranteed return. If you ask, they'll give you an answer, and if they are honest, it will sound something like this:*

*"It's an extremely selfish thing I'm doing, in many ways very wrong. No one need tell me this. But racing is my occupation, the source of my income and the thing I do best."*

*That was the way Jackie Stewart, the world-champion Formula 1 driver, addressed the question in his memoir,* Faster! *And since the Thoroughbred racehorse is every inch nature's version of the Formula 1 racecar, I'll accept Stewart's point of view. Both are highly tuned to perform at maximum speeds over varying and sometimes treacherous terrain. Also, someone has to drive, or ride.*

*The selections in this chapter stand alone as tributes to those who do the riding. However, in many cases the stories did not end.*

*Chris McCarron went on to start a school for jockeys, figuring that if a young person was determined to do it, they should learn to do it right. Russell Baze, the Iron Man of racing, passed Laffit Pincay's record on the fly and was still adding to his more than 12,000 winners as 2014 dawned. Richie Migliore fulfilled his dream of winning a Breeders' Cup race in 2008, then broke his neck again, and retired to a career as a broadcaster.*

*Eddie Delahoussaye was never able to return from his injury of 2002, as he had hoped, but the retired Gary Stevens did make a return, retired again in 2005, then made an even more unlikely comeback at the age of 50 in 2013.*

*It also is important to understand that J. C. Gonzalez was far from the last North American rider to be killed on the job. As of this writing, another dozen have died in action since Gonzalez went down in September of 1999.*

*"Courage," said Lola Montez, "and shuffle the cards."*

*Chances are, she was talking to a jockey.*

## RICHARD MIGLIORE

*October 26, 2001*

Richie Migliore has a long scar at the base of his throat dating back to early June of 1988, when he needed 8-1/2 hours of surgery to fuse three vertebrae and graft a piece of his hip to the bones in his broken neck. Sometimes, because of the nerve damage, his hands and feet still tingle and go numb.

Migliore has another long scar on the inside of his right forearm and one to match along the outside of the same arm thanks to the two operations required to repair a compound fracture sustained in July of 1999. He still has two steel plates and 16 screws in that arm, and sometimes, when he wrestles with his kids, there will be a twinge of pain he describes as the grating equivalent of "nails on a chalkboard."

Such trauma should have killed or retired Migliore long ago. And there are other, lesser dents and dings, the identifying tattoos of 21 years as a professional jockey. But none of them hurt more than the broken heart he suffered on September 11, 2001, along with millions of other native New Yorkers, when terrorists destroyed the Twin Towers of the World Trade Center.

"It didn't really hit me how emotional I was about the topic until I started putting pen to paper," said Migliore, who wrote a personal commentary about his sense of loss, and hope, for *The Blood-Horse* magazine. "I had to keep pulling up. The flood kept hitting me."

Richard Francis Migliore, the 1981 Eclipse Award–winning apprentice and nine times on top in the New York standings, was born 37 years ago in the Long Island town of Babylon. He was raised in Brooklyn, Bay Shore, and, from the age of 14, on the backstretch of Belmont Park, where he bunked in a tack room at Steve DiMauro's Barn 46.

"Steve got me started and taught me a great deal about the business," Migliore said. "But he didn't just help me to be a good jockey. He helped frame the person I am. He taught me how to be a man."

DiMauro is retired, and now John Kimmel has the barn. The twist of fate is not lost upon Migliore, who considers Kimmel his chief patron and friend.

"That's where I lived, in that room next to the office," Migliore said, nodding toward a spartan bungalow. "It was the ultimate story of running away with the circus. This was my family, and Belmont Park was my backyard."

His roots spread wide as well as deep. Migliore has one brother on the police force in Cold Spring Harbor, another brother who's a sheriff in Islip, and a best friend with the NYPD based in Manhattan South. You get any more New York than Richie Migliore, and you might as well run for mayor.

That's why the terrorist attacks on his city hit him so hard, and not just because he lost a cousin, by marriage, in the collapse of the Twin Towers. Charles Lucania was his name. They do not expect to find his remains.

"I used to take a wine course at Windows on the World," Migliore said Wednesday morning, draw day for the Breeders' Cup. "It was the year I'd broken my neck. I'd go every Monday night, kind of a diversion, because I still wasn't riding. I've been up there so many times, and again last fall, when I just wanted to go up there and look at the city."

He stopped, savoring the bittersweet memory of the breathtaking view.

"It's almost still surreal to me that it actually came down," he said. "This will take a lot of healing."

And there will be scars, just like Migliore's. They are the price he has paid for more than 3,000 wins and the security of his wife, Carmela, and their four children. Joey is 10 and the oldest. He has two younger brothers, Luciano and Philip. Baby sister Gabrielle Rose was born just last month.

"That's it," Migliore promised. "We finally got our girl."

Now, it's time for a Breeders' Cup. For all his success, Migliore has never broken through on the big day. He has had some live mounts—horses like Hidden Lake, Dollar Bill, and End Sweep—but there was only a third with Mourjane in the 1985 Turf to show for it.

He will try to change that on Saturday in the Distaff aboard Spinster Stakes winner Miss Linda, who is trained by Kimmel and owned by Leland and Robert Ackerley. If he does, there will be a genuine celebration for a hometown hero.

"People bandy about that word 'hero' way too much," Migliore said. "Sure, there are inherent risks in what I do. But the risks I take aren't selfless risks. There's monetary rewards. There's glory.

"Then here are guys who run into burning buildings to save lives," he added. "Guys who run toward the bullets, not away from them, to protect and save people's lives at the risk of their own. You can never compare an athlete to what they do, because an athlete has his own agenda. I'm just a guy who's lucky enough to get paid to do something I really enjoy."

~~~

## CHRIS McCARRON

*May 6, 2001*

There are a few things everybody knows about Chris McCarron, beyond the news that just last week he became the latest of only seven jockeys to hit the giddy 7,000-winner mark.

They know about his two Kentucky Derby winners, Alysheba and Go for Gin. They can recite many of his all-star partners, including John Henry, Sunday Silence, Flawlessly, Precisionist, and Glorious Song. And they probably are aware that—at $251 million and counting—McCarron's
~~~

mounts have racked up more money than any other jockey who ever lived.

Those who dig a little deeper know McCarron as a tireless spokesman for jockey welfare and safety. They appreciate the fact that he is a rock-solid family man with a 25-year marriage and three bright daughters, the youngest about to graduate from high school. They recognize him as a thorough professional who tends to his business, makes the right kind of headlines, and admits to no substance abuse more serious than a chronic dependency on golf.

He sounds almost too good.

But then there is the Chris McCarron who once was fined for smacking another jockey with the whip during a race, even though McCarron said it was an absolute accident and every other rider said the transgressing jock had it coming.

Or the Chris McCarron who dressed for a Halloween party in a green leotard, tight green shirt, pointy green hat, and green makeup, then had a great time telling everyone he was the "Jolly Green Condom."

Or the Chris McCarron who was laid out in an Inglewood hospital on the day after breaking both legs and his right arm at Hollywood Park, moaning softly, his hands folded and clutching a rose on his chest. He was milking the moment until his friend, comedian Tim Conway, peeked into the room.

"Is he gone yet?" Conway said, playing along. "We need the bed."

That was 11 years ago. McCarron isn't gone yet. In fact, at the age of 46 he is still very much at the heart of the game, riding top horses, winning the best races, and adding to a personal history that looks pretty good from all angles.

Even when he does not ride, McCarron makes news. Earlier this year, he rode Kentucky Derby contenders Dollar Bill to victory in the Risen Star Stakes at the Fair Grounds and Millennium Wind to win the Santa Catalina Stakes at Santa Anita. Both of them ran in the Derby without him.

"It's not the first time I've missed the Kentucky Derby," McCarron said last week. "But I hope it's the last."

His decision to ride Bienamado in the San Juan Capistrano Handicap rather than Millennium Wind the same day in the Blue Grass Stakes—and hence the Derby—was baffling to many observers. Never mind that Bienamado won his race. McCarron seemed to be giving up a bona fide chance to become one of only eight jockeys to win three or more Derbies.

"Let's just say it was one of the hardest, most complex business decisions I've ever had to make," McCarron said.

"I had very mixed feelings on my way home that day," he added. "I had just won a $400,000 race on what was probably the best grass horse in the country, and I was feeling a little dejected."

He'll get over it. He always has. In terms of sheer persistence, McCarron has few peers. On at least two occasions, he has suffered injuries that could have sent him into retirement, no questions asked.

The worst one came in October of 1986 when he went down in a three-horse pile-up on the final turn at Santa Anita. McCarron would have survived the fall relatively unscathed if he had not been struck square in the upper part of his left leg by a 115-pound projectile named Laffit Pincay. In breaking Pincay's fall, McCarron's hip joint was shattered. Three hours of surgery were required to let him walk. Whether or not he would ever ride again was open to debate.

"It was more pain than I thought was possible," McCarron once said, looking back on the accident.

Less than seven months later, McCarron was back, standing beneath the spires of Churchill Downs draped in Alysheba's Kentucky Derby roses. It was the greatest sports comeback of the year.

Fourteen years later, McCarron remains as determined as ever. His curly red hair has thinned and gone a little gray, and his business has changed to fit these times of smaller fields and richer purses. McCarron rides less now, keying on more quality mounts and riding for a regular core of top-flight trainers, such as reigning Horse of the Year Tiznow for Jay Robbins. As a consequence, McCarron finds himself spending more time watching races than riding them. It would be understandable if he let his attention wander. But then he wouldn't be Chris McCarron.

"It's not as hard for me to stay up, but it is a different challenge to stay fit," he said.

"When business slows down, I find myself going to the gym more. You can find yourself compromising your chances as far as being competitive when you're less than 100 percent fit. When you're coming down the stretch with physical specimens like Pincay and Solis, and some of these younger guys, you've got to be on top of your game."

As an athlete well past age 40, McCarron concedes that he is waiting for his body to start sending messages.

"I really didn't know what to expect," he confessed. "Maybe a diminishing of energy, or strength. But I haven't noticed anything . . . yet."

In terms of style, McCarron looks no different than he did a dozen years ago when he stepped aboard Sunday Silence for the first time and fashioned a masterpiece against Easy Goer in the Breeders' Cup Classic. With McCarron, the intellect always leads the way.

"The only change I've noticed in my riding in the last several years is in terms of attitude," he said. "I think I'm a lot kinder to horses than I used to be. I use the whip more judiciously. I try to coax a horse into doing things rather than using force. Obviously, when force is needed I can resort to that. But I think I've gotten smarter with regard to the treatment of my mounts.

"I don't know if all that equates to being a more successful rider," he added. "But I think I'm a better rider in terms of being a better horseman."

McCarron has tried to be a good citizen of the game, as well. He is a member of the board of directors of Youbet.com because he is convinced that the Internet holds the key to the future of racing. Along with his wife, Judy, he helped found the Don MacBeth Memorial Jockey Fund to aid injured riders. And he has rejoined the Jockeys' Guild as a regional vice president after resigning five years ago over possible conflicts with the aims of the MacBeth Fund.

"I regretted doing that," McCarron said. "I'm not a quitter. I decided to get involved again because it appeared to me that the Guild had not made a lot of progress on jockey issues important to me. I've got some catching up to do, but, hopefully, sometime in the future, I will be able to contribute.

"I'd like to see the Jockeys' Guild engender respect for the jockeys within the industry," he went on. "I think that's lacking greatly. For that matter, I don't think respect has ever been there to any great degree.

"In Europe, for example, and Japan, jockeys are held in much higher esteem than in this country. They are considered a much greater part of the team, and the industry as a whole.

"I'm not trying to point fingers at trainers or owners for slighting us," he added. "I think nowadays jockeys are not given the right kind of foundation at the start of their careers, to be able to have trainers say, 'I'm really grateful to have a bright young kid who's able to help me with my horses.' "

McCarron got his early lessons from the late trainer Odie Clelland, a mid-Atlantic mainstay.

"He instilled in me the knowledge and the confidence that I could converse with horsemen on a horseman's level," McCarron said. "That has really helped throughout my career."

With the boost supplied by Clelland, McCarron took it from there. He does not dwell on his numbers, but he does recall win number 1,000, simply because it came so fast in the midst of his second year of riding. Number 7,000 has put him in rare company alongside Pincay, Bill Shoemaker, Pat Day, Angel Cordero, Dave Gall, and Russell Baze.

"When you look at those names, not only are they very talented riders, they're very dedicated to their profession," McCarron said. "They have tremendous competitive spirit. What a great club to be a member of, and what a thrill."

~~~

## GARY STEVENS

*December 29, 1999*

The first time that horses, pain, and Gary Stevens arrived together at the same place was on a mustang roundup in Idaho. He figures he was about 4-years-old. He was on his mother's horse, a kindly mount, but
~~~

when they turned back toward camp that horse smelled the barn in a big way and took off like Man o' War. At some point young Gary bailed out and crashed head first into the side mirror of the family pickup. His nose wasn't very big, but it was broken, and both eyes swelled up a ripe, cherry black.

That hurt.

In October of 1985, at the age of 22, Stevens was a rising star on his way to his first riding title in Southern California. Then one morning at Santa Anita a horse named Irish Kristin bolted on the backstretch and dragged him a couple dozen yards before finally shaking him loose. That afternoon, Stevens lay in Arcadia Methodist Hospital with his right shoulder separated, his right arm broken, and the ligaments of his right knee ripped to shreds.

That really hurt.

By the summer of 1989, Stevens had established himself among the elite with a victory in the Kentucky Derby, four riding titles at Hollywood Park, two at Santa Anita, and two at the Oak Tree meet. He was battling for a third straight championship at Del Mar when, one innocent September afternoon, his horse Bin of Ice turned left in the stretch of a grass race and careened into the PVC piping that constituted the temporary rail. The piping split and speared Stevens between the eyes, opening a bloody gash, then he fractured his wrist on impact with the ground.

Oh, man, did that hurt.

The litany seems endless. October of 1987, fractured ankle. November of 1990, fractured elbow. June of 1993, fractured thumb. December of 1995, knee surgery. June of 1996, shoulder surgery. June of 1997, another knee surgery.

In August of 1998, while Stevens was taking the 2-year-old Isitever to the post in a maiden race at Del Mar, the colt suddenly ducked to the right. Stevens heard his left knee respond with a sickening pop. He could barely dismount, the pain was so great. Sitting in the track first-aid station, betrayed again by his body, he could barely look at the damaged leg.

"If this is as bad as it feels," he said, wincing in pain, "it might be all over."

It wasn't. But it was the beginning of the end. Within the week Stevens had knee surgeries number four and five. He returned later in the year—because he was expected to return—although he rode with various degrees of misery through the first part of 1999.

Then came his great European experiment, a shift to softer riding surfaces that was supposed to reduce the concussion on his ravaged knees and add a few years to his career. Sadly, the experiment backfired. The twisting, undulating English courses, with their surprising dips and changing ground, were the worst thing possible for those fragile knees, and the cold weather didn't exactly help. Surgery number six was inevitable.

It was an odd scene at Santa Anita on Sunday as Stevens explained his decision to retire. No one could recall seeing him suffer a recent injury. Athletes recover from knee surgeries all the time. He seemed perfectly healthy, neat as a pin, and walking just fine. This did not look like a worn-down jock at the end of his days. Stevens looked like a guy who needed maybe a few months off, a little golf, and a steady flow of sunshine and piña coladas.

In reality, Stevens was psychologically exhausted. Those who suffer from degenerative arthritis understand and deeply sympathize with his decision to retire. Ask Sandy Koufax, who couldn't pitch past age 31. The cartilage that the rest of us take for granted does not exist in Stevens's right knee. Bone rasps against bone with every flex and torque. As a result, the pain never goes away. It can be masked with anti-inflammatories. It can be briefly and dangerously deadened with corticosteroid injections. It may even respond to various therapies.

But the pain never, ever goes away. And there is no honest physician that will give him hope, especially if he continues to ride.

When Stevens was seven, he was diagnosed with Perthes disease. The ball of his right hip joint was deteriorating, and unless the joint was stabilized while it healed, permanent damage was likely.

They say life goes in circles. Still, there are places we prefer not to revisit. For nearly 19 months, while school kids taunted him with the nickname "Ironside," Stevens wore a brace that ran the length of his right leg. Now, at the age of 36, he is being fitted for a brace again, one that will ease the lateral pressure on his right knee until it is time to submit to the inevitable and face joint-replacement surgery.

As the sun set on the final day of the remarkable career of Gary Stevens, he stood on a camera platform at the edge of the Santa Anita grandstand rooftop, repeating the sad news for a local TV network. Watching nearby was Gary's oldest son, Tory Chad, better known to everyone as T. C.

"What's the very first thing you remember about your dad?" T. C. was asked.

"I remember him in a wheelchair in the hospital," T. C. replied.

That was in the autumn of 1985, when Stevens first injured the knee that eventually ended his career. T. C. was 13 months old at the time. He is 15 now, and with any luck he'll never need to watch his father deal with that kind of trauma again.

~~~

## RUSSELL BAZE

*August 3, 2000*

There are plenty of reasons to spend two weeks in August exploring the pleasures of Sonoma County.

You can head down Highway 116 to Monte Rio and kayak down the Russian River, or turn north at Guerneville and wander through the groves of Armstrong Redwoods, where George Lucas shot his nail-biting chase scenes from *Return of the Jedi.*

From there it's only a short jaunt to the Sonoma seacoast village of Jenner and the pleasures of Blind Beach and Goat Rock, or you can double back to Sebastopol and kill a few hours on Main Street at shops like "Incredible Records," with its rock memorabilia collection that includes unpublished photos of The Beatles and pencil drawings by a 13-year-old Jim Morrison.

Up in tiny Healdsburg (pop. 9,100), where grapevines outnumber people by about a million to one, a winery can be found at every turn of the Alexander Valley Road. Wine tasting—as well as wine swallowing and
~~~

wine purchasing—is encouraged. And then, on just about any afternoon, you can stop by the Sonoma County Fair in Santa Rosa and watch Russell Baze make blue-ribbon mincemeat out of his competition.

One year ago this week, Baze was in New York with his family, soaking up the sights of the Big Apple and basking in the glory of his Hall of Fame induction upstate in Saratoga Springs.

To make that trip, Baze had to miss half the racing meet at the fair. It was a tough decision, but then, a guy only gets into the Hall of Fame once in a lifetime.

This year it has been business as usual and back to the fair. Already at more than 7,000 career wins and counting, Baze won with 14 of 34 mounts during the first six days of the Santa Rosa meet. If there is a favorite, he rides it. If he is on a second choice, there obviously has been some kind of mistake, and he wins anyway. Shouldn't he blush at such dominance?

"Not at all," Baze replied. "I love it. And I've been accused of being greedy for quite a while. Guilty as charged.

"I only win two or three a day," he said, adding a touch of righteous indignation. "And there were a couple days here last year I didn't win any at all."

Must have eaten a bad corndog. Baze and his family always take rooms at the local Hilton and dive headfirst into the fair whenever Santa Rosa comes around. In the mornings, when there are no horses to work, there is time for tennis, swimming, and excursions into the countryside. After the races, the midway beckons.

On August 7, closing day of the fair, Baze will celebrate his 42nd birthday. What he definitely does not do is spend time apologizing for his career path, as he continues to thrive as the biggest fish in the Northern California pond. Critics say (usually while they cash) that Baze is slumming and should be going head-to-head with the marquee names at Del Mar or Saratoga during the summer months. Baze just grins and wins three more.

"Northern California is where I work and live, so riding the fairs keeps me in touch with my business," Baze said last weekend.

"Besides, I really like riding the fairs. Two weeks at each place is fun. And riding on the smaller tracks like Vallejo, with those sharper turns, helps keep you sharp."

While Baze has nothing but praise for such local colleagues as Ron Warren, Dennis Carr, Scott Stevens, and Chad Schvaneveldt, he concedes that the fields tend to suffer from a lack of depth. By the top of the stretch of most fair races, the game has pretty much boiled down to a couple of runners at most.

"Yeah, but you still have to go into each race prepared for the chance that there will be a number of horses that will be competitive," Baze said. "But a lot of times it's true that you're on a horse that's so much the best, you can mess up and still win."

And win, and win, and win. At the end of each Santa Rosa race, a flatbed pickup ferries the dismounted riders from the scale near the winner's circle back to the jockeys' room, located some 200 yards up the stretch. The last jock on board is the lucky guy who got to pose for pictures. More often than not, that guy is Baze.

More than the level of competition, though, Baze attributes his success to a run of great physical luck. He made it until last October before suffering what he considered a serious injury.

"I remember it was Halloween, because I didn't get to go trick-or-treating with the kids that night," Baze said. "I had a hairline crack in a vertebra, and some compression. If there had been any more to the crack, they would have had to operate.

"That was the T-5," Baze added. "I had compressions to T-4 and T-7 before, so if I can get T-6 I'll have a bingo."

In the meantime, he'll settle for running the table at Santa Rosa.

~~~
~~~

# JACKIE FIRES

*August 6, 2001*

Friends were dumbfounded. The audience was moved. There, standing at the podium accepting his place in the Racing Hall of Fame, the tough, cool-headed man known as Earlie Fires was fighting back tears like a mother at her daughter's wedding.

Everyone immediately circled the date. Even Fires himself was surprised. After 36 years in the profession, after riding more than 42,000 horses and winning more than 6,000 races, the man known as Little Brother had earned the reputation as the last guy on earth who would let his emotions leak. As far as anyone could remember, it had never happened before.

Jackie Fires can tell you different. Sitting in his wheelchair in the front row of the Fasig-Tipton pavilion, Jackie Fires could recall that day nearly 25 years ago when his big brother stood at his bedside in a Cincinnati hospital. The younger Fires lay paralyzed from mid-chest downward after being thrown from a horse at River Downs. He was 21, a jockey for barely five years, and he would never walk again.

"I was just laying there in intensive care, tubes running out of me everywhere," Jackie said. "Earlie looked down at me, and he was kind of like he was up there today."

The bond between brothers is complicated, a messy stew brewed from adoration, rivalry, friendship, and blood loyalty. When brothers choose the same profession, the stakes become even higher.

Jackie Fires was 10 when his brother led all North American apprentice jockeys in 1965. There was nothing else Jackie wanted to be. He never fancied himself as good as Earlie—Earlie would disagree—but he managed to lead the standings at Finger Lakes and challenge for the local titles at places like Detroit Race Course, Tampa Bay, and River Downs.

"It was kind of tough," Jackie said. "They kind of wonder why you're not doing as good as he is. But in some ways it kind of helped. Anytime you said your name was Fires, they figured you were kin to Earlie."

Jackie Fires was 16 when he boarded a plane from his home in Arkansas bound for California, where a job with W. L. Proctor awaited at Del Mar. Proctor also got Earlie started. Every rider should be so lucky. So it was a wide-eyed, excited teenager who found himself at Los Angeles International Airport that summer of 1971, looking for his ride to the track.

Problem was, he was supposed to be in San Diego.

"I got off the plane and they were announcing my name over the loudspeaker system," Jackie recalled. "I thought, 'What do they want me for? What did I do?' I wasn't exactly fresh off the farm, but I was pretty close."

Jackie finally made it to Del Mar, and beyond, to a career in his brother's footsteps. Even so, there was a chance his days as a jockey were numbered from the start. "I was bigger than Earlie," he said. "I was already having trouble with my weight."

And then came that day at River Downs. Not in the heat of a race. Not in the tension of the paddock. Not even during a full-speed morning workout. Jackie Fires was hurt while galloping a horse.

"It was the first time I saw this horse," Jackie began. "I was supposed to ride him a couple days later. I knew he was sore, so I wanted to find out how sore before I rode him. Apparently, he was too sore."

Fires is halfway grinning as he tells this, like it's a crazy racetrack story that happened to somebody else. He folded his big, strong hands in his lap and continued.

"He fell so quick that there was no time to get away. I had a hold of him and he pulled me right beneath him. He didn't stumble or nothing. He just must have got his legs crossed. I don't really remember."

A quarter of a century later, Fires lives peacefully with the injury that ended his dreams.

"Going to rehab helped me a lot," he said. "There were guys there in a lot worse shape than me. Guys who were quadriplegics, who couldn't use their arms. They'd spend an hour just trying to pull their pants up with a coat hanger."

Jackie also got lucky at home. Come October, he and his wife, Janie, will celebrate their 18th wedding anniversary. He has helped raise her two daughters by her first marriage—Donna Rae and Casey—as if they were his own.

"There's no bad feeling about racing," Jackie said. "I loved it before I started riding, and I still love it. Me, I look forward to the next time I can laugh. That's what makes me happy."

At the Hall of Fame ceremony on Monday, Earlie Fires regretted that his induction came too late to be enjoyed by people, gone now, who had been so important in his life and his career. He didn't say it, but he didn't need to. It was only by a stroke of good fortune that Jackie Fires was around to share his brother's greatest moment.

Then Earlie concluded his acceptance speech, still wrestling with his emotions. The audience jumped up, filling the pavilion with cheers and applause. Down in the front row, brother Jackie didn't stand. He floated.

~~~

# J. C. GONZALEZ

*September 12, 1999*

Johnny Barbra, Aqueduct, Oct. 13, 1940. Herbert Blackner, Sportsman's Park, Feb. 7, 1944. Roy Fiocchi, Delaware Park, June 16, 1945. George Woolf, Santa Anita Park, Jan. 4, 1946.

The flags were at half-staff Friday at Fairplex Park as the jockeys gathered in the winner's circle to pay silent tribute to J. C. Gonzalez, who was killed the day before on the final turn of the fifth race while trying to win a first-place purse worth $4,950. He would have been 24 on October 5.

Joseph Molbert, Suffolk Downs, June 6, 1949. Richard McCraw, Waterford Park, Oct. 24, 1951. William McCadden, Fair Grounds, Nov. 18, 1953. Raul Contreras, Agua Caliente, Dec. 30, 1957.

Joe Monte, a gateman and 26-year veteran of the L. A. County Fair, said hi to Gonzalez earlier in the day on Thursday while the rider sat outside the jocks' room handicapping the card, marking his *Racing Form.*

"What a nice kid, and a good young journeyman," Monte said. "When I worked the paddock at Santa Anita, sometimes he'd tap me on the leg with his whip as he walked by and say, 'My horse's got a little shot in here.' "

Jack Westrope, Hollywood Park, June 19, 1958. Richard Ferguson, Pim-
~~~

lico, Dec. 10, 1959. Phil Grohs, Bay Meadows, Dec. 6, 1965. Freddie Robertson, Del Mar, Oct. 4, 1967.

"I didn't know his family," said trainer Paco Gonzalez, no relation to J. C. but from the same hometown of Yahualica in the central Mexico state of Jalisco.

"My brother Sal knew him good, though. When he was training Quarter Horses for match races, J. C. would work horses for him all the time. He was only 14 or 15."

Joe Phillippi, Longacres, May 7, 1968. Thomas Smith, Thistledown, Sept. 27, 1969. Earl Knapp, Oaklawn Park, Feb. 19, 1973. Alvaro Pineda, Santa Anita Park, Jan. 18, 1975.

"We were the last two horses in the gate," said Fernando Toro, a close friend of Pineda. "Alvaro's horse went in. The assistant starter got out of the way. And just that fast the horse went up and I heard a loud crack."

Toro and Pineda shared a corner of the Santa Anita jockeys' room.

"I looked over and Alvaro's head was down. There was blood coming out of his mouth. I said, 'Don't move, Alvaro. Don't move. It will be okay.' But he was already gone.

"It was in the back of my mind for a long, long time," Toro added. "Even today, any time a jockey goes down, I hurt inside. Some riders say they would rather be killed than paralyzed. I don't know if I'd ever have the courage to say that."

Nelma Henderson, Churchill Downs, June 14, 1976. Bobby Pineda, Pimlico, May 3, 1978. Avelino Gomez, Woodbine, June 21, 1980. Michelle Higley, Centennial, June 29, 1980.

Tom Ward was at the beginning of his career as a racing steward when Juan Gonzalez, no relation to J. C., was killed on the first turn at Pleasanton on July 5, 1975. On Thursday he was in his usual post in the stewards' stand at Fairplex. He was asked what he remembered about the events of 24 years ago.

"Mostly, I remember the carnage," Ward said.

"Several riders went down that day. John Luckie broke his pelvis. I just so happened to have my binoculars on Juan. When he hit the ground, his head was toward the rail. When the horse came along and hit him in the head, it spun him around 180 degrees. As I recall, the horse fractured his shoulder."

Amado Credidio, Aqueduct, March 29, 1982. Nels Peterson, Turf Paradise, May 15, 1983. Kevin Lindsey, Blue Ribbon Downs, July 30, 1986. Mike Venezia, Belmont Park, Oct. 13, 1988.

Since 1941, the Jockeys' Guild has recorded 141 riding fatalities at North American racetracks. The beneficiaries of a Guild member killed at the track can collect on an $800,000 insurance policy. Beneficiaries of non-Guild members can hope for only the $100,000 negotiated by the Guild through the Thoroughbred Racing Associations. J. C. Gonzalez was not a member of the Guild.

"I don't know why," said John Giovanni, executive director of the Guild. "Gary Baze, our regional representative, helped him fill out the application forms more than a year ago and had reminded him since then. All the kid had to do is write a $20 check. It's a shame."

John Alleman, Delta Downs, Aug. 5, 1989. Luke Proctor, Bay Meadows, June 15, 1991. James Thornton, Charles Town, Dec. 11, 1994. Miguel Figueroa, Great Barrington Fair, Sept. 13, 1997.

On Friday at Fairplex Park, J. C. Gonzalez was named to ride Service Term in the first Thoroughbred race of the day. Iggy Puglisi filled in and rode Service Term to a two-length victory, then wiped a tear from his eye as he entered the winner's circle and joined in the ceremony of remembrance. In the fifth race Friday, Gonzalez would have ridden a horse named Ayer Hoy Manana.

It means "yesterday today tomorrow."

Jose Carlos Gonzalez, Fairplex Park, Sept. 9, 1999.

~~~
~~~

# KATHY KUSNER

*May 21, 2003*

Kathy Kusner was playfully alarmed to hear that Barclay Tagg, a good friend from their steeplechase riding days back in the 1960s, was being identified as the "65-year-old" trainer of Kentucky Derby and Preakness winner Funny Cide. So she gave him a call, just to make sure she heard right.

"Sixty-five!" exclaimed Kusner, who is 63. "We were screaming with laughter, wondering what happened to us."

What happened is that Tagg, now on the threshold of a Triple Crown, has joined Kusner in writing a page of racing history. And while Tagg's story is still incomplete, Kusner's impact has been chiseled in stone for 35 years as the first woman to receive a license to compete as a professional flat-racing jockey in the United States.

"I didn't set out to be the first girl jockey," Kusner protested, still the reluctant hero. "I just wanted to ride races."

Annika Sorenstam, who is playing against men this week in the Houston Open, required only an invitation from the tournament sponsors. Big deal. Back in 1968, in order to ride, Kusner had to go to court to overturn the ruling of the Maryland racing commissioners, who deemed her lacking the necessary strength to do the job.

She was strong enough, however, to be a member of the U. S. Olympic Equestrian teams that competed in Tokyo in 1964 and in Mexico City in 1968, and strong enough to win a gold medal as part of the U. S. team competing in the 1964 Pan American Games in Sao Paolo.

"Being a jockey should not be a girl-guy thing, it's whether or not you're good at it," Kusner said this week from her West Hollywood home. "It's the same with riding show jumpers. There is no advantage to be a guy, or to be stronger. But it is always an advantage to be better."

Had Kusner never done another thing other than succeed in that court case, her pioneering place in the history of American sports would have been secure. But Kusner could never hold still. The Maryland case represents only a tiny slice of her fascinating life, full of challenge and accomplishment.

After ending her career on the flat, Kusner continued as an influential presence in the show-jumping world. She became an accomplished pilot and scuba diver. She began running "ultra-marathons" and 10,000-meter races. She founded "Horses in the Hood," a Los Angeles–based non-profit organization that helps put young people from the inner-city next to horses, giving them a chance to ride them, groom them, and appreciate the care and skill that goes into horsemanship.

Kusner also developed a consultancy, with clients in the movie business, and made a name for herself as an expert witness in equine-related litigation. It's hard to argue with the credentials of someone with an Olympic silver medal at home in the bottom of a trunk.

"The medal itself doesn't mean anything," Kusner said. "What was important to me was the experience of doing it. The most fun was staying in the Olympic Village, and meeting all these other people doing such interesting stuff.

"I remember taking two boxers out to the stables one day—the light heavyweight and the middleweight—two giant black guys from Philadelphia with muscles sticking out all over the place. And they were afraid of the horses! I would have to take their huge hand in mine just to get them to stroke the horse's muzzle."

Kusner earned her medal as part of the U. S. equestrian team competing at the 1972 Summer Games in Munich. She also had a ringside seat for the terrorist attack on Israeli athletes.

"I was standing outside the Israeli compound, watching as it happened, and listening to the news on my little transistor radio," she said. "I'll never forget how, from time to time, Howard Cosell would come over to me, listen to the news from New York on my radio, then walk back in front of his television cameras and give an update. He never even said hi, or thanks."

Kusner has been blissfully unaware of the Sorenstam story unfolding in professional golf. She has better things to do, like competing in a 31-mile race with her boyfriend through the foothills of the Sierra Nevada Mountains near Lone Pine—which she was doing while the Preakness was being run—or preparing for the next horse camp for the kids from "Horses in the Hood."

Now she must set aside the time to watch the Belmont Stakes, on June 7, just in case her old pal Tagg does it again.

"There was a pipe fence somewhere on the Belmont Park backside," Kusner recalled, "and Barclay taught me how to put my hands on the fence and vault over it. I was a very poor student, so it required an excellent trainer."

Now that same trainer is going for the Triple Crown. Kusner wouldn't put it past him.

"It's not like someone you know who was a flake, or not a good horseman. Not at all," she said. "He's completely legitimate. But, of course, he's not the only one. Most of the people who are qualified will not win the Kentucky Derby and the Preakness. The fact that he is doing this is just so much fun."

~~~

## EDDIE DELAHOUSSAYE

*September 4, 2002*

Ever the gentleman, Eddie Delahoussaye was quick to recognize a lady in distress and allowed her to take his place in line.

Chivalry lives, even while awaiting a CT-scan in the trauma unit of Scripps Hospital in La Jolla, where the rider was taken last Friday after a horrible fall on the Del Mar grass.

"She was having trouble with her pacemaker, and was starting to panic," Delahoussaye said. "I didn't think I was going to die, but I thought she had a chance of dying. She looked like she needed that scan a whole lot more than me."

By Monday morning, Delahoussaye was back at his Del Mar condo. He was still sore, head to toe, as he replayed what he could recall of the crash on the backstretch of the third race, for claimers worth $55,000 to $62,500. Delahoussaye was riding a 3-year-old gelding named Seeingisbelieving, a capable maiden in against winners for trainer Mike Machowsky.

Seeingisbelieving and Delahoussaye had five horses in front of them
~~~

and three behind them as they turned onto the backstretch of the 1-1/16-mile race. That's when Seeingisbelieving snapped a cannon bone and dropped like a rock.

"Chris McCarron watched the films and told me I slid about 20 feet," Delahoussaye said. "I guess I was lucky I did, because the horse was sliding right behind me."

"I was behind Eddie," said Alex Solis, who rode Chory Four. "Just before it happened, I saw [Corey] Nakatani start to move on the outside. So I decided to follow him instead of Eddie's horse. If I didn't do that, I would have gone right over the top of him."

It could have been worse, for everyone but the horse. The injury to Seeingisbelieving was irreparable—at least in humane terms—and he was euthanized.

Delahoussaye said he sensed nothing amiss with Seeingisbelieving warming up for Friday's race, and he was traveling well right up to the moment the bone gave way. He had ridden the horse once before, in his last start at Hollywood Park on July 17, and finished second against winners under similar conditions.

Machowsky, who has been training a public stable for 12 years, said he had never had a horse fatally break down in a race before last Friday.

Three days later, he was still shaken.

"I ran a couple yesterday," Machowsky said. "It was a little tense. It can happen to anybody any time, especially if you run enough horses. But it's something I try to prevent. Every morning I go through my horses. If there's something questionable, we try to find out what's going on before taking any chances."

The loss of Seeingisbelieving is every bit as heartbreaking as the death of Go for Wand. And when 23-year-old Isiah Sala lost his life a year ago at Marquis Downs, he was taking the same risks as a 50-year-old superstar like Delahoussaye, who plies his trade on a national stage.

Still, we tend to pay more attention when the big trees fall. When a rider like Delahoussaye gets hurt, writers scramble for his bio, anticipating the end. They discover an intoxicating mix of five classics, seven Breeders' Cups, close to 6,500 winners, and Hall of Fame membership since 1993.

After 34 years in the saddle, Delahoussaye represents a level of excellence and integrity that is rare in any profession. He is a tireless advocate for the safety of his colleagues, who literally place their lives in the hands of the trainers who prepare their mounts. Seeingisbelieving could have been an example of a bad step on a good leg, no question. But that does not stop Delahoussaye from calling attention to the larger picture.

"Years ago, people would ice horses," Delahoussaye said. "They would use massage therapies, alcohol to tighten. And if they got too bad, they'd turn the horse out to give him a chance. So-called horsemen nowadays are saying they can't afford it, giving a horse that time. Well, if they can't afford it, they should get out of the game.

"If you're crazy enough to pay a million dollars for a horse, you should be smart enough to give your horse time to heal," Delahoussaye said. "Then maybe you'll have a chance to get your money back. But don't keep giving him medicine and more medicine, only covering up the ailments. The game is already dangerous enough without doing that."

Machowsky was at Delahoussaye's hospital bedside Friday night, worried sick that one of his horses might have just ended the career of an icon. Delahoussaye played it tough.

"Just put me on a good one when I come back," the rider said.

In reality, Delahoussaye will be taking stock as he mends over the next few weeks. He is already on record that 2002 is likely to be his last season. If it is not, he will have to answer to his wife, Juanita.

"I'll go home this week and let my doctor have a good look at me," Delahoussaye said. "Right now, the way this body feels, I'm going to take some time off."

He has earned it. In the meantime, Delahoussaye will celebrate his 51st birthday on September 21. Thank goodness.

~~~
~~~

# PAT DAY

*November 12, 2005*

Just as Ernie Banks meant the world to Wrigley Field, and Bill Russell owned the boards of Boston Gardens, Pat Day has inscribed his name upon every square inch of the stretch at Churchill Downs, where he reigns as the all-time leading rider.

It is appropriate, therefore, that Day should be given a day of his own at the Louisville track on Saturday, beginning with an autograph session for fans, followed by a variety of tributes, and ending with a Pat Day celebrity roast to benefit the Race Track Chaplaincy of America.

Day won four Eclipse Awards and 8,803 races during his 32-year career, which included nine wins in Triple Crown events and 12 victories in a variety of Breeders' Cup races. His career mount earnings of $297,941,912 is the monetary bar to which all other riders aspire, while his place in the Hall of Fame has been secure since his induction, in 1991.

At the age of 52, financially set and reputation intact, Day could be forgiven if he decided to fade blissfully into the scenery, allowing the game to go on without him.

Instead, Day plans to be every bit as visible on the ground as he was in the saddle. He has committed his time to work with the Race Track Chaplaincy as a representative at large, traveling to North America's racetracks, appearing at fundraisers, making himself available to the backstretch community, and, in his own way, exposing others to his Christian faith.

It is a faith that seems to inform Day's every waking moment. It is also a faith born of a self-destructive lifestyle, dating back to his 20s, when he was a hell-raising star on the rise.

"I was a very animated winner," Day said this week from his Louisville home. "When I won, I really let the world know it. Common sense, though, tells you that when you go that high when you win, you're going to go just as far the other way when you lose. The emotional and mental strain was horrific.

"And it's not just riders," Day went on. "It's anybody in any walk of life that finds himself highly successful. Look at the Wall Street guy who hits it big one day, then the next day you find him in a ditch somewhere doing coke. Nobody is immune.

"The world would have you believe that the thrill of victory, the thrill of a big sale, is supposed to give you joy, peace, and contentment," Day said. "When they find it doesn't, then they find their highs in other places, whether it's drugs, alcohol, an illicit sex affair, whatever it is. For the first 30 years of my life, and the first 10 years of my career, I was busy doing that."

What Day refers to as "my salvation" came in January of 1983, right after he made headlines with his first national championship.

"At that time in my life, I thought that once you had won the Big Kahuna, you celebrated, you partied!" Day said. "After two weeks of a drug and alcohol stupor, I took a personal inventory, and discovered I was absolutely hollow."

What transpired since then—and lasted until Day's retirement in August—was a virtually uninterrupted career of prodigious bounty. Even for those who might balk at Day's relentless message of Christian salvation, there can be nothing but admiration for his record on horseback. Blessed by a small, wrestler's physique and an uncanny touch, Day was able to set a standard of performance that translated well to any kind of Thoroughbred.

Few jockeys in the history of the sport have performed at such a high level for such a long period of time. Day attributes his success to a divinely predestined plan, along with an uncanny ability to avoid serious injuries.

"It seemed from the start, before I even knew how to tie my reins, that I was able to sense when a horse was going wrong, and possibly avoid riding them into the ground and causing spills," Day said. "I'm sure that made a difference, coupled with my experience on knowing how to fall from my bull-riding days."

Although vastly more comfortable in a stable area, Day surfaced on Capitol Hill last month to testify in a House committee hearing on jockey insurance, safety, and recent management problems at the Jockeys' Guild, of which Day was once president.

"I've always been supportive of the Guild, and very involved," Day said. "But I didn't want to be a part of it with the current management in place. The hearings made it clear that there were some radical changes that needed to be made in management.

"I will always have the jockeys' concerns in the forefront," Day added. "With new Guild leadership, if there is something I can do to help, I am not at all opposed to that."

In the meantime, Day will have his plate full working with the Race Track Chaplaincy.

"I don't know anybody more blessed than I am," Day concluded. "To have ridden for 32 years and enjoyed a successful career, and then to be able to look forward to the work I'll be doing now with the Chaplaincy, I can only give thanks.

"And the best thing is, I'll never retire from this," Day added. "What I'm doing today is what I will be doing every day until I draw my last breath."

~~~

## ROSIE NAPRAVNIK

*May 14, 2011*

Rosie Napravnik dug herself out from under last week's Derby media avalanche and came up for air, exhausted and inspired, determined to go back for more.

"Absolutely," she said. "I'll be very disappointed if I'm not there every year. What an incredible experience."

It will happen, without a doubt, given Napravnik's upward trajectory in the sport as an accomplished woman jockey in what is still very much a man's world. Someday her participation in the Derby might even be old hat, at least until that day she wins one. Then look out, especially in view of the reaction to her performance aboard Pants On Fire last Saturday at Churchill Downs.

"I never had so many congratulations for finishing ninth," Napravnik said Thursday morning.

She was back in Delaware, getting ready to ride there this weekend.
~~~

"Everybody was so happy for me in the Oaks, too," she added, referring to her close second the day before the Derby aboard St. John's River. "And I'm thinking, 'Dammit, I lost!' When is it a good thing to lose?"

Napravnik is a ferocious competitor who is learning when to turn it off and on. Not that the mass media version of Napravnik on display last week was a false front. Far from it. She was poised, articulate, and gracious by turns, finding herself, at the age of 23, targeted as one of the stories of the 137th Derby. None of the six Derby horses ridden by women had ever finished better than 11th—not exactly a high bar—but the fact Napravnik was in her first Derby and riding the Louisiana Derby winner sent reporters swooning over the possibilities.

"I don't really thrive on attention, so it definitely wore me out," she said. "It was all kind of overwhelming. I know the media is a key part of the sport, and my mom definitely enjoyed being on TV. There were times, though, I just wanted to take a nap."

As the Derby approached, Napravnik got plenty of advice from fellow jocks on how she would feel when she heard "My Old Kentucky Home" and paraded onto the track. Get ready for the tears to flow, she was warned.

"Getting choked up like that is not really me, so I really didn't get emotional at any point," she said. "But I was very excited. I kept thinking, 'This is so cool.' I remember Ramon looking over at me in the post parade"—that would be Ramon Dominguez, on Stay Thirsty—"and saying, 'Pretty exciting, isn't it?' "

Her reply: "Awesome!"

As far as the race itself, Napravnik did just about everything a jockey is supposed to do to give a horse a chance to win the Derby.

"Even with all the attention on me for being a girl riding in the Derby, the most important thing was to keep my focus and do my job right, to get my horse a good trip," Napravnik said. "It was important I proved myself capable of competing at that level."

Mission accomplished. Napravnik got Pants On Fire away from the gate like a champ and was able to secure an ideal position into the first turn, just in behind pacesetters Shackleford and Comma to the Top.

"I was so thankful for the demeanor of my horse," she said. "It was one less thing I had to worry about. He was never nervous, never rank, although he did act up a little in the gate."

There was a point approaching the far turn that Napravnik let herself think something special might be happening.

"At the half-mile pole I still had horse when I nudged him," she said. "I thought, 'I guess we're going to find out how much.' I was really excited to not be going backwards at the point of the race where it really begins."

Around the turn, as Napravnik and her colt continued to keep the lead in their sights, Nehro and Corey Nakatani made a huge move on the outside to attack the leaders.

"That horse moved so early and so fast, it was kind of like we had to go with him," Napravnik said. "That's when I discovered I didn't really have what I needed at that point."

Pants On Fire seemed to go through the motions after that, losing ground gradually to be beaten just under eight lengths by Animal Kingdom. It was later reported by trainer Kelly Breen that Pants On Fire had bled.

"The only thing that went wrong was the bleeding I guess," Napravnik noted. "Hopefully that's why he didn't finish well, but it's not like he stopped completely and was beaten many."

Aside from the thrill of the race itself, Napravnik came away with plenty of souvenirs and a bag full of goodies, among them the traditional group photo taken of the Derby jockeys before the race.

"It's always unfair, because the guys don't have to do their hair," Napravnik said. "I try to look good, but I just gave up.

"I also got a $105 jock's mount fee, and a gift bag with lots of nice things," she added. "They must have done one especially for girls, because one of the gifts was a Kentucky Derby purse, which is very nice. I'm sure the guys didn't get a purse.

"I also got five long-stemmed red roses—Derby roses," Napravnik added. "I ended up putting them on the dashboard of my car. Somebody said, 'No, you should take them home and dry them. Don't let them get wrecked.' I mean, they're ninth-place roses! What the heck do I want them for?"

~~~
~~~

# MIKE SMITH

*May 1, 2012*

Mike Smith knew something was wrong the second the music stopped. It was Derby Day 1994, and as far as Smith was concerned, the 120th running of America's most famous horse race was Holy Bull's to lose. Only trouble was, as the gray colt took his place in the post parade in front of 100,000 fans, he clearly was not the keen, looking-for-trouble Holy Bull who blew away his opposition in the Florida Derby and the Blue Grass.

"I was extremely high on him that day," Smith recalled, the disappointment still palpable. "I thought this was it—if I'm ever going to win one it's today. My main concern was actually staying on him in the post parade, because he was very difficult. He liked to play so much that I knew when they got through singing 'My Old Kentucky Home' and the crowd went wild, I better really be tied on."

Then the music stopped.

"He didn't even move," Smith said.

And that was that. Holy Bull left the gate spinning his wheels over the cuppy Churchill Downs track, never picked up the bit, and finished a distant 12th to Go for Gin.

At the time, Smith was the leading rider in the land, winner of the Eclipse Award in 1993 and a dozen years into what was becoming an exemplary career. But even the most successful jockey understands that a colt like Holy Bull is a rare beast. With Smith on board, Holy Bull swept through the rest of 1994, winning the Met Mile, the Travers, the Woodward, and Horse of the Year. Rewarding, yes. But the Derby still hurt. It's the Derby every jockey wants to win.

Which is why it will surprise absolutely no one to know that in this day of instant access to all manner of digital delights, Mike Smith carries a recent photo of the gray stallion Giacomo on his iPhone, a handy reminder of the day Holy Bull's most famous son carried Smith to victory in the 2005 Kentucky Derby, at odds of 50-1.

"Look at him, almost white now like his daddy," Smith said with a flash of his familiar grin. "Damn right he's got a special place in my heart."

Of course, there's always room for more. To that end, Smith, 46, will be riding the lightly raced Arkansas Derby winner Bodemeister in the 138th running of the Kentucky Derby on Saturday for owner Ahmed Zayat and trainer Bob Baffert. They could go favored, even in the face of the formidable Union Rags and the unbeaten Wood Memorial winner Gemologist, not to mention the fact that Bodemeister will attempt to become the first Derby winner since 1882 without racing experience as a 2-year-old. Then again, Smith is the last guy who needs to be told the Derby is a tough nut to crack. If Holy Bull couldn't get the job done…

"Some of them get discouraged, and they just quit running," Smith pointed out. "But some of them get over the track extremely well, and that's what you're hoping for. Bob said he likes the way the colt has been handling the track, which is great to hear. I'll find out pretty quick on Saturday."

Bodemeister will be Smith's 19th ride in the Derby, dating back to 1984 when he and Pine Circle chased home Swale and Laffit Pincay. On June 12, Smith will celebrate the 30th anniversary of his first win aboard the 4-year-old gelding Future Man at Santa Fe Downs in his native New Mexico. The winning purse that day was about $1,400.

At the time, the profession was dominated by veterans Laffit Pincay, Angel Cordero, and Jorge Velasquez, along with the emerging talents of Chris McCarron, Pat Day, and Eddie Delahoussaye. Even the ageless Bill Shoemaker, 49 at the time, was to be reckoned with as the regular rider of 1981 Horse of the Year John Henry, among others.

Breaking into the New York market, Smith eventually took his place among the game's elite competitors. He rode with regularity for the name trainers at Belmont and Saratoga, including Shug McGaughey, Bill Mott, Nick Zito, and Allen Jerkens, a living legend who's been known to let his post-race emotions show.

"He only got mad at me once," Smith said of Jerkens. "But he got the wrong horse. He yelled at me for going wide. 'It wasn't me, Chief,' I said. 'I was laying second.' 'No you weren't!' he said."

Smith's reply?

"Okay, if you say so."

This is classic Smith, going along to get along, accommodating a personality more suited to the chorus than his starring role on center stage. He confesses to a shy reluctance early on to join the adult world.

"Heck, I left home when I was 14, so I was growing up everywhere I went," Smith said. "And it took me a long time to grow up."

To hear Smith tell it, he loved every minute, a small kid in a big world, beating the bushes for mounts in Nebraska, riding cold winters in Chicago at Hawthorne, even dodging the INS on the backstretch of Minnesota's Canterbury Downs, natural-born citizen that he is. He laughed at the memory.

"They were doing a raid one morning and I was just walking down the road," Smith said. "A trainer up ahead yells out at me, 'Run, Mike, run!' I thought there was a loose horse, but he was just goofing with me. When they tackled me from behind, I thought I'd been hit by the horse, but it was the agents. I had me a moustache and a lot more dark hair at the time, so I guess I was what they were looking for. I told them, 'My name's Mike Smith.' They said, 'Sure, that's what they all say.' "

In the shorthand of horse racing, Smith has found himself pigeonholed at one time or another as being a specialist with top fillies. This was supported with a list that includes Inside Information, Sky Beauty, and Heavenly Prize, as well as Azeri and Zenyatta, both voted Horse of the Year. But a rider does not make it to the Hall of Fame without the whole package. You don't win more than 5,000 races—including 15 in Breeders' Cup events—just riding good fillies.

Besides the father-son combo of Holy Bull and Giacomo, the list of Smith's memorable colts includes the tempestuous Coronado's Quest, the durable Devil His Due, turf freak Lure, Preakness winner Prairie Bayou, sprint star Cherokee Run, and the opportunistic Drosselmeyer, winner of the Belmont Stakes and Breeders' Cup Classic with Smith at the wheel.

In Bodemeister, Smith has found a partner who fits neatly with his Kentucky Derby experience. Twice in the past decade, the rider ended up at Churchill Downs aboard fast, tractable colts who did everything right on the most important day of their lives. It wasn't their fault Smith doesn't have two more Derbies to his name.

In 2002, riding the Lexington Stakes winner Proud Citizen, Smith gave chase to the fleet War Emblem through what turned out to be crawling fractions, at least by Derby standards. Proud Citizen never caught the leader, but was best of the rest.

In 2004, Smith was savoring his trip aboard Hollywood Futurity winner Lion Heart, cruising easily on the lead over a sloppy track only a few in the field of 18 could truly handle. One of them, unfortunately, was Smarty Jones, who pursued Lion Heart at a dangerous arm's length.

"I had so much horse under me," Smith said. "At the three-eighths I honestly felt like I couldn't lose. Then Smarty Jones came to me and went right on by, like he was in a different league." Lion Heart was easily second.

Beyond his Derby record, the last decade of Smith's life has been the stuff of a juicy biopic. In no particular order, he was elected to the Hall of Fame, ended his marriage, restlessly migrated from California to the East Coast and back again, starred in a TV reality show with his girlfriend, founded a wine label with fellow jockey Alex Solis, rode Zenyatta to the top of the racing world, and ran briefly afoul of the law.

The wine—"Jinetes"—Smith describes as an "expensive hobby." He recommends the syrah. The reality show was *Jockeys* on Animal Planet, and the girlfriend was Chantal Sutherland, a headline jockey in her own right.

"I said no to the show at first," Smith said. "When we decided to do it, I warned her it would be the end for us." He was right.

Zenyatta's unbeaten run, right up to the bittersweet moment she narrowly lost the 2010 Breeders' Cup Classic at Churchill Downs in her 20th start, curried more attention for Smith than he'd received his entire career. His ongoing relationship with the great mare remains one of racing's great love stories—Smith visits Zenyatta in Kentucky whenever possible—and he was ever graceful in deflecting all the praise in her direction no matter what major media came his way.

The heat of celebrity can sting as well as warm, though. Smith made a different kind of headline in July of 2011 when he was charged with a DUI on opening night of the Del Mar meet. The penalties included a driver's license suspension, a series of classes, and 10 days of house arrest.

"I was able to keep working, but I had to wear the tracking signal on my ankle," Smith said. "I went straight home from the track, which in a way was good for me. I've got a nice house, but I get awful restless just being in it alone. The experience forced me to stay home and think about what happened."

Smith was lucky and knows it. Whatever alterations he subsequently made in his personal life have seemed to translate well on track, for he is riding with the flair of jockeys half his age.

"I'm in a good place right now—mentally, physically," he said. "I just want to keep that going. For whatever reason, it's all working, and I just want to keep it that way."

Smith concedes self-reflection is not his favorite pastime, although as an athlete in a dangerous profession, this might be a good thing. The navel-gazing Hamlet could not have hit the same hole Smith did with Giacomo in the 2005 Derby stretch. While Smith has the luxury of riding less now—500 mounts or so a year in the best possible events his agent, Brad Pegram, can find—the reduced activity finds his mind sometimes wandering.

"I was at Del Mar not long ago, just enjoying the beautiful view, waiting to meet some friends for lunch," Smith said. "I got to wondering about what I'd do when I retire. I mean, I don't really do anything except go to the track and go to the gym. I never played golf. I suppose I might want to try some racing TV. But I'd really never given it any thought."

The reason, Smith conceded, is probably because he's still very much a professional Thoroughbred jockey, with mountains yet to climb. The last 10 years of Smith's career have been, in many ways, more fulfilling than the first 20. Nothing would be better than to add a second Kentucky Derby with Bodemeister, an exceptional colt who would appear to lack for nothing except experience. Smith responded with a knowing gleam in his eye.

"I guess that's where I come in," he said.

*(Bodemeister and Smith finished second in both the 2012 Kentucky Derby and the*

*Preakness, then, in 2013, he won the Belmont Stakes aboard Palace Malice, the high point of a banner season. "The best year I ever had was 1994," Smith said. "But I'll take a season like 2013 anytime.")*

Six

# LITTLE BIG WOMAN

*Julie Krone was inducted into the Thoroughbred Racing Hall of Fame in August of 2000. Our wedding was in May of the following year. Just to be clear, the one did not lead to the other. And for the record, I did not marry a jockey. I married a horse-racing broadcaster and former* Sports Illustrated *cover girl who just happened to be a retired professional athlete of some repute.*

*Upon agreeing to our marriage, Julie made sure that as part of the deal I was okay with the idea of adding a child to our mix. Her concern was well founded. It was my second time around, and I already had fathered a perfectly wonderful son. But I agreed to her terms before the words left her lips.*

*When the stars did not at first align, and motherhood wasn't immediately in the cards, all bets were off. Julie got fit, got an agent, and went back to work with the same ferocity of purpose that had inspired the first 18 years of her groundbreaking career. Over the ensuing season I was asked, more than once, "Don't you worry? Aren't you scared? How can you watch?"*

*Fair questions, I suppose, for a guy whose beloved was putting her life on the line several times a day, never mind that she was consorting with ruffians like Gary Stevens, Pat Valenzuela, and Laffit Pincay. Usually I'd let the cold-eyed journalist in me do the talking. "I think by now she knows what she's doing," I'd say. "And besides, it's fun to watch."*

*At least most of the time it was. There were those emergency trips to the hospital and a few to first aid, but a whole lot more ended up in the winner's circle. About a year after her second injury, she was feeling fresh again and ready to pick up where she left off. Then nature intervened, and in September of 2005 our daughter was born.*

## LONE STAR

*April 21, 1999*

It was half past six at the end of a warm and windy Texas afternoon that Julie Krone finally realized it was over.

No more hauling her bag full of tack through airports.

No more horseplay in the jocks' room.

No more moments of sweet communication with a racehorse ready to run.

She checked herself, shook her head as if to clear the background noise, and flashed her trademark smile.

"Don't expect me to cry," she told a gathering of media Sunday at Lone Star Park. "I wanted to go out with a lot of pride, on a bright light, with a big day."

So ended the career of one of America's most successful female athletes and one of Thoroughbred racing's most enduring stars, not with a whimper of pain and debilitating injury, but with a loud bang of triumph and celebration on a day that delivered all that it could have reasonably promised.

Five mounts. Three wins. Scores of autographs and photos. And a ferocious second-place finish in her final ride, the $300,000 Lone Star Derby, aboard a colt named Desert Demon, who came within 1-1/4 lengths of giving Krone victory number 3,547 in her 18-year career. Typically, Krone felt bad for the horse.

"He tried so hard," she said, her face still flecked with red sand and her hair matted with sweat. "I was screaming, 'Please, win!' "

By that time, it hardly mattered to the Lone Star crowd of 21,124. They arrived hoping for a glimpse of Krone and ended up with a tale to tell their grandchildren. From the moment she emerged from the jockeys' room shortly before noon—to an ovation from the long line of people snaking around the paddock railing waiting for her autograph—to the last of the hero-worshipping kids she pulled out of the crowd for special attention, Krone rewrote the book on how to retire with grace, dignity, and unfettered joy.

Krone came through with her very first mount of the day, the 3-year-old filly Dance to Fit, who broke from post 14 in the 6-furlong second race and drew off to win by 1-1/2 lengths at odds of 3-1. Afterwards, Bill Stice, Dance to Fit's trainer, stood beneath a grandstand monitor admiring Krone's ride and wished out loud, "I hope it's not her last one."

It wasn't. The next race on the card was dubbed the Julie Krone Classic, again at 6 furlongs. Krone was home and dry by 5-1/2 lengths aboard Executive Girl, favored at 8-5, before the fans knew what hit them.

"I wish I could tell you we wrote the script this way," said Lone Star president Bob Kaminski as he stood in the winner's circle, looking a little shell-shocked.

Krone took a break during the fourth race and spent some of the time cleaning up a face full of three-layered sheet cake, courtesy of her fellow Lone Star riders.

She got her revenge in the fifth aboard Paris Jet, a 6-year-old gelding whose previous claim to fame was a victory in the Spirit of Texas Stakes last December. On this particular day, he had been dropped into a $20,000 claimer by Bill Stice, but he ran like a champ for Krone, winning by 2-3/4 lengths at odds of 3-1.

With that, Krone's career win total had reached 3,546, tops among women and better than most men. And there it stayed, despite good efforts by third-place Allen's Oop in the Texas Mile and her near miss on Desert Demon in the Derby. When asked where Desert Demon might run next, trainer Mike Stidham replied, with tongue in cheek, "I have no idea. I've lost my rider."

In the end, Krone's final day will be remembered as much for what happened on the ground as what took place in the saddle. Older fans regaled her with stories of when they first saw her ride. Young kids, especially girls, pressed close to the railing and shrieked with glee as Krone posed for pictures and signed their programs.

"The best, most rewarding thing is like what happened today," Krone said, "with 50 little girls, and all their energy. I just like to think they can read something about me, and some of the adversities and problems I've had, and say, 'Julie Krone got through that, so I can, too.' "

But in truth, Krone's appeal is universal. It will be two young boys who will take away some of the most cherished memories of the day.

Gary Palmisano, Jr., son of Fair Grounds trainer Gary Palmisano, celebrated his 11th birthday on April 18 at Krone's side for most of her public ceremonies, basking in the glow.

"Gary spent a lot of time with her on the backstretch at the Fair Grounds," said the elder Palmisano as he watched his son with pride. "She called him her unofficial agent. He's usually kind of shy, but just look at him."

Then, late in the day as Krone finally made her way back to the jockeys' room, Clay Mello, an 11-year-old diehard Krone fan from Austin who insisted his family make the trip to Lone Star, caught her eye and asked her for one last autograph. Krone signed his T-shirt with a flourish and a happy face, then said, "Come with me. I'll get you a pair of goggles."

When Krone was asked by Lone Star management for a list of special people she would like in attendance on her final day, she named only one: her mother.

Ailing and weak from her battle with cancer, Judi Krone was wheeled like a queen from the jockeys' room—where she had spent a few quiet moments with her daughter—to the winner's circle so she could watch Julie's last ride.

"The first time she was on a horse, she was in here," Judi Krone said, patting her stomach. "I've always been in awe of my little girl."

Judi Krone was strong enough to stand alongside her daughter for post-race interviews and photos. When they were finished, a security guard approached with Judi's wheelchair. Julie looked at it with mock alarm.

"Not for me, thanks," Julie said. "That's why I'm retiring, so I don't have to ride in one of those."

In the end, it was the beating her body had taken through a career of 20,481 mounts, 11 riding titles, and her 1993 Belmont Stakes victory aboard Colonial Affair that finally inspired her to set a retirement date.

"The reasons are multi-dimensional," Krone said, "and I actually decided in February. Because I'm a professional athlete, though, I had to keep it in confidence for a while.

"There was that day I got banged around in the starting gate," she went on. "My ankle hurt, my arm hurt, my stomach hurt. It didn't revive the old fears. But it did make me think, okay, this is not what I want to have happen. I do not want to be hurt again. It's your life, and you can do what you want with it."

Krone tossed out a number of things she wants to do now, ranging from earning a doctorate in psychology to teaching Sunday school.

"For starters, I think I'll sleep in for about two years," she said.

"I'm probably a lot more hyperactive than I think I am," Krone added. "I feel kind of sorry for the people around me for the next couple months, at least until I figure out how to channel this energy."

~~~

## A NEW LEAF

*April 21, 2000*

The sight was vaguely familiar, but the setting was all wrong.

It was definitely Julie Krone aboard the big liver chestnut. There was no mistaking the best female jockey in the history of the sport. But instead of barreling around the turn at Belmont, or splitting horses deep in the Saratoga stretch, here she was on a racing day in suburban Los Angeles, in an arena just 25 minutes from Santa Anita Park, flawlessly sending her big horse through a series of jumps, just for the fun of it.

What's wrong with this picture? Absolutely nothing.

On April 18, 1999, Julie Krone ended her 18-year career in the saddle and rode into the sunset with three winners at Lone Star Park near Dallas. That gave her a lifetime total of 3,546 wins, including the 1993 Belmont
~~~

Stakes. In a flash, her full-speed lifestyle came to a screeching halt. She said farewell to the limelight, vowing to sleep in, teach kids, eat what she wanted, and work on her college degree.

Now a year has gone by, and the 37-year-old Krone has packed more into the last 12 months than most people could handle in a lifetime. Among other things she has:

Moved 3,000 miles and started a new television career in a new town with a new network, TVG.

Become the first woman nominated to the horse-racing Hall of Fame (election results to be announced May 2).

Sold her dream house in Saratoga Springs and ended her marriage in divorce.

Begun teaching a weekly class of preschoolers at a San Fernando Valley church.

Continued her quest for a PhD in psychology.

Become a regular at the show-horse stable of trainer Rosey Reed at the Los Angeles Equestrian Center.

Launched a career as a voice actor for animation programming on the Nickelodeon network.

Signed with the pharmaceutical company Pfizer as a spokesperson for the awareness of post-traumatic stress disorder (PTSD) and the efficacy of the drug Zoloft in its treatment.

It is estimated that as many as 13 million Americans suffer from PTSD stemming from natural disasters, injuries, assault, or sudden death of loved ones. Pfizer got Krone on *Good Morning America* last week with Diane Sawyer.

Krone is also hitting the speaker's circuit, and she has agreed to Friday night simulcast appearances at the upcoming Hollywood Park meet, while continuing her earlier promotional work for Connecticut OTB.

"Yeah, it sounds like a lot," Krone said last weekend before getting aboard her 15-year-old jumper, Peter Rabbit. "But compared to what I went through with my mom, everything else just fades into the background."

Judi Krone died near her New Jersey home last December. The last time she was seen in public was at her daughter's retirement. Weak from her long battle with cancer, Judi Krone pulled herself out of a wheelchair to stand alongside her daughter in a winner's circle ceremony that day.

"Two days after that was the last time she ever walked," Krone said. "At the end, when she was in the hospice and you could literally smell the cancer eating her from the inside, me and my brother Donnie were with her 24-7. We prayed and talked about heaven, and sometimes she'd open her eyes and be right there with us for a while."

Since it was Judi Krone who put Julie Krone on horseback as a toddler and encouraged her passion for jumpers as a girl, it was a strange karma that ended the life of the mother and the racetrack career of the daughter in the same calendar year.

Krone continues to struggle with the memories, even when she does the thing she loves most.

"When I rode in a show I always called my mom," she said. "But the first one I rode in after she died, I blanked out completely. I didn't even know where the first jump was. I just turned around and rode out of the arena."

Then she laughed. "My mom would have said I just wasted the $35 entry fee."

Right now, Krone is happiest working with kids and horses. Yet she seems proudest of her connection with Pfizer. While still competing, she was diagnosed with PTSD and severe depression, symptoms stemming from her many injuries. She underwent a year of therapy before she began taking Zoloft, which is also used in the treatment of panic disorder and obsessive-compulsive disorder.

"There's a macho mentality attached to athletes that they are immune to something like PTSD," Krone said. "The thing I hope to do is de-stigmatize psychic illness."

In the meantime, it has become increasingly easier for Krone to watch a horse race without riding it in her head.

"There is nothing in the world like that feeling, when the horse is reading your mind and wants to win as bad as you do," she said. "I miss that part.

"But now I am no longer willing to trade a body part, or experience another trauma, for the chance to do all that wonderful stuff."

And that's just fine. She put in her time, and there is no chance she will disappear soon.

~~~

## SHE'S BACK

*October 30, 2002*

My wife intends to return to competition in Friday's fifth race at Santa Anita Park. On Saturday, she has two mounts in the 13th edition of the Cal Cup, the biggest day of the Oak Tree meet. Beyond that she is looking forward to the opening of the Hollywood Park fall meeting next Wednesday, November 6.

I have reviewed our vows with care, and frankly, I am stumped. I found the part about richer or poorer, in sickness and in health. That was clear enough.

There was some plighting of troth, whatever that is, and promises back and forth of loyalty and love. But at some point my mind must have wandered, because nowhere in the words we exchanged on our wedding day do I find anything referring to exactas and quinellas.

Still, I should not have been surprised. No one ever loved her job more than Julie Krone. When she walked away from race riding in April of 1999, it was hard, but it was necessary. I was there when it happened, at Lone Star Park, and when she said "that's a wrap," I had no reason to doubt her. I was a reporter. I wrote it down.

Three and a half years have passed since that day. Things change. And while I do not profess to be an expert on the first 37 years of Julie Krone's life, I have borne close witness to the last two. One thing, if anything, is absolutely certain: If she does not ride, she will surely explode.

There were signs along the way, commencing last summer. Pre-dawn disappearances to ride horses in workouts at Del Mar. A bale of hay in the backyard, rigged up with a saddle and reins. Then came the whips, bun-
~~~

dled and brightly colored. "One for every kind of horse," she explained. I like the red one.

My friends are worried. But not about her. They wonder if I can take the heat. They picture me hiding in a grandstand alcove, curled in a fetal position with a *Racing Form* over my head, waiting for Trevor Denman's voice to subside.

How will I react, they ask, when I hear the name-calling from disgruntled gamblers, flinging expletives at my one true love after losing a race at even-money? My wife, thank goodness, already gave me the answer.

"Just agree with them," she said. "They won't know what to think."

My editor has suggested that this has never happened before—a sportswriter married to a Hall of Fame athlete. Perhaps that is true. I promise to take notes. As a celebrity couple, however, we leave something to be desired. In the greater world, we come off more like the baseball brothers Hank and Tommie Aaron. One of them hit 755 home runs. The other hit 13. Call me Tommie.

"You've just become the Bill Clinton of horse racing," cracked Hollywood Park's Allen Gutterman, who used to be a friend. "The only questions you'll get now will be about your wife."

So far, he's right. The return of Julie Krone is headline news, and I am obliged to acknowledge its impact on the game. My favorite reaction, however, comes from the well-meaning cavemen still roaming the landscape, ever baffled by issues of gender. They want to know why I would let her do such a thing. Don't I know a girl like her could get hurt out there? I checked the calendar. Yep, it's 2002.

And then there are the guys who cut through chromosomes and reach right to the heart of the matter. Guys like Paco Gonzalez, who trained the great Free House, and who knows what it is like to devote heart and soul to a profession of passionate choice. When informed that Julie Krone would be resuming her career, he said, simply, "Why not?"

On February 11, 1969, at age 37, Bill Shoemaker returned to competition after spending 13 months on the sidelines, recovering from the worst injury of his career. It took that long to repair the femur of his right leg, which was broken in two.

"You wonder if you're going to be able to do it as good as you did before," Shoemaker said. "You might not show it, but the nerves inside are jumping up and down."

On the day Shoemaker returned, he won with all three of his mounts. After the first one, those nerves stopped jumping up and down. He was back to work, doing what he loved.

"Work is not man's punishment," wrote George Sand. "It is his reward and his strength, his glory and his pleasure."

Sand, it should be noted, was born Lucile Aurore Dupin, a woman who took a man's name in a man's world and became one of the most famous novelists of the 19th century.

Julie Krone was born Julie Krone and is still Julie Krone.

~~~

# OUCH

*March 12, 2003*

Mark Johnston is an Eclipse Award–winning jockey of respectable reputation and healthy common sense who has made a name for himself on the Maryland circuit competing against the likes of Edgar Prado and Rick Wilson. Johnston knows how to win (3,038 to date) and works hard for his money, so it is no surprise that he has decided to pick up stakes and try California at the prime-time age of 32. Only one real question remains.

Is he nuts?

Hasn't he heard? Doesn't he realize that Southern California has been replaced by the Bermuda Triangle, a place of dark karma and terrible dread where jockeys are being eaten alive? Riders walk around feeling like they have targets painted on their silks. Compared to this, ice hockey without a helmet is a stroll in the park.

"Not another one," said Leonard Rodriguez as the racetrack ambulance pulled up again at the emergency entrance of Arcadia's Methodist Hospital last Saturday afternoon.

Rodriguez is sort of the ER's concierge, a friendly, familiar face who
~~~

can usher the helpless guest to the right window for faster service. For the past three weeks he has been greeting a steady stream of riders from across the street at Santa Anita, prompting Rodriguez to shake his head in numb wonder.

"Man," he said, "they're dropping like flies."

Julie Krone, my wife, thought she got away lucky after last Saturday's first race when all she did was take a nasty blow to the nose from a tightly packed clod of dirt as she rode the $12,500 claimer Like Flying into the first turn.

The blow opened both nostrils and sent blood flying into her goggles. Thus blinded, she had to rely on the mercy of fellow riders and the survival instincts of her filly to complete the course. When she came to a stop, blood covered her mouth and chin, like Hannibal Lecter after an especially good meal. Nick Hines, who trained the filly, took one look and thought his jock had been hit by shrapnel.

"I was sick, man. I was speechless. Or maybe I was awestruck," Hines said. "I didn't know if the horse had hit her or what. But if I took a hit like that, I would have fallen off the horse."

Hines, it should be noted, is built like a pulling guard.

Krone shrugged it off— " 'Twas only a flesh wound," she said—cleaned up the blood and got ready to ride the rest of the card. Then two hours later she broke her back.

On a scale of 1 to way-out-there, the circumstances that sent Krone hard to the ground at the start of the day's fifth race were definitely strange.

She was on the French horse Sublet for trainer Ian Jory in a race beginning at the top of the hillside course. When the gates opened, Sublet took his first step with his head, hitting the turf face-first and spiking his jockey like a football after a touchdown.

"I've never had a horse do that in my life," said Krone. At last count, she had ridden more than 20,000 races.

"That horse just disappeared," said Jay Slender, Santa Anita's starter. "It was like he was standing on glass. Then he stumbled, and when that happens, your heart just stops, because these riders get hurt the most when they go down like that and end up underneath the horse."

The damage, as widely reported, was bad enough: three compressed vertebrae in the mid-back and fractures to the transverse process bones on the left side of lumbar vertebrae 2 and 3, where the muscles ripped away from the spine. She also has a sore shoulder, a bruised elbow, and an abiding gratitude that she still can move all 10 fingers and all 10 toes.

So the adventure has commenced, with a front-row seat at the healing of a professional athlete. In nearly 30 years of covering the sport, this reporter has paid plenty of visits to the hospital rooms of fallen riders—Gary Stevens, Eddie Delahoussaye, Fernando Toro, Chris McCarron, Laffit Pincay, Jr.—in order to bear witness to the damage that the game can inflict on the human anatomy.

Last Saturday was the first time, however, that I was invited to spend the night. There was a lounge chair in Julie's room, manufactured sometime during the 1970s and contoured like a coach seat in a cut-rate airline, offering the only chance for rest.

I should have checked with an expert. I should have sought the advice of Jeanine Pincay, for instance, who had just left the hospital with her husband, Laffit, after his treatment for a fractured cervical vertebra.

"He was there three nights when they finally said I could stay," Jeanine said. "Laffit took one look at that recliner and told me, 'Go home. You'll never get any sleep on that.' "

Pincay was wrong. I had a series of three or four restful, 15-minute naps, pretzeled into a chair designed for anything but comfortable repose.

Thank goodness, though, we got to go home by Monday. Now Julie can heal and be good as new again, just as she has done so many times in the past.

Only problem is, I've got this pain, right here in my back . . .

~~~
~~~

# DREAM RIDE

*August 29, 2003*

As a writer I was trained to avoid using the word "I" as much as humanly possible. This has been fairly easy, since what I think about Thoroughbred racing has not been nearly as important as what I have seen and heard. Besides, the "I" is never necessary when it comes to the reporting of fact, and in the end, I think writers who use the "I" to extremes tend to be tedious and self-indulgent. Who is this "I" guy anyway?

Sometimes, however, events cut close to the bone. To deny the "I" ends up appearing dishonestly coy. But I protest too much. And I have just exhausted my yearly "I" allotment. I apologize.

You see, last Sunday my wife, Julie Krone, went to work and won the Pacific Classic at Del Mar, the marquee race of the California summer. It took a few days to sink in.

She won it for Ron and Debbie McAnally, no less, and Sid and Jenny Craig, while filling in for the injured Gary Stevens. And while it is always an option to focus strictly upon a horse like the suddenly exciting Candy Ride, this time it is impossible. I surrender.

When my son, Ed, was born early on the morning of October 2, 1982, the first person I called to tell the news—outside of the immediate family—was Ron McAnally. The trainer was already a regular subject of my writing (John Henry was the reigning Horse of the Year), and he had become a friend as well. I also knew McAnally was sure to be awake at 4 a.m. Trainers.

Jump nearly 21 years, to the night before the 2003 Pacific Classic, and there is my son and his step-mom in our family room watching his digital videotape of Candy Ride's victory in the American Handicap at Hollywood Park with Stevens. She watched it four or five times, then she described how Candy Ride would get her to the quarter pole at the throat of Medaglia d'Oro, and then how the best horse would win from there.

It is never quite that simple, but it happened exactly as she described. When it was over, she sought out Gary Stevens in the winner's circle for a victory embrace. She knew exactly how he felt, being forced to digest the bitter pill of your horse winning a million-dollar race for somebody else. It is part of the price a jockey must pay.

It happened to Julie Krone in the fall of 1990, when she had just teamed with Safely Kept for back-to-back stakes wins in Maryland and New Jersey. Then, one morning at Monmouth Park, she fractured her ankle in a freak accident. Two starts later, Safely Kept won the Breeders' Cup Sprint.

It happened in the worst way, 10 years ago this Saturday, when Julie Krone was nearly killed in a race at Saratoga. Her right ankle was shattered, seemingly beyond repair. Her left elbow was sliced open to the joint. Her heart was bruised from the impact of a horse's hoof. There is no telling how many good horses she lost in that transaction, for 1993 was the year she not only won the Belmont Stakes, but led the standings at the Belmont springtime meet as well.

Is it worth it, the sacrifice of health and body parts in pursuit of success, the thrill of the chase? Hall of Fame jockeys like Stevens and Krone will answer yes without blinking, and stick to their story until "yes" no longer makes sense. Both of them have "retired" before, and no one begrudged their decision. Both of them came back.

Watching from a box near the sixteenth pole last Sunday, I put my binoculars down when Candy Ride collared Medaglia d'Oro at the head of the stretch and took in the sweeping panorama, the packed grandstand apron, the fans cheering the sight of one very good horse beating another on a perfect summer day.

As Candy Ride hit the wire, and the celebration commenced, a hand reached out and lightly squeezed my shoulder. The hand belonged to John Stewart, who was watching his new friend Julie Krone with a combination of curiosity and awe.

Back in the early 1960s, when Stewart was busy being one-third of the Kingston Trio, Julie Krone was just learning how to climb on a horse. As the San Diego–born son of a Standardbred and show-horse trainer, Stewart also spent his share of time in the stalls, mostly at Pomona, where his father kept his stock.

Stewart went solo and wrote songs like "Daydream Believer," "California Bloodlines," "July, You're a Woman," and "Gold." When so moved, he dipped into the trough of his horse-filled youth to write "Mother Country," "Back in Pomona," and his ode to Secretariat, "Let the Big Horse Run." He has just written a song inspired by the movie *Seabiscuit.* He calls it "Tanforan."

On the night before the Pacific Classic, John Stewart called Julie Krone at home, gabbed for a while, and then signed off with a little four-line ditty, a mere suggestion of a chorus that went something like, "Candy Ride, Candy Ride/Oh, Candy Ride/Candy Ride, Candy Ride/Gotta let him fly."

Now he can finish the rest of the song.

Seven

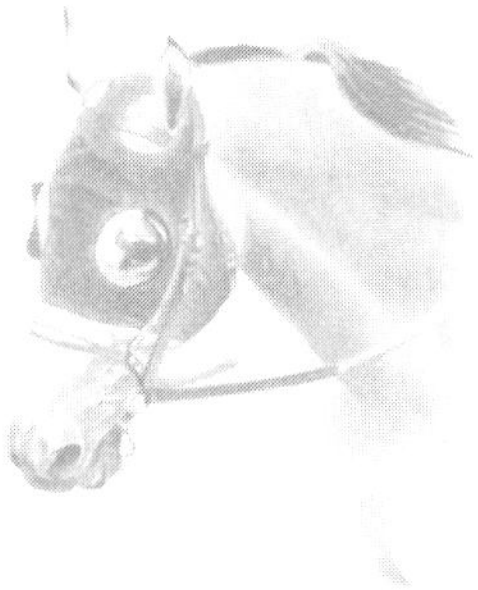

# ANYTHING GOES

*Charlie Whittingham meant no harm. I had written his biography, he liked it, and in gratitude he gave a horse my name. How he turned out on the racetrack was hardly the issue. I was honored…and anxious to see the colt run.*

*The day came at Del Mar, on a brilliant summer afternoon when the sunlight played with the spray of the fountain in the large grandstand plaza. As I entered the plaza, the voice of Trevor Denman was filling the air with the late changes in the official program. A scratch here, an overweight there, and then, in the fourth race, Trevor announced for all to hear, "Make Hovdey a gelding."*

*Thanks Charlie.*

*Then there was the time we were sitting in McCarthy's Irish pub in Fethard, halfway between Ballydoyle and Coolmore, glued to the TV while waiting for the start of the historic Grand National steeplechase at Aintree. The field of 40 was milling around behind the barrier when suddenly all hell broke loose, the tape went up, and horses were lurching around like sheep in a pen. Officials immediately called a false start, so we did the only reasonable thing and ordered another round.*

*Just about then McCarthy's front door opened and the parish priest burst in, breathless, from his church across the street. "Be praised," said the padre, seeing the race had been delayed. "I was fearful I'd missed the start."*

*Whether or not divine intervention was involved is beside the point. In the world of horse racing, it is best to leave the heart and mind open to all possibilities. A writer need only find the right place at the right time, then hold still and let the unusual occur.*

# SUMMER ROMANCE

*August 11, 2000*

It is easy to get them confused, Saratoga and Del Mar. After all, they both open in the midst of summer and refuse to end until that last good 2-year-old either breaks your heart or makes your meet.

They both are based loosely on the philosophy that people, when living in temporary conditions, will spend money like they don't have a real mortgage back home, and that actually cooking and serving a meal is downright un-American when so many seasonal employees rely on 40 straight days of total restaurant dependency.

There are, however, dramatic differences between the summer scenes, and not just the obvious fact that you could drop Del Mar—track, backside and all—into the Saratoga infield and still have room for the rowboats. Spending time at both Del Mar and Saratoga, within the span of a few days, is enough to burn those differences into the mind forever:

At Saratoga, fans must come prepared for sweltering heat, sudden torrents, thunder, lightning, and even hail. At Del Mar, the greatest weather risk is a day when the ultraviolet rating creeps above a 10.

At Saratoga, you are not allowed to wear short pants in the saddling paddock. At Del Mar, you are not allowed to remove your pants in the saddling paddock.

At Saratoga, Bill Mott trains around a private golf course at the Stonerside property where he stables his blue-ribbon band of runners. At Del Mar, Richard Mandella's valuable string of horses has a view of the pavilion where prize swine compete during the county fair.

At Saratoga, Nick Zito can spend an afternoon sitting in his clubhouse box with the mayor of the town on one side and the commissioner of racing on the other. At Del Mar, anybody can hobnob with such celebrities as Eddie from Alhambra, Angeline wannabes, and Karl, the guy who put in your driveway.

At Saratoga, if you time it right, you can see both a beautiful sunrise and later a memorable sunset over the dark waters of Saratoga Lake. At Del Mar, a Pacific sunset from the beach is tonic enough for any soul, but if you are still there for sunrise you've probably got some explaining to do.

At Saratoga, horsemen have the option of working their horses on the popular Oklahoma Training Track, thus relieving the pressure on the main track. At Del Mar, horsemen can hold their breath and dive into the main track mob each morning, or simply release their horses into the San Dieguito wetlands and pray for low tide.

Del Mar fans get mariachis in the courtyard. Saratoga has that damn bell . . . all day long.

Del Mar is made of concrete, steel, stucco, and tile. Saratoga is made of wood, wood, wood, and more wood.

At Saratoga, you park on lawns, alleys, porches, and driveways just to get within a few blocks of the track. At Del Mar, you check your watch at 1:30, dust off the beach sand, and stroll down the road in plenty of time to set up shop near the rail and get down on the first of the rolling pick threes.

Saratoga has trees in the parking lots, trees in the infield, trees on the backside, and trees growing through the blacktop behind the grandstand. Del Mar has plenty of trees, too. Some of them are even green.

At Saratoga, a good race is an open maiden event with 12 horses by Danzig, Saint Ballado, Carson City, Polish Numbers, and Storm Cat. At Del Mar, sirens sound and balloons fall from the rafters for a field of 10. Never mind that it's made of horses who have yet to win for a $15,000 tag.

At Saratoga, after the races, Marylou Whitney goes home with her party riding in horse-drawn carriages, accompanied by mounted police who stop traffic on Broadway to let them pass. At Del Mar, after he's had enough for the day, Mike Pegram puts his grandson Gator on one shoulder, his cooler on the other, and walks up the hill to the Solana Gate and down the street to his summer place on the cliffs overlooking the track.

Saratoga, in all its glorious history dating back to the Civil War, is a grand place to visit, to soak in the traditions of the game, and to bask in the glow of names like Bill Travers, Lillian Russell, and "Diamond" Jim Brady. You feel special just walking around.

But Del Mar is a deep breath of fresh air, where nobody cares if you wear khaki pants or a cardboard belt. Traditions don't go back 100 years. They go back to last week, when you found that great margarita bar run by the cast from *Coyote Ugly* and valet parking for free. And besides, they always save my spot on the beach.

~~~

## TIGER AND BIG RED

*June 22, 2000*

Writers deal in metaphors. Call it an occupational weakness. Everything reminds us of something else, or else we get confused, frustrated, and driven to desperate adjectives.

So it was last Sunday night, in the press tent near the 18th green at Pebble Beach, that a collection of the best sportswriters in the business wrestled with the challenge of placing the U. S. Open victory of Tiger Woods into perspective. They summoned the images of Michael Jordan, Babe Ruth, Jim Thorpe. They trotted out home-run kings and lopsided Super Bowls. One writer went from laptop to laptop, polling his colleagues with the question, "Have you ever seen anything like this?"

"Yes," answered Tom Callahan, contributing editor of *Golf Digest* and former sports editor of *Time* magazine. "I saw Secretariat win the Belmont by 31 lengths."

That was the name, the common thread, that kept cropping up in story after story as writers tried to describe Woods's 15-shot humiliation of the world's finest golfers:

"This was Tiger Woods, a gale force in his own right, who turned the final day of the 100th U. S. Open into the biggest runaway since Secretariat in the 1973 Belmont Stakes." —Chris Dufresne, *Los Angeles Times*.
~~~

"It was reminiscent of Pedro Martinez reeling off 17 strikeouts and shutting down the Yankees in the Bronx last September. Or Mark McGwire swatting No. 68 and 69 and then 70 two years ago. Or Secretariat, 31 lengths ahead, 27 years ago." —Gerry Callahan, *Boston Herald.*

"Tiger Woods could have had John Daly and Jean Van de Velde play his final hole and he still would have won the 100th U.S. Open on Sunday. Thankfully, Woods finished the round himself, so now we have an updated version of Secretariat romping home to win the Belmont by a country mile." —Michael Mayo, *Florida Sun-Sentinel.*

Mayo, also an accomplished racing writer, embellished his theme later in the paragraph by describing Woods as ". . . grinding along, moving like a tremendous machine," in homage to announcer Chic Anderson's unforgettable description of Secretariat's most famous race. And there truly was something Secretariat-like to the isolated splendor of Woods last Sunday, other than the fact that they both wore red.

"It was a one-sided, one-man show," wrote Gerry Callahan. "But it was sports history, and how can that not be a great show?"

Golf fans lucky enough to walk the fairways at Pebble Beach last weekend will be able to tell their grandchildren the same kind of tales shared by racing fans who were at Belmont Park on June 9, 1973, when Secretariat separated himself for all time from all other four-legged creatures.

For this particular father and his very special son, the 100th U. S. Open was always in the cards. He had been there before, sort of, while being carried by his pregnant mother around Pebble Beach in June of 1982 when Tom Watson beat Jack Nicklaus with the shot heard 'round the world. To expect a more exciting tournament 18 years later was unreasonable, and completely unnecessary.

Five years ago, when it was announced that Pebble Beach would be the site of the 2000 Open, we made plans to go. As far as we were concerned, it seemed a perfect way to celebrate what was going to be a high-school graduation. Never mind who showed up or what happened. For all we cared, the 2000 Open could have ended up golf's equivalent of the colorless 2000 Belmont Stakes. Andy North and Lou Graham in a playoff at eight over par. It still would be golf heaven.

Instead, we got history. Day after day, through the fog and the wind and the startling Monterey coast sunshine, the grin on my son's face grew in proportion to the red numbers posted by Woods on the big scoreboards. We searched the field for our personal Sham, some worthy opponent to push Woods into new dimensions. But in the end, the search was pointless. Like Secretariat in the Belmont, Woods was in competition with Woods. Or, as Charles Hatton wrote of Big Red:

"His only point of reference is himself."

"Both experiences for me were otherworldly, but they were also very different," said Bill Nack, Secretariat's biographer, who was glued to his TV for the entire Woods performance.

"One was a physically astonishing act in terms of heart, stamina, speed," Nack said. "The other was like watching a guy cutting the Hope diamond. It was so precise. Woods's accomplishment required a toughness of mind. Secretariat's, on the other hand, was a feat of sheer athleticism . . . one that I'd never seen before nor will ever see again."

Such moments tend to push the mundane aside, for it is not every day you get to witness history. At the end of the afternoon, as we skirted the stands at the 17th to take a place along Tiger's 18th and final fairway, my son stopped, looked at me, and with great concern said, "Wait a minute. Today is Father's Day!"

I had to laugh. He was forgiven.

"Yeah," I said. "Today is Father's Day, too."

~~~

## DUCK!

*February 25, 2000*

Racing is a dangerous game, and not simply for the horses and jockeys. Mutuel clerks risk carpal tunnel syndrome and paper cuts. Turf writers live in fear of salmonella from all that free food. And one of these days, a redundant racetrack executive will discover, to his horror, that his golden parachute failed to open.
~~~

It can be risky down in the pits, as well. Consider this item from the foreign desk, courtesy of the *Racing Post*, filed earlier this week from Wolverhampton Racecourse in England:

"They say a horseshoe is lucky, but bookmaker's clerk Ray Turner was left counting his blessings after being hit by one at Wolverhampton on Saturday night. The plate was thrown from one of the runners as they passed the betting ring, where it just missed several people before thudding into Turner's left shoulder.

"Turner, 50, who works for Merseyside-based bookmaker Terry Higgins, was straightening the money in his boss's bag and unaware of the potentially lethal missile heading his way. Although his jacket cushioned some of the blow, he was taken to the racecourse medical room and given painkillers, while an ice-pack was applied to the shoulder. He was still complaining of a tingling sensation in his left hand more than 90 minutes later.

" 'I've been working in the ring for 25 years and have never heard of anything like this,' Turner said. 'I was just doing my job, and suddenly this thing struck me on the shoulder. It could have been much worse if it had hit me, or someone else, on the head.' "

Or someone else . . .

Jack Perry was fed up with English food, English theater, English weather—all things English, for that matter, except for the horses. At an English racecourse he was in seventh heaven, far from the humdrum ovals back home. This was real racing, not some glorified video game.

When he arrived in London, it had taken the yobos at British Airways two days to find his lost bag. Now here he was, 24 hours left on this vacation from hell, and all he could think of was how to get from Euston Station to Wolverhampton in time for the 7:30 Saturday night.

"At least the trains run on time," Perry thought as he grabbed a *Telegraph*, a greasy bag of fries ("Okay. Gimme some chips!") and a warm Coke before settling into a standard-class car heading north.

Perry was a hardcore horseplayer from Chicago who was convinced he could beat the English game because he studied tapes like a maniac back home. It cost him to keep up, with conversion to American video, expensive form books, and a subscription to the *Racing Post*. But so far, it had been worth it.

He loved to play cheap horses on the flat in the winter. He figured it was easy pickings. Besides, there was something about English claimers running on wood chips that hit home with Perry's blue-collar sensibilities. These were tough nuts relegated to the back room of the racing scene, not the sleek, sheikh-bred darlings trotted out two or three times a year and otherwise kept wrapped in cotton.

Like Dahlidya. She may have been bred by Arabs to win the Oaks, but she was a working stiff now. Perry watched her run at Wolverhampton on Thursday afternoon from the shelter of a Coral betting shop near Buckingham Palace. The mare was overmatched, and ran like it, but then she turned up the next day—the very next day!—in a 6-furlong claimer at Southwell. Back at the Coral shop, Perry took the 7-2 and watched her win by a length, then went around the corner for a pint at the Gobsmack Pub.

Saturday was Perry's last day to play. He had a good feeling about a horse named Sharp Shuffle, and he wanted to watch it happen in the flesh. He made Wolverhampton in plenty of time to hit the tote and box Sharp Shuffle with a couple of longshots—one of them an Irish animal named Doberman who had just won for the first time in 33 starts.

Perry was still shopping for straight bets in the bookie ring when the race went off. The best he could find on Sharp Shuffle was 5-1, same as the tote. He took up a spot in front of the stall occupied by a bookmaker named Higgins, and by the time the field came into view around the final turn of the pear-shaped course, Doberman was leading at 25-1 and Sharp Shuffle was closing fast. As they flew past, it looked like Doberman held on.

Perry jumped in the air and upon landing doubled over in excitement. He felt something whiz past his ear. Behind him, beneath the cheers, he heard a thud and a voice.

"Ow!"

And a man with a bag of money grabbed his shoulder.

~~~
~~~

# THE DOCTOR IS IN

*December 13, 2006*

Joe Steiner was introduced to Dr. David Seftel in the usual manner. That is to say, Steiner was flat on his back, on the clubhouse turn of the Bay Meadows turf course, dazed and gasping for breath.

"I was there to ride the stake, and I picked one up in the last race," Steiner said not long ago. "The horse fell after the wire. Next thing I know, I'm lying on the ground, the wind knocked out of me, and there he is, standing over me. I asked him how he got there. He said, 'I ran.' "

For Steiner, such mundane tumbles were par for the course. In Seftel's experience, though, as medical director of the two major Northern California racetracks, there is a certain amount of urgency attached to even the most innocent looking fall.

"You've got about 90 seconds to get someone breathing again to have a chance to avoid major brain damage," Seftel said. "And after three minutes, they're brain-dead. There is no luxury of time."

In the harsh economic reality of the racing world, there is really no room for a luxury like David Seftel. His presence in the medical mix of the Thoroughbred world is nothing short of amazing. When Bay Meadows management was looking for someone as a temporary replacement for a retiring track physician during the 2000 San Mateo County Fair, their specifications did not read like this:

Wanted—Board-certified internist, currently on staff as pulmonologist at San Mateo Medical Center, preferably trained at Harvard's Beth Israel Hospital and Loyola University, also with a Master's degree in business administration from Harvard. Other interests should include research directorships in areas of macular degeneration and disease surveillance technology, as well as the application of NASA tele-medicine technologies in making prenatal ultrasound screening available to the impoverished, AIDS-riddled rural female population of South Africa.

But that's what they got.

"I was fascinated," said Seftel, 38, of his first reaction to the racetrack. "It was like walking into a totally different world. There was so much about horse racing that I did not know. But it was very familiar in that it was family. No matter what their petty conflicts might be, the objective every single day was to put forth their best performance.

"It was also an environment in which people wanted to be well," Seftel said. "This is different from a lot of clinical practice, particularly in hospitals these days, in which you have a category of people which I term the institutionally sick, the people who wallow in the sick role, who keep coming back to the hospital and actually become comfortable with that role. At the racetrack, people get ill, but they want to get better, because they're passionate about what they do."

Seftel's mandate is to care primarily for the jockeys in his practice, but that has not stopped him from treating the ills of the backstretch community and even the occasional fan. Pete Tunney, president of Golden Gate Fields, marvels at Seftel's generosity.

"The running joke has been, someone with a cold will want to go see Seftel, but they can't, because he's doing open-heart surgery," Tunney said. "He's a real humanitarian, who also happens to be a genius."

A more or less typical week in Seftel's very atypical work life recently included a trip to his native South Africa for hands-on administration of the prenatal ultrasound project, then a presentation at the Jockeys' Guild meeting in Las Vegas on the riders' health survey, and then back to his clinic at Bay Meadows, where he attended to a pair of riders who went down last Sunday in the mud. Both of them got up.

"I've always been drawn to unusual challenges," Seftel said. "But I pale in comparison to my parents. They always say I'm bone idle and lazy."

Seftel is a son of doctors, both professors of medicine. His father, Dr. Harry Seftel, puts in 14-hour work days that include being radio host of one of South Africa's most popular call-in health shows.

Harry's son, on the other hand, makes headlines only when he is called on to comment about serious injuries to jockeys—injuries that might have been worse without the rapid response provided by Bay Meadows and Golden Gate through Seftel's clinic.

"There is very inconsistent medical and emergency care at racetracks throughout the country," Seftel said. "I was taken by the fact that there are very few racetracks that actually have a doctor on-site and have trained paramedics. Most tracks have basic life-support ambulance crews—young kids just out of college with a few weeks of training in CPR, but absolutely no experience in the extreme kind of trauma that we see at the racetrack.

"Sometimes, when I look at my records, the repertoire of cases and conditions is more bizarre than the most extraordinary fiction," he said. "I remember a day at Golden Gate when we had five riders down. One with a punctured lung, one with a fractured spine—literally a classic triage situation. That's a scenario that all racetracks have to plan for and be ready for, but unfortunately very few are."

If Seftel has anything to say about it, that will eventually change.

~~~

## MEN OF LETTERS

*August 11, 2012*

Heroes serve a purpose, though one size does not fit all. Mine are mostly literary for the simple reason, I suppose, that it is natural to aim for even the loftiest of targets once you've settled on a certain path in life.

I lost three heroes from my living pantheon this week, making it a bad week by most standards but a good time to embrace the reasons they were there in the first place.

Robert Hughes was Australian, as loud and as flamboyant as many of the artists he both loved and loathed as the longtime critic for *Time* magazine. His 1981 BBC series, *The Shock of the New*, raised the bar forever for those who fancied themselves perceptive observers of modern culture, while his books took the reader on bracing journeys to Barcelona, Sydney, and Rome, as well as to his adopted land in the monumental *American Visions*.

Writing with "precise and vivacious eloquence," in the words of his friend and fellow critic Leon Wieseltier, Hughes was praised by contemporaries as "the most famous art critic in the world," for what that's
~~~

worth. For me, he was always the most lyrical of writers who could say what needed to be said because—in historical terms—he knew where the bodies were buried, and how they got there. He was 74 and lived in a New York loft.

I signed on early for the long ride with Gore Vidal when I realized he was the guy who wrote *The Best Man*, both the play and screenplay. If there is a better political drama, the floor will entertain nominations. Nominations closed.

With Vidal you got egg roll, and every other dish on the intellectual menu, plus politics. When he ran for the Democratic nomination for the U. S. Senate in California, in 1982, he reasoned, "I don't want it written on my tombstone that he always complained but he never did anything about it." He lost, even with my vote.

As a historical novelist, Vidal has few peers, as *Lincoln*, *Burr*, and *1876* attest. As a media raconteur, he could slice and dice the most formidable rivals. Little pieces of William F. Buckley and Norman Mailer still litter the studio floors where they clashed. As for his trenchant commentaries on America's place in the world, let's just say that history gets to decide if Vidal was on the right side of things after all. He died in Los Angeles and was 86.

Pete Pedersen, my third man of letters, would blanch at the idea of being tag-teamed in the same space as Hughes and Vidal. Pedersen knew the good stuff when he read it, but he was not a writer by trade—only by early inclination and necessity—and he lived his long life with a writer's sensibility, always attuned to the good story, the sad tale, the ironic twist.

This quality gave Pedersen a bulletproof defense against the absurd extremes of his profession. As a racing steward, he was charged with a lot more than calling balls and strikes. The concerns that crossed his desk ranged from the deadly to the petty—cocaine positives, parking fines, financial fraud, brawls. Once, he and his fellow stewards had to deal with a man who had sexually assaulted a goat.

"There's no accounting for taste," Pedersen said later with a straight face. "But the concern here is for the well-being of the goat."

Pedersen knew the lot of the steward was to be criticized from all sides, sometimes all at once. To honor his retirement in July of 2005, Hollywood Park officials asked Pedersen to descend from the stewards' stand and present the trophy for the Hollywood Gold Cup to the winning owner. He hesitated.

"I told them they were really taking a chance," Pedersen said. "If I were shot, there would be many suspects."

The exaggeration was amusing, but wide of the mark. At the end of the day, Pedersen was one of those individuals who commanded respect because he treated others likewise. To Pete, it was a rare fellow who ever did anything wrong on purpose.

"Eddie Arcaro didn't like officials much," Pedersen once recalled. "But he said if you didn't have them, the jocks would go out and kill each other. I know they can't run in lanes—there has to be competition—but the safety of the horse and rider is something we have to be concerned with all the time."

Pedersen celebrated his 92nd birthday this year on the Fourth of July. A few weeks later he fell on the walkway in front of his home in Arcadia, suffered a severe head injury and never regained consciousness. He will be laid to rest at Forest Lawn in Hollywood Hills, not far from the gravesites of Bette Davis, Lucille Ball, Gene Autry, Jack Webb, and Buster Keaton. According to his family, Pedersen would want memorial donations to go in his name to a Thoroughbred retirement organization or a local animal shelter.

That's fine, but first I need to come to terms with the fact my friend is gone. In retirement, Pedersen was restless, a vital intellect. He read voraciously, fiddled with his archives, and vowed to learn how to surf the net. From time to time he'd write a piece for a trade publication, sharing anecdotes with the literary touch of a latter-day Red Smith. He would turn up at Clocker's Corner, the Santa Anita morning hangout, if only to bask in the delight of shared memories with familiar faces. He'd make a regular pilgrimage to witness the Santa Anita Handicap, anonymous in the crowd until someone called out, "Pete!" and his cover was blown.

"What do you think, Pete?" he was asked on a March day in 2011, while the stewards were agonizing over their inquiry into Game On Dude's narrow Handicap victory.

"It's a tough one," he replied, then allowed himself a grin. "I think I'm glad I'm down here instead of up there."

~~~

## WHO'S ON FIRST?

*May 12, 2001*

Let's see if I've got this straight. Kent Desormeaux began the season with Tony Matos as his agent, then left for Japan in April. Matos already had Victor Espinoza and Julio Garcia, and now he will be representing Gary Stevens, while Garcia has been picked up by Rene San Miguel, who also has Matt Garcia, no relation.

Stevens began the 2001 season represented by Corey Black, the former rider who had once been represented by Bob Meldahl, among others. Stevens then switched from Black to Meldahl, who also had Laffit Pincay, who used to have Tony Matos, but that was a long time ago.

Meldahl had room for Stevens in his stable because Corey Nakatani, no relation to Corey Black, left California to ride in Kentucky. He didn't like it there, so Nakatani returned to California, and Meldahl took him back, and Stevens switched to Matos. As far as anyone knows, Desormeaux is still in Japan.

If all of this is confusing, don't sweat it. The last thing a racing fan needs to remember is the name of the guy who is booking the mounts for the jockeys who are out there doing all the heavy lifting. And yes, they are mostly guys, except for Michelle Barsotti, who used to have Brice Blanc but now works for Garrett Gomez, who used to have . . . oh, never mind.

Given the recent flurry of agent-hopping out West, which is beginning to resemble a French farce with a long hallway and lots of slamming doors, the profession of jock's agent would appear to have no more stability than that of Italian prime minister. There are, of course, exceptions to the rule. Harry Silbert and Bill Shoemaker were inseparable, certainly a smart move on Silbert's part. Scotty McClellan is going on 20 years with Chris McCarron. "People would always say I was always jumping around,
~~~

taking jocks away from other agents," said Charles "Chick" McClellan, Scotty's father, now retired. "I never took a jock away from anybody in my life."

McClellan had a good run with Alvaro Pineda in the late 1960s and early 1970s, then took the book of Fernando Toro for 11 years.

"Eleven years, eight months," McClellan corrected. "And I probably made a bad move there at one point, because I could have taken Pincay, and I didn't do it. I thought too much of Fernando. I might be giving myself more pats on the back than I deserve, but I liked him and his family so much, I thought his business might suffer."

Loyalty. What a concept. But it happens, even in the hyper-competitive world of jockeys and their agents. One of the best was another guy named Chick—Charles "Chick" Lang—who has had just about every job that exists on the racetrack, frontside and back. Lang, now a consultant for the Jockeys' Guild, had Bill Hartack's book for six years at the beginning of the jockey's Hall of Fame career.

"It was the best job I ever had," Lang said. "In fact, I think that every trainer, before they get a trainer's license, should have to be an agent for 60 days. That way they can learn to read a condition book."

Lang booked mounts for Hartack in the days when an agent got 10 percent of the jockey's customary 10 percent. Today an agent gets anywhere from 20-30 percent of his jock's take, depending on the deal he cuts. Lang licked his lips at the thought of a money-rider like Hartack roaming the country in the year 2001, gobbling up the stakes cash.

"What a lollipop that would be," Lang said.

The job does look pretty simple, at least at first glance. Pete Wilson, gone now but never forgotten as an all-around racetrack character, boiled down the job of the jock's agent thusly:

"All you need is a nickel pencil. The condition book is free."

Wilson hustled book for a lot of riders, including Hartack near the end of his career. But even Wilson would admit that the best agents work for their money, especially if a rider is in demand.

"I wouldn't call it hard work, but it's not a job for a lazy person," said Corey Black, who now represents Luis Jauregui in addition to Blanc.

"It's time-consuming," Black went on. "And it's getting a little more sophisticated now. I use the Ragozin Sheets, and when I had Gary, I had to have a secretary to handle billings. And because of simulcasting, I'm watching a race every five minutes instead of every half hour."

Still, for all the technology, it comes down to people skills. Lang insists that an agent needs to be a salesman, first and foremost. The ability to juggle also helps.

"I used to give everybody I could second call," Lang said. "You try to hang them up as long as you can. I would give them a definite maybe."

At last, it all makes sense.

~~~

## EAU DE ROSES

*May 10, 2005*

Who needs a Triple Crown winner? Or all those Rip Torn racing commercials? Or even a *Seabiscuit* sequel? Horse racing suddenly has a lovable longshot named Giacomo, an overnight major media magnet providing both high drama and low humor.

Those who didn't hit at 50-1 can at least laugh in the aftermath. Save the bitter tears for real tragedies, like a war without end, or the next album by Bjork. After all, it's only horses running in a circle. In the wake of last Saturday's dizzy Kentucky Derby, some of the best and brightest are stepping up with Giacomo jokes and routines, led by America's foremost closet horse-racing fan, David Letterman.

Letterman devoted a significant amount of valuable late-night network time on his Monday show to Giacomo's Derby upset, beginning with videotape of the race, slightly doctored, that depicted a horse with an ignited tail zooming past the field.

"Immediately after, a stewards' inquiry went up," Letterman deadpanned. "What it looked like to me was that the horse had some sort of rocket strapped to its ass."

Biff Henderson, Letterman's blue-collar version of Charles Kuralt,
~~~

shared his Derby adventure at Churchill Downs that included a mint julep drinking binge and lines like, "Did you know that the ladies consider me the most exciting two minutes in the bedroom?" and, "Do you mind if I try on your hat?"

There was a touching moment in the jockeys' room as well, when Biff, surrounded on a couch by Mark Guidry, John Velazquez, and Mike Smith, confessed, "You know, you guys are so cute, I'd like to put you in my pocket and take you home."

To no one's surprise, Biff bet on Giacomo. Whether it was before or after the race, it didn't really matter.

Back in the studio, Letterman's "Top Ten Tips for Winning the Kentucky Derby" was inevitably read by Mike Smith, Giacomo's jockey, wearing his white pants, boots, and the silks of Ann and Jerry Moss. The best of the Ten were No. 6 ("Starter will let you out of gate early if you slip him a twenty"), No. 4 ("Two words: vibrating saddle"), and No. 2 ("To eliminate wind resistance, shave your horse"). And the No. 1 tip for winning the Kentucky Derby: "It helps if your trainer is Jose Canseco."

For those who find joy in a glass half-full, Giacomo also contributed to a bad day for the owner of a certain professional baseball team, as Jay Leno noted in his *Tonight Show* opening monologue Monday night. The zingers went like this:

"Let's see, it's about 11:40, so George Steinbrenner's horse should be crossing the finish line any time now." (laughs) "I think he was hoping to use the horse to distance himself from the Yankees." (laughs) "The Kentucky Derby winner was Giacomo." (smattering of applause) "Yankee owner George Steinbrenner's horse Bellamy Road finished seventh." (cheers) "In fact, George gave the horse a new name today—Yankee Stadium Hot Dog." (groans and laughs)

Humor, of course, is in the eye of the beholder. One man's belly laugh is another's stifled yawn, and Derby winners, as a rule, are not particularly funny. Once in a while, a horse comes along to crack the deadly serious facade of the whole Triple Crown enterprise, yet it is impossible to predict which one it will be. As a test, compare and contrast recent Derby winners for automatic laughs:

Fusaichi Pegasus—not unless Buddy Hackett says the name.

Monarchos—ran too fast to be funny.

War Emblem—lone front-runners are never funny.

Funny Cide—made Barclay Tagg smile; now that's funny.

Smarty Jones—more way cool and hip than ha-ha funny.

Giacomo—see, there. . .you smiled!

New York satirist Andy Borowitz took time off from daily taunts directed at politicians, Fox News, and Ben Affleck to report the pseudo-news headline, "Derby Winner Launches Fragrance," a perfume to be called Whoa by Giacomo.

"Giacomo's decision to launch a celebrity fragrance caught many in the perfume industry by surprise, since no horse-based scent has ever had mass-market success at the nation's cosmetic counters," Borowitz noted.

"But Jesse Diblanco, who heads up the consumer products division of Team Giacomo, dismisses such naysaying, claiming that Giacomo is an exception to the rule: 'He's not a horse, he's a brand.'

"Within the racing industry, some observers are voicing their concern that Giacomo's sudden plunge into the world of celebrity culture may hurt his chances of winning the second leg of racing's Triple Crown, the Preakness.

"In addition to launching his fragrance, Giacomo has been seen partying in recent days with such staples of the club circuit as Paris Hilton and white-hot teen starlet Lindsay Lohan. Late Monday night, for example, reporters spotted Giacomo stumbling back to his stall, trailing empty bottles of Cristal champagne in his wake.

"Racing insider Dobie Grossman worries that for Giacomo, the Derby success was a case of too much, too soon: 'Remember, at the end of the day, he's only three years old.' "

Racing fans, enjoy it while you can. Something like this can happen only once a year, if at all, no matter how much time Letterman spends in wishful thinking.

"It's such an exciting event," Letterman said. "It kicks off the Triple Crown, and it's so successful that they're talking about having it every Saturday."

~~~
~~~

# ENGLAND SWINGS

*September 17, 2011*

It was confusing enough, driving in England, what with the steering wheel where my dachshund usually pokes her nose out the passenger-side window. The accelerator was down there where it belonged, but the gear shift required operation by my left hand, which is normally about as useless as a placing judge in a walkover.

Driving on the left side of the road is easier than you'd think, though, once you learn—the hard way more often than not—from which direction the danger comes. Eventually, the American pilgrim grows accustomed to the deeper meaning of signs such as Diversion, Way Out, Give Way, and Roundabout (the last of these an obvious homage to the 40th anniversary of the song from Yes), and takes comfort in the knowledge that the British think the way they drive is nuts, too.

Yep, I was doing fine until I stopped for petrol—or "gas" as some call it—and presented my cash at the convenience-store counter, requesting "twenty pounds on number five," as if I knew what I was doing. The clerk checked his machine, cleared his throat, and looked at me with an expression normally reserved for an otherwise well-behaved child who's just wet himself.

"But you haven't pumped any gas yet, sir," he explained.

"You mean I don't pay first?"

"Well, no," he replied. "No you don't."

Obviously, this is no way to run a country. But I was in Yorkshire, far from the breakneck bustle of London Town, and by then I was growing accustomed to a more relaxed way of doing business. Perhaps it was because it was St. Leger week at Doncaster Racecourse, celebrating a classic race that had been around since Washington crossed the Delaware. Maybe it was the broad fields dotted with horses and hay rolls, or the vast, roiling Yorkshire skies, or the fact that no one panicked when I wandered into their lane while admiring the view. Wherever the magic came from, it worked.

It is a fact, however, that such brief, wide-eyed visits tend to obscure the true texture of the times. The British people are experiencing the same economic woes as Americans, and British horse racing is likewise struggling to maintain any semblance of health in its historically rich corner of the sporting and entertainment world.

Of course, you wouldn't know it from the 30,000 or so warm and windblown fans who turned out on St. Leger day last Saturday to cheer home Masked Marvel in the big one, giving trainer John Gosden and jockey William Buick their second straight victory in the mile and three-quarter event. Even the most cynical observer of the scene would have been likewise encouraged by the response of the racing industry to the Leger Legends event that kicked off the festival three days earlier for the benefit of the Injured Jockeys Fund and the Northern Racing College, also located in Doncaster.

"We're serving two very good causes," said Tim Adams, head of the Leger Legends organizing committee. "The mandate of the Northern Racing College is to provide quality training for young people to work in the industry—jockeys, work riders, stable hands—and of course the Injured Jockeys Fund is necessary to care for the unluckiest of the many riders injured in the line of duty. You might say between the two of them they represent the hopeful beginning of a career in racing and the very real possibility of how things might end up in a very dangerous sport."

Adams, an accountant by trade, is a horse owner and a passionate supporter of his local Huddersfield rugby league team whose international business adventures have taken him to Australia, Africa, and the Orient. He tries hard to be optimistic in the face of the numbers necessary to operate the Northern Racing College (of which he is a trustee) or build a rehabilitation center for injured jockeys in the Yorkshire region. But in the end, Adams and his allies must confront the same challenges facing their American counterparts when trying to support such unfunded moral mandates as nurturing a viable work force and caring for the injured among them.

"We get funding from the government, but that's getting tougher," Adams pointed out. "There's a small amount coming in from the racing authority, as well as private funding from loyal benefactors. But you can only go back to them so many times. And then there are fundraisers, like the Leger Legends, which also help raise awareness."

The centerpiece of the Leger Legends event was the second running of a race featuring 16 retired jockeys at a mile down the Town Moor straightaway at Doncaster. Among the participants were such popular personalities from both the flat and the jumps as John Reid, Kevin Darley, and Charlie Swan. With betting sanctioned and everyone playing for real, the many bookmaking companies stepped up to pledge a minimum contribution to the cause, with more possible based on handle. Adams noted that upwards of 100,000 pounds was likely raised, a very loud and satisfying drop in a deep bucket.

In the spirit of full disclosure, my wife, Julie Krone, was among the 16, and not only did she have way too much fun, she had the good fortune to finish first, which means she now has followers in places called Scunthorpe and Barnsley.

"I don't think I've ever ridden for free in my life," she beamed afterward, "and I was never happier to do it."

Credit where credit's due, though. Somehow I got her to the races that day without hitting anything … of consequence.

~~~

## CURTAINS

*December 12, 2013*

It was a big deal at the time, my first trip to Hollywood Park, but not so much because of where I was going with my dad but who we were going to see that summer afternoon.

We were going to see Hill Rise, my Thoroughbred hero, who had seduced my fertile teenage imagination with his towering physique and commanding presence—and that was just on TV. I had survived his bittersweet spring of 1964, when Hill Rise hurtled through the Santa Anita meet unscathed before Northern Dancer ruined his/my day in the Kentucky Derby. Now I was ready to behold the big guy for the first time in
~~~

the flesh, as Hill Rise tried to be the first horse since Noor in 1950 to win the Santa Anita Handicap and the Hollywood Gold Cup in the same year. I knew enough to know a horse doesn't get much better than that.

Details of the day are sketchy. I was 14, so give me a break. It turns out that the official crowd count of 58,971 on that July 17, 1965, ended up the largest ever for a Hollywood Gold Cup. But to me, big crowds were no big deal.

By then, I'd been to a World Series at Dodger Stadium (October 2, 1963, Game 3, the house filled to its 55,912 capacity), a USC–Notre Dame game at the Los Angeles Coliseum (November 28, 1964, attendance: 83,840), and the 1965 Rose Parade on a chilly New Year's Day morning with about a million other souls lining Colorado Boulevard in Pasadena. Arnold Palmer was Grand Marshal.

We watched the Gold Cup from the apron, standing at about the sixteenth pole, with Harry Henson's gravelly call barely audible above the 58,970 fans screaming around me. Whoosh went this black thing by us, topped with blue polka dots on white, followed a couple of beats later by the rest of the field, including Hill Rise. Native Diver won by five. My horse finished third.

The Hollywood Park of 1965 has been gone for quite some time. Horses saddled back then in paddock stalls by the track. There was no turf course, the racetrack was only a mile around, and it would be years before the monstrous casino building would be tacked on to the west.

Also, those were Canadian geese adorning the infield, instead of the current tribe of forlorn flamingos.

I'll always regret that I missed the original Hollywood Park, which opened in 1938 and rivaled crosstown Santa Anita with its high-end art-deco touches of stylish curves, polished woods, plush alcoves, and reflecting pools. It was all ritzy Hollywood for a Hollywood crowd, and it burned like an oiled torch one night in May 1949.

It was rebuilt with some of the original style and then maintained as neat as a pin through the 1950s and '60s while considered nothing less than one of California's finest sporting venues.

Californians of a certain age (mine) commenced their affair with Hollywood Park during those heady years when Native Diver won three straight Hollywood Gold Cups. His reign as the West's most popular Thoroughbred provided some consolation for coming along after the eras of Seabiscuit, Noor, Citation, and Swaps, when the bar was set as high as a horse can reach.

Within the decade, I went from rabid grandstand fan to a dream job as a third-rung racetrack publicity flak, then from there to the ranks of the ink-stained wretches who lived out their racing fantasies on the printed page.

The oldest Hollywood Park memories are scattered and disorganized, snapshots tossed in a shoebox.

Here's one of me (lord, that hair) working for Bob Benoit and Nat Wess in the publicity department when I would every so often go for a jog on the flat, firm Bermuda grass turf course and imagine myself treading in the hoofprints of Pretense, Pink Pigeon, Fort Marcy, and Fiddle Isle.

Here's another of my Camaro pulling up lame no fewer than twice in neighborhoods surrounding Hollywood Park, leaving me at the mercy of what were supposed to be roaming bands of vicious youths. Instead, I got lifts from locals, one of them with his own tow truck.

Here's the day I stopped by John Henry's stall in one of the older wooden barns not long after he returned from winning the Sword Dancer in New York. I dared to give him a playful hug, but only because he was still feeling the quieting effects of a travel-size dose of acepromazine. Ron McAnally looked on and grinned.

"Be careful," he said. "It'll wear off in about five minutes, and then you're in trouble."

And in this one, I'm standing alongside some bald dude peering through a viewing window at the Hollywood Park equine hospital as Dr. Greg Ferraro removed two bone chips from the right knee of Sunday Silence. It was just 13 days after the black colt had beaten Easy Goer in their version of Ali-Frazier at the Breeders' Cup Classic.

Charlie Whittingham, the bald dude who trained and owned a piece of Sunday Silence, wondered how the other guy felt.

Will I miss Hollywood Park? Of course I will, especially when I think of those moments shared there with trainers like Willard Proctor, Thad Ackel, Ian Jory, Lewis Cenicola, and Joe Manzi. I will miss the sprawling backstretch and the casual access to Zenyatta, Affirmed, Lava Man, Best Pal, Bayakoa, Ancient Title, Crystal Water, Flawlessly, and Quack.

If you were lucky enough to stand next to one of them, especially in the morning when they trained, their presence was so overwhelming, their spirit so deep, that you literally forgot where you were. It was Hollywood Park.

Anyway, I already miss standing with assistant trainer Humberto Ascanio on the clubhouse porch overlooking the winner's circle as one of his Bobby Frankel runners held forth. I will miss hanging with Neil Drysdale or Dick Mandella at the patio rail of the stable cafeteria, decoding their tics and twitches as their horses worked in front of us.

I will miss the long walk down the bridle path around the home turn to meet Cigar or Sandpit or Azeri coming over from the barns to the paddock. I will miss Grace in the press-box kitchen, Ruben in the Turf Club, and Rudy at the fountain gate.

In the end, it was the people and the horses who made Hollywood Park special, not the other way around. At the peak of its success, Hollywood Park provided a wonderful stage for some of the finest racing that California—and the nation—could ever expect. Now the stage comes down, but the show goes on because no matter how hard you swing it, you can't touch a memory with a wrecking ball.

~~~

## HOME OF THE BRAVE

*September 18, 2001*

Once, when they were both still young, Gary Stevens and Pat Valenzuela squared off in the jocks' room at Hollywood Park after a race filled with strife. Words were exchanged, then Valenzuela sent a punch in the general direction of Gary's firm, patrician chin. He barely flinched. Valenzuela held his hand in pain.
~~~

"That all you got?" Stevens said.

As the miles went by last Thursday night, the scene kept coming to mind, a metaphor—clumsy but pertinent—for the resilience of the American jawline. Civilization should never have to endure such an awful blow.

But now it was America's turn. America's turn to see if it could recover from its own London blitz, its own siege of Stalingrad, its own Nagasaki.

"That all you got?"

All night long, past the truck stops and the roadkill, the speakers of the dark-green Mustang rattled with the voices of talk-show hosts. It was Radio Free America, and it was all I had to get me through the darkness of 747 miles, from Des Moines to Dallas–Fort Worth, in time to make a flight back home.

The events of September 11 found this reporter on a brief holiday, celebrating a special family event near the eastern shores of Lake Michigan. Then the planes went down and the towers fell, freezing the country cold with fear and anger. So far away from lower Manhattan, feeling helpless and emotionally at sea, there was nothing to do but grieve and rant and finally try to find a way back home. The inconvenience was trivial, but, suddenly, being home became very important.

So the search began, through the heart of the country, looking for an open airport and an available flight to just about anywhere, as long as it was headed west.

The road signs passed like Scrabble tiles: Onomonowoc, Towanda, Makquaketa, Shickasha. "Pat, I'd like to buy a vowel." There was Belmont, Wisconsin, pop. 866, and Derby, Kansas, pop. 17,807. Just after sunset, a few miles east of Highway 61, sat Clinton, Iowa, the birthplace of Allen Paulson. A little while later, off to the west of I-35, the deep Missouri night sheltered tiny Parnell, where Jimmy Jones had been recently laid to rest.

I am now fairly certain that I can identify at least two of the Quad Cities. But I did not know that the National Teachers Hall of Fame was in Emporia, Kansas, or that the National Balloon Museum was in Indianola, Iowa, or that a skunk smells decidedly different if you are driving the car that hits him first. That was just north of Guthrie, Oklahoma.

Maybe the stink was coming from the radio. Sometimes it was hard to swallow. For every sober minute of Dan Schorr, there was an hour of Michael "Just Like My Dad" Reagan blaming the Trade Center tragedy on Bill Clinton, or Mike Savage and his *Savage Nation*, demanding nothing less than a nuclear apocalypse to be rained down upon Afghanistan.

At one turn in the road, a new station beamed in, bringing a classic radio episode of *The Green Hornet.* It was called "Murder Across the Board," a fine piece of theater set at a racetrack. There was a scam, a ringer, and a damsel in some sort of petty distress. I turned back to *Savage Nation.*

An all-sports station found its people arguing back and forth over the same point: To play or not to play. The announcer read the list of cancellations. "Major League Baseball, NFL football, the PGA, NASCAR . . . even horse racing!" Even horse racing, the game that never stops, bowed its head for a moment out of respect for the nation's loss.

Most of the talk-show callers were honestly conflicted, although such a moment flushes out the bitter cynics as well. In Oklahoma City, where terrorism is not an abstract, one caller suggested that canceling football games just because something bad happened back East was pure hogwash. His logic?

"I'll bet when the Federal Building was bombed, they didn't miss a beat in New York." The talk-show host agreed.

It was warming up on a bright Texas morning by the time I found the rental car lot at Dallas–Fort Worth International and pried my backside out of that fine green Mustang. She never missed a beat, or an oat, and she wore her New York license plates with honor.

The painful delays expected at airport check-in were temporarily alleviated by a light schedule of flights. Only the desperate and the stranded seemed to be travelling. I confessed to both. And since the pull of home was stronger than any fear of flying, there was only a wave of relief when—at 10:47 a.m., Central Daylight Time—Capt. Patrick Palmer lifted our Delta MD-90 off the runway, banked westward, and opened the throttle.

It was only then that I stopped to consider my fellow passengers, something travelers will be doing now with a new, anxious intensity. And that's when I saw them. Four or five young men scattered throughout the coach cabin, well-muscled and wearing T-shirts, jeans, tattoos, and identical haircuts.

Breathe easy. They were U. S. Marines, called back quickly from leave to their base at Camp Pendleton, just north of Del Mar. Soon they would be following their own dangerous orders, placing themselves in harm's way, acting out of duty and honor, and generally behaving like New York City firefighters. The kind that rush headlong into flaming, 110-story towers to save lives.

That's what we've got.

# Eight

# A SHOE FOR ALL SEASONS

*Forget about those photos of Bill Shoemaker draped in roses after winning the Kentucky Derby on Ferdinand or perched lightly aboard Spectacular Bid in full flight. The coolest ever Shoemaker image could be found in a high-class magazine advertisement making the rounds in the late 1980s. The ad features the 4-foot-10 Shoemaker and 7-foot-1 Wilt Chamberlain posed on a spit of seaside sand. Chamberlain is gazing off-camera and into the distance, while Shoemaker is leaning casually against Chamberlain's right hip and looking straight into the lens. They are both wearing white.*

*For the longest time, Bill Shoemaker was Thoroughbred racing, as far as the public was concerned, in the same way Wilt Chamberlain was basketball, Johnny Bench was baseball, and Jack Nicklaus was the first name to come to mind when anyone thought about professional golf. Shoemaker could be found on* The Tonight Show *joking with Johnny Carson, at Hollywood parties with Cary Grant and Elizabeth Taylor. He mingled the accessible star power of George Clooney with the artistic grace of Baryshnikov. He was also a scamp.*

*Until Bill Shoemaker sent some kind of practical joke in your direction, you really did not feel like part of the tribe. I was initiated with a hot spoon, recently dunked in scalding coffee, on the back of my neck as I sat in the jockeys' room debriefing Fernando Toro after a race. I turned to see Shoemaker in deft misdirection, demonstrating a wedge shot to a worshipful apprentice with an invisible golf club. Toro, my only witness, looked at me without sympathy.*

*Shoemaker began life prematurely born, wrapped in a blanket and placed in a shoebox at the mouth of a warm oven. At the end he was a prisoner of paralysis, the victim of a one-car freeway crash. He will be recalled for those operatic extremes, of course, but also for all that he accomplished in between.*

## LIFE OF THE MIND

*October 22, 1998*

Bill Shoemaker shrugged his shoulders, up and down, three, four, five times. He twisted his head hard to the left and back to the right. Then, with visible concentration, he raised his elbows about half an inch from the arm rests of his heavy black wheelchair.

"If I can do that now, who knows?" Shoemaker said. "Maybe someday I'll be able to use my upper body again."

It has been more than seven years since Shoemaker lost control of his Ford Bronco on the evening of April 8, 1991, while driving home from a golf game and rolled down a freeway embankment 10 miles east of Santa Anita Park.

The resulting damage to his spinal column left him a quadriplegic, unable to fend for himself and requiring around-the-clock, live-in care. He even had to learn how to breathe.

At the time of the accident—barely a year after he retired from riding with a world's record 8,833 wins—Shoemaker was building a clientele as a trainer. That career was effectively nipped in the bud, although a number of clients—Allen Paulson and Burt Bacharach among them—continued to send Shoemaker horses while he attempted to run the stable from his wheelchair.

Last winter, the effort finally took its toll. Shoemaker officially retired and gave up the stable to his assistant, Patrick Gallagher. At the age of 66, the most famous personality in modern Thoroughbred racing stepped once and for all into the background.

"Just trying to stay healthy is a full-time job," Shoemaker said earlier this week in his San Marino home, not far from Santa Anita. "I know guys in my situation that let themselves go. Don't take care of themselves at all. They've pretty much given up."

Shoemaker's voice was strong, or at least stronger than it had been in recent memory. The paralysis extends the length of his torso, making it difficult to breathe deeply enough to talk for an extended period of time. He describes the feeling like "a tight band wrapped around my chest."

He found he could develop his diaphragm, and he was able to learn to use it as a bellows to force air into his lungs. When he first rejoined public life, back in the fall of 1991 at the Oak Tree meet, he could utter only a few words at a time, and those words came with great difficulty. Today he can chat for more than an hour and hold up his end of the conversation. Silent Shoe? Not if he can help it.

"At first I had the tracheal tube to breathe," Shoemaker recalled. "It was awful, but I didn't have much choice. I remember the time I was in a special hospital bed that turned you automatically to prevent pressure sores. Once it turned me the wrong way, and my trach tube felt out. An alarm was supposed to go off at the nurses' station, but I guess it didn't right away. I was laying there, not getting any air, thinking this was it."

No such luck. Shoemaker was eventually weaned from the tracheal tube and artificial oxygen. "That was about the hardest thing I've ever done," he insisted. Tougher than riding against Arcaro, Longden, or Pincay? "Heck, that was fun."

But the physical challenges did not end. Breakdown was the greatest danger—and not the kind that happens to a racehorse below the knee. Quadriplegics, unable to manipulate their own bodies, suffer from a degeneration of skin tissue if their weight is not regularly shifted to relieve pressure. Shoemaker explained:

"When you can feel your feet, you're not going to let them point down, on the toes, or some other way that's not normal," he said. "I wouldn't know if that was happening. When it does, the bone puts pressure on the skin from the inside. That's when you get infection. Sometimes gangrene."

He was speaking from experience. Three years ago, Shoemaker came close to losing his right foot, the infection from pressure sores was so severe.

A friend at a local Veterans Administration hospital told Shoemaker about a new procedure—a variation on hyperbaric oxygen therapy developed originally for scuba divers suffering from carbon-dioxide poisoning. It was eventually discovered that the infusion of pure oxygen could also enhance healing and the growth of healthy skin tissue, hence its application to major burn victims and serious skin disease.

Topical hyperbaric oxygen therapy substitutes the full body chamber with a localized bag secured to the patient and inflated with oxygen. It was still in the experimental stages, but Shoemaker jumped at the chance. "What did I have to lose?"

He didn't lose his foot, and the results were so dramatic that Shoemaker eventually invested in a company that is marketing the procedure to hospitals. Shoemaker is not only honorary chairman and spokesman for Numotech, Inc., but he is also a satisfied customer. Last June he journeyed to Albuquerque, New Mexico, to appear at the launch of a research deal with Sandia National Laboratories to develop a portable oxygen unit.

It is clear that the project has invigorated Shoemaker. Life, he says, can get very boring. His physical needs are handled with smooth efficiency by home aides Harry Thein and Alvin Lwin. He can eat what he wants, but he tries to stay away from fatty foods, and alcohol has lost all appeal. He falls asleep easily at night, usually around 9 o'clock, but he wakes at odd hours.

He is surrounded in his L-shaped, ranch-style home with the trophies and memorabilia of his 41 years as a jockey. He can read the *Racing Form* or *The Blood-Horse* if someone turns the pages. A large TV gives the sports nut in Shoemaker as many games and racing shows as he can handle. There is no way, however, to fully appreciate the isolation of his existence.

"My life is pretty much all in my head," he said. "There are times I think, what's the use? Why am I trying so hard to stay healthy? It's hard not to think that way. I have to think about all the good things that have happened in my life. I think about my daughter."

Amanda Shoemaker is 18 and a freshman at the University of Colorado. Her parents divorced about four years ago and Amanda remained with her father, who is going through the usual separation anxiety. "I miss her a lot," Shoemaker said. "The house is quiet without her. But she's a big girl now."

Shoemaker appears at fundraisers for the Shoemaker Foundation, formed to assist seriously injured and financially strapped racetrack workers. He was on hand two weeks ago for a benefit concert at Hollywood Park.

He also visits the racetrack every week or so. Santa Anita management has chained off a small terrace in the clubhouse mezzanine section for Shoemaker. Sipping and puffing on the control tube of his automated wheelchair, Shoemaker will navigate through the crowd, spin a hard right, and come to a perfect stop at his usual spot.

Shoemaker remains convinced that someday he will regain the use of his upper body. In the meantime, he is keeping track of other options.

"There are voice-activated things I'm looking into for around the house," Shoemaker said. "Sometimes I end up alone, when I send Harry or Alvin out on an errand. They could get in an accident and I could be here two days—just sitting here—before anyone noticed.

"With voice-activated I could use a computer. I could control the lights and the thermostat. I could answer the phone and even make calls."

He grinned at the thought. "I'd be bothering people at all hours, calling up jocks or reporters and telling them just what they did wrong."

Somehow, that sounds like a call worth taking.

~~~

# TAKE A BOW

*February 3, 2000*

Robbie Davis has won more than 3,000 races. His mounts have earned more than $100 million in purses. But for all his collection of glittering mementos, the most cherished treasure in his trophy case is a framed pair of photographs depicting eerily similar scenes.

In one, the young Davis is being hoisted aloft by his fellow jockeys while he proudly displays a belt buckle freshly won at an Idaho county
~~~

fair. In the other, a more mature Davis is doing the hoisting, and the man perched on his shoulder is Bill Shoemaker.

That was on February 3, 1990, the day of Shoemaker's last ride.

"It was one of the highlights of my life," said Davis, one of 10 jockeys who rode against Shoemaker in the Legend's Last Ride at Santa Anita, 10 years ago on Thursday.

Shoemaker's last ride was a piece of history that attracted 64,573 fans to the track and a national television audience as part of ABC's *Wide World of Sports*. Santa Anita Park paid Shoemaker a reported $100,000 for the privilege to host the event, but to the men who rode against him that day, the experience was priceless.

"It was kind of emotional," said Fernando Toro, who retired less than five months later. He was 49. Shoemaker was 58.

"Believe me," Toro said, "after that day, going to the jocks' room, there was something missing. The next day, everybody was very quiet, but nobody wanted to say anything. The room was kind of empty."

So was the game. Even into his late 50s, as his business flagged, Shoemaker's presence lent the California riding colony an incomparable touch of class. This was where The Shoe hung his tack, and those who competed against him on a daily basis felt privileged to ride alongside.

Of course, they were also subjected to Shoemaker's guile at racetrack rummy and his endless catalog of practical jokes, from shaving cream in a sleeve to a hot spoon on the back of the neck.

"He'd put a bar of soap in my boot," Toro recalled. "I'd say, 'Bill, I don't mind you put the bar of soap in my boot. But you don't have to get it wet first.' "

On the day of his final ride—number 40,352—Shoemaker floated through the room, low-key as ever. He had been pointing for the day, riding only six times in the first month of the new decade, while winning twice to put his total at 8,833.

The Legend's Last Ride was a one-mile handicap on the grass for a purse of $100,000. Shoemaker had his pick of the field and chose Patchy Groundfog, a hard-knocking New York horse trained by Julio Canani.

Along with Davis and Toro, the race drew future Hall of Famers Eddie

Delahoussaye, Sandy Hawley, Russell Baze, Chris McCarron, and Gary Stevens, along with Corey Black, Pat Valenzuela, and Gary Boulanger.

"I remember thinking how the boo-birds were saying we were gonna let Shoe win the race," Stevens recalled. "It couldn't have been more the other way. I rode it like it was a million-dollar race. To me, the perfect outcome would have been me winning it and Shoe second."

"I was trying to win the race so bad," said Davis, who rode Shining Steel. "We all felt that way. We were taking chances that normally we wouldn't really take. I remember getting in trouble about three times."

Down the backstretch, Shoemaker was cruising along in second, just off the pace set by Stevens and Splendor Catch. Shoemaker and Stevens were still in front at the eighth pole, while behind them the others jammed together. Somehow, Delahoussaye found a way through aboard Exemplary Leader.

"That race was like riding the Kentucky Derby," Delahoussaye said. "Everybody was so intense, wanting to win the race and beat him. I know I really wanted to win."

Delahoussaye did, by a half a length over Toro's horse, Happy Toss, with Corey Black and Oraibi finishing a close third, just ahead of Shoemaker. Davis finished fifth.

"After the race, Shoemaker was walking along, through the crowd back to the jocks' room," Davis said. "I thought, 'Here's a guy who's won 8,000 races. It's his last ride.' I looked at Toro and said, 'He can't walk home. Let's pick him up!' "

And what was Shoemaker's reaction? Toro laughed.

"He yelled, 'Don't drop me!' "

Less than a year after his retirement to a life of training, Shoemaker was paralyzed from the upper-chest down when his Ford Bronco rolled off a freeway embankment. He has been confined to a wheelchair ever since, but that has not stopped him from regular visits to the racetrack. His favorite hangout is still the jocks' room.

"You never know when to quit, at least most jocks don't," Shoemaker said, reflecting on his final ride. "A rider never wants to quit. There's no easy way to say, 'This is it.' "

Were there any lingering regrets about the way he went out?

"No, I guess I did it as good as you could do it," Shoemaker said. "Except that I did have a chance to ride the winner."

~~~

## STILLNESS

*October 12, 2003*

Paddy Gallagher leaned on the wood railing at the mouth of his stable shedrow and gazed up at a huge pepper tree swaying gently in the soft autumn breeze. In the distance, Trevor Denman's voice could be heard calling a race near the end of the Santa Anita program. It was almost four o'clock. Gallagher's horses were hungry, and they were letting him know.

"I remember the day I showed up to go to work for Bill at Hollywood Park," Gallagher said. "There was him and me, and just two horses. And a groom, if I remember. I'm not sure what we were thinking, but before too long there were 35 horses in the barn. That was March of 1990."

It had been nine hours since Gallagher had learned that his best friend had died. Nine melancholy hours to deal with the fact that Bill Shoemaker would no longer be on the other end of the telephone for their daily calls, that Shoe would never again summon a tale from the good old days, nor laugh at one of Gallagher's famously off-color jokes.

"It was just like him, wasn't it?" Gallagher said. "Going quietly in his sleep. Never making a fuss."

When Bill Shoemaker closed his eyes and took his last, labored breath, some time between 4:30 and 6 a.m. Sunday in his San Marino home, a curtain softly descended upon the life of a man whose signature grace was the untroubled defiance of insurmountable odds.

He survived a premature birth weight of about two pounds. He defied the conventional prejudice against small jockeys. He survived the public pounding of a misjudged Kentucky Derby finish that dogged him for years. His answer, in the end, was 8,833 victories, four of them in the Derby, including his last at age 54.
~~~

In recent years, Shoemaker had all but disappeared from public view. The lonely freeway accident that left him a quadriplegic occurred in April 1991, cutting short what was destined to be a successful second career as a Thoroughbred trainer.

Shoemaker continued to work alongside Gallagher, lending his name and considerable insight to the operation. But in the end, the hard work of mere survival became too great. Shoemaker officially retired in 1997.

"Here's the kind of horseman he was, the kind of trainer he would have been," Gallagher began.

"One morning that first season, he went by the barn at Hollywood to get on a couple young fillies. On the way back to Santa Anita, he calls me and says, 'You're gonna get mad at me when you see the work tab. They went kind of fast. But the one filly has more natural speed than maybe anything I've ever been on. And the other one is all class. She could be very special.'

"The one was Glen Kate," Gallagher said. "The other was Fire the Groom, and neither one had started."

Let the record show that Glen Kate went on to win the Laurel Dash and the Hong Kong International Bowl, and that Fire the Groom won the Beverly D.

Shoemaker, by then confined to a wheelchair, had to miss those races. He was busy learning how to deal with life without the ability to move his hands, arms, or legs.

"I could never imagine what he went through, just to get from one day to the next," Gallagher said. "He had to be handled for everything. Picked up to be showered, put in his chair, put in bed. They had to move his arms and legs to keep the circulation going, and breathing exercises to help him cough, to keep his lungs clear.

"But I never heard him complain," Gallagher said. "And he could still laugh. Laughed so hard sometimes that tears would come to his eyes. Only thing was, someone would have to reach over and wipe those tears away for him."

In what turned out to be his final visit, Shoemaker dropped by Santa Anita Park earlier this month and spent the afternoon in the jockeys' room. That evening, he joined Gallagher for dinner in nearby Sierra Madre.

"He was talking about the new rider, Ryan Fogelsonger," Gallagher recalled. "Bill thought the kid looked pretty good on a horse. Thought he might make it out here. Then he said he was kind of mad at himself for not going over and introducing himself to the kid. Imagine that. Imagine being Bill Shoemaker, and being so humble."

In the coming days, Shoemaker tributes will pour forth. A memorial service is planned. Bill would be a little miffed at all the bother, but it's not for him—it is for his friends, his fans, his family, and especially for his daughter, Amanda. Not surprisingly, Shoemaker's preference was to keep things low-key.

"We were talking about it one day," Gallagher said. "I don't remember what brought it up, but Bill said that for sure he wanted to be cremated. I told him not to worry, and for no extra charge I'd scatter his ashes on the finish line at Churchill Downs so he'd never forget where it was. That made him laugh."

He laughed so hard he cried.

~~~

## BEST OF THE BEST

*October 14, 2003*

It can be argued that Bill Shoemaker's greatest ride came on the summer day in 1991 when, in the first months of his quadriplegic existence following his one-car wreck, he successfully negotiated the hallway of a Colorado rehabilitation hospital using the sip-and-puff mechanism of his customized wheelchair. Later, he became so adept at its operation that he could run right over the tip of your shoe and make you think it was an accident.

Shoemaker spent more than 12 years in that wheelchair before his death last Sunday. He leaves behind a wealth of memories—Shoemaker stories have been flying this week—and there are some that even the humble Shoemaker enjoyed chewing on more than others.
~~~

First and foremost, there was the 1986 Kentucky Derby aboard Ferdinand. Shoemaker was 54 at the time, making moves like a kid without a care.

"It was probably his greatest ride, but I wish he'd saved it for another day," said Chris McCarron, who finished second in that Derby on Bold Arrangement.

"Shoe made three perfect decisions that day," McCarron began. "First, he took his horse back to last from the inside post, otherwise he might have been put over the fence on the first turn. Then he made a move down the backstretch, cutting inside horses when he needed to. Finally, there was his move to the rail in the stretch. My colt was busy battling Broad Brush, and we had him beat. Then I look over and there's that little sonofagun going by us. I thought, 'Where'd he come from?' "

The companion piece to the 1986 Derby was the 1987 Breeders' Cup Classic at Hollywood Park, which hopefully will be highlighted during the NBC telecast of the Breeders' Cup on October 25. Ferdinand and Shoemaker teamed to defeat Alysheba and McCarron in history's most exciting clash of Kentucky Derby winners.

"I could have gone to the lead at any time," Shoemaker said. "But I knew Ferdinand liked to pull himself up when he was in front. I knew Alysheba would be coming, but I had to wait as long as I could."

The sight of Shoemaker sitting chilly with barely a sixteenth of a mile to run in a $3 million race was unforgettable. When Shoemaker finally roused Ferdinand, the big red colt gave him just enough to win by a nose.

It was Shoemaker who rode Buckpasser to a nose victory over Abe's Hope in the 1966 Flamingo Stakes, dubbed the "Chicken Flamingo" because Hialeah management thought Buckpasser was such a lock that they made it a non-wagering event. Shoemaker was not fooled.

"The hardest race to win is the race you're supposed to win," he said.

John Henry was supposed to win the inaugural running of the Arlington Million in 1981, but all bets were scrambled when the course came up muddy and deep. John Henry hated the going, and Shoemaker knew it. But Shoe also knew his horse. Instead of pressing the issue, searching for good ground, or asking for too much, Shoemaker let John Henry get his sea legs. Ol' John found his rhythm just in time to catch The Bart on the line and win by a nose.

Shoemaker's work on Exceller in the 1978 Jockey Club Gold Cup ranks with his best. That day, in the wind and rain, Seattle Slew (under Angel Cordero) and Affirmed splashed through the Belmont mud in fast early fractions, while Shoemaker found himself more than 30 lengths off the pace halfway through the race. Then they began to move.

"I knew Cordero would be looking for me," Shoemaker said. "He'd try to shut me off or carry me wide like he always does. So I put my horse right behind him, in his blind spot. When he looked for me over his right shoulder, I took my horse to the inside and went to the lead. Still, Seattle Slew came back to make it close." The margin was a nose.

Shoemaker's all-time favorite ride came in the 1962 San Juan Capistrano Handicap, when he nursed the hardcore miler Olden Times to a narrow win at nearly 1-3/4 miles. It was a race later that year, however, that will always rank among the greatest in the Shoemaker canon, when Shoemaker rode Belmont winner Jaipur for Moody Jolley in the Travers against the brilliant Ridan, under Manuel Ycaza.

"Maybe there was never a race like it," wrote veteran turf journalist Russ Harris. "It simply isn't possible for two horses to throw hooks into each other for a solid 1-1/4 miles, going as hard as they can every inch of the route, without giving way in the stretch. . . . It isn't possible, but Jaipur and Ridan did it. I never saw a horse race like it, and I couldn't find anyone at Saratoga who had."

Jaipur beat Ridan by a bob of the nose.

"Jolley proclaimed that Shoemaker was worth five pounds over any other rider, and Jaipur had finished well behind Ridan in earlier starts with other riders," Harris added. "If you switch the riders, would Ridan have won the Travers? I would have run on that ticket."

~~~
~~~

# ETERNAL FLAME

*October 21, 2003*

Southern California is on fire again, so it must be time for a Breeders' Cup at Santa Anita Park.

When the international racing carnival last hit the Santa Anita side of town 10 years ago, the mountains rimming the L. A. basin were alive with the flames of a dozen distinct conflagrations. More fires burned to the south in Orange County, but the most dramatic—at least from the vantage point of Breeders' Cup participants—was the Sierra Madre fire that destroyed 151 homes in the foothills above the racetrack.

Hot and tinder-dry conditions were ripe for another outbreak this week, so it came as no real surprise Tuesday afternoon when the skies to the east, west, and south of Santa Anita filled with the sickly, reddish-gray smoke of brush in full burn. October in Southern California can be a very mean season.

The drama was not lost on the thousand or so faithful fans and friends of the family who gathered in the Santa Anita stands late Tuesday afternoon to spend a few precious moments in remembrance of Bill Shoemaker. Natural disasters mixed well with the emotions of personal loss.

The indomitable spirit of Bill Shoemaker permeates Santa Anita, from the histories of its greatest races, to the statuary in the paddock gardens, to the oldest corners of the jockeys' room, where Shoemaker reigned as a benign, accessible king and played his schoolboy pranks.

Shoemaker's death on the morning of October 12, at age 72, trumped the sense of loss pervading the Southern California racing world since the summer of 2002, when a healthy Chris McCarron retired from riding. That was followed by career-ending injuries to Eddie Delahoussaye and Laffit Pincay, and the near-fatal experience of Gary Stevens in August at Arlington Park. Suddenly, everyone felt very mortal.

Shoemaker's death, however, rang a bell of finality. An era had ended, one populated by such formidable personalities as Charlie Whittingham, Eddie Arcaro, Johnny Longden, and Lazaro Barrera. The history of Thoroughbred racing had come to a natural divide—those lucky enough to have lived in the time of Bill Shoemaker now had to deal with what comes next.

Tuesday's ceremony was anchored with dignity by Hollywood Park's Mike Willman. Amy Zimmerman's Santa Anita television team put together a full-blooded video montage of Shoemaker's life, highlighted by priceless archival film shot by the late Joe Burnham. An eloquent eulogy was delivered by John Gosden, the British trainer whose California career was graced by Shoemaker's friendship, as well as his active participation in a number of stakes wins.

The congregation was shaken briefly by the tearful appearance of Don Pierce, Shoemaker's closest running mate for 40 years and a ferociously competitive jockey in his time. Pierce could barely deliver his tribute, leading once again to the nagging question: What happens when the tough guy cries?

It was, however, a modern Mount Rushmore of riders—Pincay, Delahoussaye, McCarron, and Stevens—who stepped up to say what needed to be said, leaving no doubt as to the impact of their departed friend.

"Before Shoemaker, with very few exceptions, jockeys got little respect," McCarron said. "Shoe forced people to respect jockeys. They couldn't help respecting jockeys after what he did on the track, and off the track."

True to form, Delahoussaye offered no frills. "I love him, and I'll miss him," he said. Then he read a poem titled "I'm Free," which contained the lines, "If parting has left a void/then fill it with remembered joy."

"He was a great friend," Pincay said. "He's probably laughing at all of us sitting in the sun sweating, while he's having a drink with Charlie."

Ten years ago, when the Breeders' Cup was at Santa Anita Park, trainer Bill Shoemaker sent out Diazo, who finished sixth in the Breeders' Cup Classic. Shoe had been in a wheelchair for two years, but that did not stop him from being part of the biggest day of the season.

Pincay, in addition to riding Diazo, won the Juvenile Fillies that day aboard Phone Chatter. Delahoussaye won the Distaff on Hollywood Wildcat (after dropping his stick) and the Sprint on Cardmania from out of the clouds. McCarron endured tough losses in both the Distaff, on

Paseana, and the Turf, aboard Bien Bien, while Stevens took the Juvenile with Brocco and thought he was home and dry in the Classic on Bertrando, until the French longshot Arcangues ran them down.

It was Stevens who sounded the sweetest note as he concluded his remembrance of his days as a young kid from Idaho learning the ropes at Shoemaker's knee. Everyone knew that Shoemaker lasted as long as he did in a quadriplegic state because he did not want to miss the formative years of his daughter, now 23.

Looking down at Amanda Shoemaker, a poised young woman who trains hunters and jumpers at a San Francisco–area stable, Stevens spoke for all of racing when he said, "Thank you, Amanda, for giving us 12 more years with your dad."

## Nine

# NOT FORGOTTEN

*On more than one occasion I have been asked to deliver a eulogy. This is not as much fun as it sounds. I am honored, of course, but always baffled at my choice as someone whose task it is to embellish a funeral service with fond remembrances of the dear departed. I can only assume it is because I own a dark suit and refrain from drinking until sundown.*

*Saying farewell in print, however, is another matter. A columnist loves a story that comes equipped with a ready-made ending. All the evidence is in. No need to hedge. The selections in this chapter marked losses of significance to the racing community, across the board, from the stalwart groom of Sunday Silence to the man who made me a lifelong fan.*

*Affirmed would have been the horse of a lifetime even without his historic rivalry with Alydar. John Henry felt like part of the family. Chris Antley, Bobby Frankel, and Eddie Gregson were gone too soon, but that does not mean the loss of Warren Stute, Willard Proctor, or Bill Hartack stung any less just because they had reached the twilight of their years.*

*"All that lives must die, passing through nature to eternity," Shakespeare wrote.*

*But not before a writer gets to take one last swing.*

# W. L. PROCTOR

*November 4, 1998*

The last living creature to see Willard Proctor alive was a horse he had just fed. Her name is Our Dreamer. She is a daughter of Storm Cat out of Breeders' Cup Distaff winner One Dreamer, and Proctor said she was going to be the best horse in the barn.

There is something so truly and perfectly right in that simple fact that there is barely anything left to say. Still, there is a volume to write about Willard Lee Proctor, and what he represented, and what it means now that he is gone.

When a man like Proctor dies, the cosmic books get all out of whack. We talk about what he left behind, all the memories and the lessons. There is comfort in such sentiments, but somehow that's not enough. We need him here, that lighthouse of a Texan, maybe now more than ever.

Proctor defied definition. Conventional wisdom does not apply, so don't bother looking for a simple explanation to the magic of his spell. He never won a Triple Crown race. He never trained a champion. He started only two horses in the Breeders' Cup and neither one hit the board.

And yet, on the strength of his threescore stakes winners and unwavering integrity, he commanded a respect reserved only for the elite of a generation—a generation sadly disappearing from our midst. The Proctor name is synonymous with Woody Stephens, Buster Millerick, Bob Wheeler, and Buddy Hirsch. The late Stanley Rieser, Proctor's pal and running mate in considerable mischief, once came away from a visit out West shaking his head in awe.

"I have never known anyone who demands so much attention with so little effort," Rieser said. "I see how he affects these guys. He'll be sitting on his pony, and you'd think they was talking to the President."

Proctor's gift was his absolute self-confidence. Only the greatest trainers make their decisions with such breathless clarity. Proctor knew exactly what horses would do and why.

He began paying heed, long ago, as a kid in Lampases. Long and lean, young Willard Lee would strap himself onto the fastest horse he could catch and ride match races through the oil fields of central Texas. They used the drill rigs as pole markers.

In a life so filled with adventure—from the South Pacific of World War II to the backroads of American racing—it is significant what sticks in the head. Proctor never forgot the slaughter of his father's cattle when Depression-era prices went through the floor. Good meat gone worthless.

His Army buddies included Ralph Neves and Oleg Cassini, and when his outfit suited up for a rodeo in Australia, Proctor called himself the Cowboy from Hollywood and Vine.

"I had to be careful, though," he said. "Those Australians knew a lot more about Hollywood than I did."

Proctor always gave the horse the benefit of the doubt. In the morning, it was the rider's fault if something went wrong. In the afternoon, Proctor himself took the heat. There were no shortcuts, no overnight wonders, no secrets to his success. He trained for men like Leonard Lavin, Ralph Lowe, J. Graham Brown, and Bull Hancock. Expedience was not in their vocabulary. Easy answers were usually wrong.

To watch the Proctor stable in action was to appreciate an efficient machine with a quiet, humming engine. Proctor always demanded pride in the workplace, and he was there to set the example. Three horses to a groom—not the more cost-effective four or five. No visitors, no horseplay, no radios in the mornings.

"I know I've had a reputation as being hard to work for," he once said. "It doesn't bother me one bit. I mean, if you ain't gonna be the boss, then you shouldn't even be there."

It seemed as if Proctor was always there, at the barn, among the horses. "Hell, I like coming back in the afternoons," he said. "What else am I going to do?"

And so it was that Willard Proctor, a month and a half shy of his 83rd birthday, was mixing hot feed for a 2-year-old colt last Friday afternoon, straightened up, keeled over backwards, and left this world a better place. The gray filly named Our Dreamer lifted her nose out of her tub to check the commotion and peered down into the face of her trainer, lying in front of her stall.

Those closest to him knew he was not well. "I'm just glad he could spend his time right here," said Patricia Johnson, Proctor's assistant and best friend. The cause of death was cardiac arrest from the disease that had enlarged his heart to several times its normal size.

But then, we already knew that W. L. Proctor had more heart than most.

~~~

# EDDIE GREGSON

*June 9, 2000*

Monday morning. The fifth day of June, and in the first stall of the parking lot of an office building on Mission Street in the Los Angeles suburb of South Pasadena there is a black Mercedes S500 with a Hollywood Park turf club sticker in the window and backstretch mud splashed behind all four tires.

The Mercedes was clearly parked in a hurry. The wheels are still raked hard to the left where the driver made his turn into the lot. The interior of the car is practically empty, save for a bottle of water in the backseat, racetrack dust on the floor mats, and a black-and-white 5x7 photograph, propped on the console behind the gearshift knob, depicting a show-jump rider being pitched head over heels from the top of a reluctant horse.

"Eddie loved that picture," said Trudy McCaffery, one of Eddie Gregson's best friends. "Whenever he was having a bad day, he would look at the photo and be reminded that it was never going as bad as it was for the guy in the picture."

Last Sunday it got that bad.

The gunshot suicide of Edwin Janss Gregson, at his South Pasadena office only hours after he saddled two promising young horses at Hollywood Park, has sent shivers of mortality through the racing industry. Friends and colleagues struggled to make sense of an act committed by a man who, at first, second, and third glance, seemed to have had the world by the tail.

"I've gone through all the emotions," said Jon Kelly, Gregson's principal
~~~

patron, for whom the 62-year-old trainer was crafting a quality-packed racing and breeding stable.

"I would talk to him every day," Kelly said. "I can make no sense of it at all. I'm mad at him for doing it. And I'm terribly sad for how he must have felt to do such a thing at all."

"The guy had everything," said Eddie Delahoussaye, who gave Gregson his victory in the 1982 Kentucky Derby aboard Gato Del Sol. "I've been trying to rack my brain for a reason. I can't believe he would do this to us."

Neither Kelly nor Delahoussaye was being selfish in their indignation. Rather, they were expressing the heartfelt agonies of those left behind when a loved one chooses suicide. We only know the world in which we live, and so we define such moments in terms of what we can touch, see, and feel. To remove a rich, full-flavored existence such as Gregson's creates a shockwave that rattles all reason.

"I know this for a fact," Delahoussaye said. "The game won't be the same without him."

Gregson was the driving force behind the rejuvenation of the Del Mar yearling sale. As president of the California Thoroughbred Trainers Association, he was a tireless advocate for better conditions for both the horses and the people who cared for them. As a public trainer of impeccable reputation, he fought the hard battles against the spread of racing medication, and he told more than one owner things they did not necessarily want to hear.

"We took a lot of flak for not running Gato Del Sol in the Preakness that year," said Arthur Hancock, who owned the Derby winner with Leone Peters. "But Eddie was really a good horseman. I had to figure he knew best."

In truth, the game today is different from the one in which the Gregson stable thrived. The stands have gone empty. The nature of patronage has changed. Traditions of horsemanship are being overwhelmed by encroaching economics. Burdened with an old soul and a longing for a bygone era, Gregson struggled with those differences.

"He loved the game and the people in it," said Gail Gregson, his wife of 32 years. "But that circle was shrinking as the game changed."

Gregson was also an extremely proud man who was handsome enough in his youth to try a film career. Even at a youthful 62, he was not anxious to settle into anything resembling senior years. He battled chronic eczema, a painful skin condition, and he always had hanging over him the suicide of his uncle, the famed Southern California land developer Edwin Janss, Jr., in March of 1989.

"They were very close," said friend Mike Hirsch, son of Hall of Fame trainer Buddy Hirsch. "He patterned himself after Ed Janss—his business sense, his taste in art."

Wine connoisseur, art collector, antique expert—arbiter of good taste in an otherwise tasteless world—Eddie Gregson many times felt himself out of time and place. And so he tried to create the world in which he wanted to live, which more recently included the renovation of a piece of property in Rancho Santa Fe to be used for the budding Jon Kelly stable of racing and breeding bloodstock.

"He was on top of every detail," Kelly said. "Every inch of ground. Every fence. He wanted it to be perfect.

"When we first started out together about three years ago, we had some bad luck with a couple of starters," Kelly went on. "Eddie told me to have patience and reminded me of our master plan. I told him, at this rate, I'd be a 75- or 80-year-old man before I'd make it to the winner's circle, and he'd probably be in a walker."

And Gregson's reply? Kelly shook his head at the memory and smiled.

"He said, 'Jon, can you think of a better way to spend that part of your life?' "

We may never know why Eddie Gregson would leave such hope behind.

~~~

## CHRIS ANTLEY

*December 6, 2000*

He was hanging around at the edge of a fishing pond located on the property of a South Carolina training center. He was just 14-years-old. A
~~~

local trainer thought he had the size and the look of a kid who could ride a horse.

"You ever ride a horse, kid?" the trainer asked.

"Nope," the kid answered.

And so it began.

A small boy from a small town, blessed with natural ability and thrust into a world of high-rollers, is often a walking recipe for disaster. Predators come in all shapes and sizes. They bring tempting treats and sweet diversions. Christopher Wiley Antley, dead at age 34, played his unfortunate part to the hilt.

But we can't stop there. Nothing is quite so simple. Antley was nothing if not a very complicated man.

He read philosophy, wrote poetry, and doodled strange and wonderful drawings in the margins of his *Racing Form* each day before he rode.

He was computer literate and fluent in cyberspace years before the rest of us even knew there was such a thing called the Internet.

He was built like an old-fashioned athlete, like a guy who could roll out of bed and win five. His muscles were rounded, not etched. His shoulders sloped to a powerful back that supplied relentless push.

He had the face of a choirboy, dimpled and scrubbed, and lit by a smile that could seduce total strangers. If he shaved, no one ever knew.

He had swagger by the bushel, and a knack in the saddle that could back up any boast. To watch Chris Antley ride was a privilege. Low over the animal, he seemed always on the move, getting things done, in search of an edge. With more than 3,400 wins—two of them in the Kentucky Derby—it is hard to pick the highlights.

But just for a treat, just to watch the real thing in action, take a look sometime at Antley's 1990 CCA Oaks with Turnback the Alarm, or his 1988 Gotham Stakes with Private Terms, or his work in the 1996 San Pasqual aboard Alphabet Soup. Young riders will learn from him for years.

At the same time, they must also understand that Antley had a paper-thin psyche, susceptible to tearing and shredding under the pressure of his work. His publicly confessed use of drugs and alcohol became a chronic reference, as if it were part of his name. In that sense he lumped himself in with a modern sports pathology. But unlike many athletes who become chronic abusers, burning bridges along the way, Antley's unabiding charm and extraordinary talent seemed to keep harsh judgments at bay.

It didn't help. All the friendships and support systems in the world failed in the end. And in the end, Chris Antley was never a happy man. How could he be? When he was riding, he was reducing so drastically that his body became the enemy, rather than the reason for his success. When he stopped riding—to clean up or slim down—his heart constantly ached for the day he could compete again.

William Feather did not know Chris Antley. The author died two years before Antley began to ride. Still, it is Antley who comes to mind when reading Feather's words: "One of the indictments of civilizations is that happiness and intelligence are so rarely found in the same person."

Antley was smart, but his most fervent search was for happiness. Conventional trappings did not soothe Antley's soul. A dream house, a loving wife, a child on the way—these things are supposed to do the trick. But he died in that house. His love is left alone. His child will never know him.

The investigation will continue to unfold. Sooner or later, we will know if Antley brought the killer to his own doorstep, or if his death was caused by a random brush with evil.

In the meantime, we should be grateful that the everlasting image of Chris Antley will not be the garlands of yellow police tape draping the front of his Pasadena home. Instead, it will be the jockey, on his knees in the Belmont Park sand, comforting the brave colt Charismatic and cradling his badly injured leg in the grim moments at the end of the 1999 Belmont Stakes.

In 1989, when Antley was in the midst of his recurring battle with cocaine and alcohol, he shared the following letter with journalist Susan Finley in a story for the *Thoroughbred Record.* The letter was addressed "Dear God . . ."

"When I am old," Antley wrote, "will I sit and think about the things that just flew by unnoticed and the things I passed not doing and the people who sometimes feel imaginary? God, you have given me much talent, opportunity, money, friends, and people who really care for me. And now do I really push all of this to its right fulfillment? Am I truly happy?"

Whether or not he was ever truly happy, we will never really know. Only one thing is for certain as we struggle with the story. Chris Antley is truly gone.

~~~

## AFFIRMED

*January 14, 2001*

A large red tree just fell in the forest, and everybody heard. Affirmed is dead. There will never be another.

"It's the end of an era," said Patrice Wolfson on Friday between the tears.

She bred and raced Affirmed with her husband, Louis Wolfson, and for three solid years their Harbor View Farm colors never flew higher than they did aboard their graceful chestnut colt.

Take all of his accomplishments and stack them in a pile. It hurts the neck to see the top. Champion at the age of two. Triple Crown winner of 1978. Horse of the Year in 1978 and 1979. First to break Kelso's record of earnings. Successful as a stallion and sire of champions. Affirmed could never replace himself, but no one really expected it to happen.

These eyes first beheld Affirmed in the flesh in the walking ring at Santa Anita on a quiet Wednesday in March of 1978. He was coming out as a 3-year-old after a long, wet winter of anticipation. And as he strolled around the ring under Steve Cauthen, impervious to the crowd, you could hear the fans whisper his name. Affirmed.

He raced for 29 months and won 22 of his 29 races. Once, his saddle slipped. Once, he was disqualified from victory for merely doing what he was asked to do. And twice, but only twice, he was beaten by Alydar on the square, which took nothing away from Affirmed and always reflected well upon Alydar.

Remove Alydar from the picture—yes, an impossible task—and Affirmed would have won the first 18 starts of his life. Little wonder that his
~~~

trainer, Lazaro Barrera, gave him the highest possible compliment when he said, quite simply, "Affirmed always runs a good race."

His skills were complete. There were never excuses needed. He could sprint with the sprinters and gallop the routers into the ground. He broke like a rocket, rated with a fingertip, and carried weight as if it were nothing but truffles and brie.

Affirmed legends abound. Many of them are true. One morning at Santa Anita, in an uncharacteristic fit of pique, Affirmed lost his rider and headed down the stable road. Panic ensued, as Barrera's weak heart took another hit. But apparently Affirmed knew what he was doing all along. When he stopped, allowing himself to be caught, he was on the doorstep of the Charlie Whittingham barn.

In a rough game where everyone gets dirty, Affirmed could come off as aloof, a bit of a dandy. Practicing high artistry, groom Juan Alaniz would plait the base of Affirmed's shimmering red tail, then twist his mane into delicate ringlets to create a sweeping line of Botticelli curls.

Only fools were deceived. Affirmed was no fop, no perfumed pretty boy. Once loaded into the gate, he went from a courtly Don Diego to a vengeful Zorro in the blink of an eye. Opponents came away sliced and diced, robbed of their delusions and wondering what happened.

While it is hopeless to choose from among flawless gems, Affirmed's best race may have come on June 24, 1979, in the mile and a quarter Hollywood Gold Cup. You will get no argument from Darrel McHargue.

Laffit Pincay was on Affirmed and McHargue was on Sirlad, a champion from Italy trained by Charlie Whittingham. Affirmed carried 132 pounds, while Sirlad carried 120. Locked together from the start, with Affirmed on the inside, they went the half in :45.60, the three-quarters in 1:09.60, the mile in 1:34.20.

"When two horses hook up like that, one of them usually drops out long before they hit the stretch," said McHargue, now a steward in Northern California.

"But when it's just you and another horse, and things don't change, you get in kind of a zone. It didn't seem like there was anybody else in the race. Just Sirlad and Affirmed."

At the end, it was just Affirmed, by three-quarters of a length in 1:58.40. McHargue was sorry he lost, proud of his horse, and not the least bit surprised.

"The year before, in the Belmont Stakes, I remember watching him in the gate," McHargue said. "He was like a caged animal, just looking for an opening. Not fractious, but alert. A professional in every sense."

That was Affirmed. Always on the clock, bringing honor to the hard work of being a racehorse. There were never any hammy displays of rampant personality, never any endzone antics. But there was a time, one memorable moment, when Affirmed dropped his guard.

It was July 4, 1979, just 10 days after his Hollywood Gold Cup, and the California fans were being granted one last look at the champ. With his legs wrapped in Barrera's bright orange bandages and Pincay in the saddle wearing the Wolfson silks, Affirmed emerged from the paddock and strolled down the stretch to the cheers of more than 65,000.

"Then he did something he never did before," Barrera later recalled. "Halfway down the stretch, he turned and looked right at the public. He looked everybody over, acting just like a movie star."

That's because Affirmed was a star, bright and everlasting.

~~~

## CHARLES CLAY

*November 5, 2009*

Twenty years ago the stare was there, in the Florida twilight, as Charles Clay and Sunday Silence stood together at the top of the Thoroughbred world. They had just won the 1989 Breeders' Cup Classic, with help from Charlie Whittingham and Chris McCarron. But make no mistake, it was the man at the shank—a proud, glowering virtuoso of his craft—who had every bit as much to do with what happened that day.

The piercing eyes of Charles Clay closed softly October 25, in a Pasadena hospice not far from Santa Anita Park, where he came to the end of a battle with the throat cancer and liver failure probably preordained
~~~

by the cigarettes and I. W. Harper he consumed in sometimes intemperate amounts. He was 76, or so, depending on who was talking and how long they'd known Charles Clay. And in the days and weeks before the end, a lot of the people who knew precisely the worth of the man made sure they told him one last time.

"He didn't really say much when I saw him. Couldn't toward the end," said Eugene "Snake" McDaniel, Clay's oldest friend from when they were kids working at Charles Town Racetrack. "But then, he was always a loner."

"He'd say, 'I'm not doin' too well, but that's another story,' " said John "Short Man" Flakes, who looked upon Clay as an older brother. "Then he'd change the subject."

In truth, that was pretty easy to do, as long as the subject was Thoroughbreds. The black grooms and riders of Clay's generation who migrated to California laid hands upon some of the finest racehorses of their time. McDaniel, who still works for Ben Cecil, rubbed Ack Ack and Forli. Joe Merriweather, now with John Sadler but no longer in the saddle, was the morning man for Social Climber, Old Mose, and King of Cricket. Flakes, who works for John Shirreffs, groomed Sarsar for David Whiteley when she swept the table at Santa Anita and then beat colts in the 1975 Withers.

All of them worked at one time or another for Charlie Whittingham, but it was Clay who lasted the longest, to the day Whittingham died in April of 1999. For Charlie, he rubbed the solid stakes winners Craelius and Swink, Kentucky Oaks winner Goodbye Halo, and a little mare from France named Estrapade, who won the Arlington Million and an Eclipse Award in 1986. In 1991, Whittingham stayed home and sent Clay, along with assistant trainer Tim Yakteen, with Golden Pheasant to Tokyo to win the Japan Cup.

"When we trained at Hollywood, I drove Clay to work every morning," said Yakteen, now a trainer on his own. "I did a lot of listening."

If you were smart, and just a little brave, you got past Clay's forbidding exterior to the generous heart of a man who held his work in the highest esteem. No one took better care of their horses, which is why Whittingham gave Clay many of his best.

"If you could mold an ideal groom—all the qualities you'd want in an individual who takes care of your horses—you would want Clay," Yakteen said. "He didn't just communicate with his horses. He talked to them. I'd hear him in the stall all the time, talking to them like they were people. And they'd listen. He loved them, but he also knew how to impart the discipline they need, because without it they can be hurt. Like a child you teach to look both ways before crossing the street. If you don't, sometimes you don't get a second chance."

Yakteen's recollections brought back Clay's voice, gruff and sharp above the quiet of Whittingham's barn, profane and gentle by turns, still bearing a trace of his West Virginia roots.

"Here now, Sunday," he'd snap, when the rangy colt would misbehave. "Get serious."

Clay's work with Sunday Silence was his masterpiece. The near-black colt had a tempestuous streak, and in Clay he found a mentor who brooked no nonsense. Together they won the Santa Anita Derby, Kentucky Derby, Preakness, and Super Derby before their memorable Breeders' Cup victory over Easy Goer.

"At Keeneland, in the dining room, there is a painting of Clay leading Sunday Silence," Yakteen said. "It's a fitting tribute. I stop and look at it every time I go back there."

Clay's stern visage also gazes down from a photo gallery of noteworthy grooms and exercise riders decorating the walls of the card room in the Santa Anita backstretch recreation center. This week, a handwritten note was taped to the frame:

"Mr. Clay, I love you. You will be missed forever. Jetta."

That would be Jetta Vaughns, the 31-year-old daughter of Short Man Flakes, who recalls following Clay around like a puppydog as a kid, when her father worked for Whittingham.

"I was scared of him, but it wasn't too long before I figured out he was a softie," Vaughns said.

"Girl, he changed your diapers!" Snake McDaniel said. They both laughed.

It was only in the last few days that word got around to Clay's old friends that he had passed away. They are not exactly in the text and Twitter crowd. But Breeders' Cup is a bad time to die, especially if you deserve some attention. Vaughns was intent that there be some kind of memorial service, and there probably will be, once the dust settles.

"When I got to Santa Anita, in December of 1964, the first guy I ran into was Clay," Short Man said. "I ran into him at the stable gate. He asked me what was I doing. I said, 'Nothin',' so he said, 'Come on, I'm goin' to the store.' We hung out with each other ever since. Did a lot of jobs together, and had some fun.

"I learned from Clay that if you treat your horse like a piece of crap, he'll be a piece of crap," Flakes added. "But if you treat him like an equal, give him some confidence, that horse will win a race for you. I learned a lot from him. He was a good man."

~~~

## WARREN STUTE

*August 11, 2007*

Noble Threewitt once had an owner tell him to claim a horse that was trained by Warren Stute. Fat chance.

"He's about the last guy on earth I'd claim a horse off," Threewitt told his patron. "He's a very close friend of mine."

"What do you mean, close friend?" the owner wondered. "I've never even seen you talk to him!"

Threewitt shot the guy a cold eye.

"I don't see what that's got to do with it," he replied.

So there it is, the snapshot version of Warren Stute, a Thoroughbred trainer so respected by his peers that he could be your best friend without you even knowing it, mostly because he'd never bother to make a fuss, but at some point you had impressed him enough to put you in tight for life, which was a very good spot. And anyway, as far as Warren was concerned, actions speak louder and more honestly than any number of words.

Stute's death this week, at the age of 85, brought to an end a career
~~~

dating back to 1940, when the son of Indiana dairy farmers Herman and Edith Stute went into business for himself at the old Caliente racetrack in Tijuana. Opinionated, brusque, and honest to a fault, Stute was the classic tough guy with both bark and bite. His owners deferred to his will with their horses or they hit the road, a style that has few practitioners today. But for a precious handful of patrons through the years—men like Clement Hirsch, Travis Kerr, and Wayne Hughes—Stute was just what they needed, a horse-training version of Lincoln's General Grant, willing to stick out his neck and make the tough decisions—stop or go—without a flinch.

Which is why no one was really surprised during the summer of 1969 when Warren unveiled a South American 3-1/2-year-old named Figonero, winning an allowance race, the American Handicap on grass, and the Hollywood Gold Cup at a mile and a quarter in the space of 15 days. Nor were there gasps of wonder the following year when Stute beat the boys in the Del Mar Futurity with the filly June Darling, then won three stakes with her during the five weeks of the Oak Tree meet at Santa Anita Park.

American males born in 1922 are not necessarily supposed to make it all the way to 2007, so in that sense Warren Stute bucked the odds. But it wasn't as if he wrapped himself in cotton and tried to nurse himself to the wire. He was still galloping his own horses into his 80s. He'd broken enough bones to rattle when he walked. Once, when he was schooling an exercise rider on how to handle a problem horse, he was dumped into a coma that had friends and family shopping for black crepe. When he finally came around, he wisecracked, "See, that's how you do it."

Stute exposed himself to a whole new audience during the spring of 2005 when he took Illinois Derby winner Greely's Galaxy to the Kentucky Derby. During the traditional dinner for Derby trainers, Warren snagged one of the biggest laughs when, undaunted by the glib deliveries of Wayne Lukas and Todd Pletcher, he shrugged, "I can't out-talk them, so I guess I'll just have to out-train them."

From his victory in 1951 with Great Circle in the $205,700 Santa Anita Maturity ("I lived for a year off what I made on that one," Warren said.) to his 2002 triumph in the desert of Dubai in the $1 million Godolphin

Mile, nothing was more important to him than personal loyalty. And no one could raise the protective mother bear in Stute quicker than his little brother Mel, whose own training credits include Snow Chief, Brave Raj, Very Subtle, and Fleet Nasrullah.

"We just made a hell of a lot of money, Stevens," Warren said to his jockey, that guy Gary, after winning in Dubai. "And I made enough to take out a full-page ad in the *Daily Racing Form* and tell all these people just how many good horses Melvin Stute has trained."

If Warren Stute had any regrets at all, it was the fact that his brother was not recognized by the Thoroughbred Racing Hall of Fame.

"A friend of ours likes to say that Mel has made it this far in spite of me," Warren said once, poking fun at his fierce reputation. "I guess I did kind of let go of a few owners, and it built up from there. But I'm not near as bad as they make me out."

No, not half as bad. And a romantic at heart, to which Trudy, his wife of 51 years, will gladly attest. Early each morning, for as long as she could remember, she found an affectionate note from her husband, scribbled in the pre-dawn darkness before he tiptoed out the door and headed for the track. During the recent months, when the accrued effects of small strokes began to take their toll, Stute's routine may have been interrupted, but his spirit rarely flagged. A few days before his death, Trudy told friends that her husband tried to write her one last note, but darned if the pencil wouldn't cooperate.

"It's my last love note from Warren," Trudy said.

~~~

# JOHN HENRY

*October 11, 2007*

When Queen Victoria died on January 22, 1901, after a 64-year reign over the British Empire, traffic stopped, church bells tolled, stores were shuttered, and theaters closed in mid-performance. Tens of thousands packed the streets of London on the day of her funeral, wearing black
~~~

and mourning the passing of the only monarch most of them had ever known. In death, she was described as "the magnetic idea that drew the passionate affection and allegiance of her subjects to the centre."

When Franklin D. Roosevelt died on April 12, 1945, war-weary Americans staggered at the news. Teenagers had never known another president, and many adults never wanted another. In Chicago, the young reporter Studs Terkel wrote, "I'm walking south on Michigan Boulevard and I can't stop crying. Everybody is crying." In Greenville, North Carolina, a large bell originally installed as an air-raid signal was rung every ten seconds for twenty minutes beginning at 6:15 p.m.

The following day, Chief Petty Officer Graham Jackson, Roosevelt's favorite musician, took up his accordion to play "Goin' Home" as the train bearing the president's casket left Warm Springs, Georgia, headed for Washington, D.C., and then on to the Roosevelt home in Hyde Park, New York, where the president was buried in a rose garden. Thousands lined the tracks along the way.

In his own manner, insistent and steady, the Thoroughbred known as John Henry has been every bit as important to his own constituency as are the great leaders of human civilization. He was a performer of unflinching honesty, generous in victory, gallant in defeat. Horse racing could count on John Henry, year after year, to put the game in headlines and people in the seats.

Now that he is gone, after a long and accessible retirement at the Kentucky Horse Park, he is still impossible to forget, even though his last competitive appearance was 23 years ago, when he won for the 39th time in a career of 83 starts.

For those lucky enough to enjoy the ride, it is impossible to erase the images of John Henry through the years, yanking the heart out of very good horses as they came at him in waves—Spence Bay, Galaxy Libra, Flying Paster, Majesty's Prince, Caterman, Balzac, Royal Heroine, Relaunch, Win, The Bart, Relaxing.

The point of the Thoroughbred endeavor is to breed horses like John Henry all the time. So far, there only has been the one, just as Kelso, Forego, Damascus, Dr. Fager, Secretariat, Ruffian, Seattle Slew, Affirmed, and Spectacular Bid each have come and gone without hope of replacement, the constellations in racing's vast sky.

And yet, at the end of the day, John Henry was no more and no less than a hard-working performance animal. He needed the care and conditioning of any great athlete playing at the pinnacle of a sport. Ron McAnally, his most successful trainer, would lay awake countless nights wondering, "Did I do enough? Did I do too much?"

Of all his accomplishments in a Hall of Fame career that has spanned parts of six decades, McAnally views his handling of John Henry leading up to the 1982 Santa Anita Handicap as his training masterpiece.

John Henry had won the Handicap in 1981 and was the reigning Horse of the Year, but he had not raced since his fourth-place finish in the December 6 Hollywood Turf Cup. He spent a month of R&R at the Galway Downs training center, then returned to Santa Anita on January 7, 1982, and recorded the following collection of formal works:

January 15, three-eighths, :35 4/5...January 22, half mile, :49 3/5, track slow...January 30, three-quarters, 1:12 2/5...February 9, seven-eighths, 1:27 3/5, turf...February 15, mile, 1:37 2/5, breezing...February 21, mile, 1:36 4/5...February 28, mile and one-eighth, 1:47 2/5 (Shoemaker up)... March 6, three-eighths, :35, breezing.

In the race itself, on March 7, John Henry was beaten a nose by Perrault, but then elevated to victory on Perrault's clear-cut disqualification. The prelude, though, was nearly as satisfying as the climax, and the mile of February 21 was especially memorable, underlying John Henry's grip on his environment.

It was late on a cool Sunday morning when John Henry and exercise rider Lewis Cenicola stepped onto the track. More than 300 fans and horsemen lingered, enjoying breakfast and the sunshine. But they fell silent when Cenicola broke off at the wire, after which the hush was broken only by workout host Terry Nelson announcing the half and three-quarter splits. When John Henry crossed the line, and Nelson reported the final time, the crowd snapped back to life.

"Just like E. F. Hutton," McAnally said, allowing himself a grin. "When John Henry talks, everybody listens."

In its issue of May 1985, *Equus* magazine analyzed the John Henry phenomenon from stem to stern. The most telling observations came from Dr. George Pratt, the noted MIT engineering professor who made a lifetime study of the equine in motion.

According to *Equus*, Pratt noted that John Henry's gait was "characterized by a minimal overlap time—the period when two legs are on the ground—and low action. He doesn't fold his legs up much in preparation for the next stride. As a result, his legs don't have to absorb so much of the shock and vibration that trigger unsoundness."

John Henry's famously exaggerated head bob—described by McAnally as an oil well in action—was actually an important part of the package, since a horse's head naturally rises and falls to counterbalance the rise and fall of the body.

John Henry's head bob reduced body movement and allowed him to achieve an unusually long stride for his height of 15.2 hands. The typical horse of that size, according to Pratt, has a 23-foot stride. John Henry's stride measured 25.45 feet.

But even with his beneficial stride, his vigorous constitution, and his youthful outlook, John Henry was not immune to the ravages of racing and training. At one time or another, he had to deal with a calcified ankle, an osselet, near-fatal colic, a severe hip muscle pull, strained suspensories, and a blind splint.

And yet, with the help of McAnally and his staff, he kept coming back for more.

The thing that finally grounded John Henry as a racehorse, at the age of 10 in July of 1985, was damage to the deep flexor tendon, just below and behind his right knee. Even then, Dr. Jack Robbins, his most attentive vet, gave John Henry the benefit of the doubt.

"With John Henry," Robbins warned, "if you don't leave the back door open, he'll make you eat your words every time."

It was the same story written by John Henry in retirement, turning back the infirmities of age, defying the relentless calendars.

"He was such a fighter, even when his body was giving out, he just kept right on," said Cathy Roby, John Henry's primary caretaker at the Horse

Park. "But the last few days, you could tell he was just tired. He was saying, 'Let's get this over with. I don't want to fight anymore.' "

And finally it was okay, at last, to softly close that door. John Henry is goin' home.

~~~

## BILL HARTACK

*November 30, 2007*

To take the measure of a man in the days immediately following his death is patently unfair. Either he has made his mark, and it was worth the trouble to mention while the subject was still living, or he was a cipher, having no real impact beyond his immediate circle. End of story.

For someone like Bill Hartack, a contentious man of sweeping contradictions, there is also the very real possibility that were he around to suffer the post-mortems, he would take exception to just about everything read or said, beyond a handful of irrefutable facts.

He would no doubt agree that he won five Kentucky Derbies, beginning with Iron Liege in 1957 and ending with Majestic Prince in 1969. He would admit that he had been a member of the horse racing Hall of Fame for 48 of his nearly 75 years. And he could hardly argue with such core numbers as 4,272 victories and six national championships, although he'd probably demand an audit.

Hartack also might concede to a rough Pennsylvania childhood, what there was of it, defined by a mother who died in a car wreck when Bill was only eight and a father who was generous with nothing but the lash. Neither could Hartack deny the lavish lifestyle he methodically acquired as his riding success soared through the 1950s, complete with a West Virginia horse farm, a speedboat, luxury cars, and closets stocked with the finest threads, along with a posh pad in Miami Springs.

As for the rest, it would depend on which Hartack showed up—the angry, driven competitor who suffered fools not at all, or the selectively social bon vivant of his later years as a racing official, sometimes willing
~~~

to entertain whoever would listen with stories from racing's bygone days.

"He never did lose that tough attitude of his," said Louisiana trainer and fishing buddy Gary Palmisano, who welcomed the lifelong bachelor into his home during Hartack's tenure as a Fair Grounds steward. "When we'd go out, before I could even drop anchor, Bill would have a line in the water. He had to catch the first fish, the biggest fish, and the most fish.

"When he'd come over, he loved nothing better than to play checkers or chess with my son Gary," Palmisano added, "or get on the computer and play all kinds of video football games. Then they'd shoot some pool, and of course Bill had to win."

Hartack was a big name when racing was a big game, on a par with baseball and collegiate football, and reigned as the fourth head on the sport's Mount Rushmore alongside Eddie Arcaro, Bill Shoemaker, and Johnny Longden.

It happened quickly, too. Hartack was all of 23 and still eight months from his first Derby win when the young turf writer Joe Hirsch supplied the prose for a *Sports Illustrated* cover story, published September 17, 1956. At the time, Hartack was well on his way to taking the season's titles for both money and races won.

Hirsch's story in *SI* begins with the scene of an ebullient Hartack celebrating a victory, chatting amiably with fans and valets as he makes his way from the winner's circle to the room, the picture of a personable star on the rise. One race later, after losing on a favorite, the same Hartack was surly, mean, and impatient, a sullen Mr. Hyde wearing Dr. Jekyll's white pants and boots.

"He does indulge himself in the vilest of black moods, during which he refuses to speak to close friends, scowls and glowers at almost everyone," wrote Hirsch, retired now as *Daily Racing Form* executive columnist.

"Bill feels his position as one of America's leading riders quite keenly, and hates to give bad performances or be beaten on a favorite," Hirsch's story continued. "Since nearly everything he rides is heavily supported, the pressure is tremendous, and occasionally he gives vent to his feelings by sulking. However, when things are going right, he's full of natural charm, discusses things intimately and frankly with even casual acquaintances.

"This is no simple boy, this Hartack," Hirsch's article concluded. "He hasn't fully learned to accept all the many obligations of success as yet. But then Arcaro, too, was a renowned wild one in his youth and matured into quite a man, respected wherever there was racing in this country. Hartack is the Arcaro of tomorrow, and tomorrow is almost today."

History will note that Hartack was never anyone but Hartack, and even though he did not rise to Hirsch's challenge—to become as widely embraced as Eddie Arcaro—Hartack left an indelible mark upon American racing because of his mark on America's most famous race.

"He was the best Derby rider who ever lived," Hirsch said this week from his home in Manhattan. "It's so much of a rider's race, and he always seemed to be in the right place, making his move at the right time."

Only one of Hartack's five Derby winners was favored, the unbeaten Majestic Prince, owned by Canadian lumberman Frank McMahon.

"Once, while we were out on the boat, I asked him who was the best horse he ever rode," Gary Palmisano said. "And believe me he had never answered that question. He'd always give some smart-aleck answer like, 'If they know the best horse, they only rode one horse.' Like that.

"He stopped fishing for a minute and said that Majestic Prince was absolutely the best horse he ever rode, just a machine," Palmisano said, "and that the owner ruined him running in the Belmont after he bowed winning the Preakness."

Blunt, honest, and proud, Hartack exhibited all the attributes of a man on guard duty 24 hours a day, lest someone poke a nose in front.

"When the *Sports Illustrated* story came out, Bill was riding in New Jersey," Joe Hirsch said. "He came into the city one day, and we walked around, just to have dinner and see a movie. Bill stopped at every newsstand, just to see the display of his face on the covers."

Did anyone mention he was also human, with friends both loyal and long-suffering?

"I have a pen-and-ink of Hartack drawn by LeRoy Neiman," Hirsch added. "He caught him beautifully, in kind of a sulking pose, which he often assumed. It's probably the best thing I have."

~~~
~~~

# BOBBY FRANKEL

*November 18, 2009*

Bobby Frankel died Monday still owing me a night's sleep.

I only mention this because Frankel was a man who tended to settle his debts, balance the books, and move along to the next race on the card. But there was that time, heading to the 1998 Breeders' Cup at Churchill Downs, when he kept me awake for the whole four hours of the L.A.-to-Cincinnati red-eye, chattering in the seat next to me about the races, the movies, books, restaurants, current events, and the people we had in common, though from vastly different angles.

At one point the stewardess said, "Shhh. People are trying to sleep." She had no idea.

We landed, and then it was, "Forget about your car. You're driving with me." So that went well, too, and the conversation continued unchecked until we realized somebody missed the turnoff and we were apparently heading to Louisville by way of Lexington, or West Virginia. But who hasn't done that? Rather than point fingers, Frankel took the responsibility, I took the blame, and we enjoyed an extra hundred miles or so of verdant Kentucky countryside.

Anyway, he felt right at home. The city boy in Frankel always breathed easier when he could look out over a field of Thoroughbreds doing more or less what nature intended them to do, which is eat grass and make little Thoroughbreds, along with the occasional frolic. If pinned down, Bobby was never entirely comfortable with what racing asked of its equine athletes. This, more than anything else, prompted his evolution from a peerless claiming hustler to a meticulous handler of rare equine jewels.

"In claiming, you've got egos involved," he told me in a 1995 interview. "I knew how that was. And the horses were the alter-ego. People weren't thinking of them as animals who feel pain. I'd see guys lose a horse and clapping because somebody else got stuck with a bad horse, or a horse breaks his leg and somebody claims him, and they're giving each other high-fives. That's the worst. I didn't feel like being part of that anymore."

He was never really meant to be part of the claiming world in the first place, even though the young Frankel was a horseplayer, and a whiz, aided and abetted by inherent talent. He always described his mother, Gertrude, as a "real good handicapper," although his father, Melvin, "couldn't pick his nose."

His first mentor was Johnny Campo, assistant to Hall of Famer Eddie Neloy at the time, when their barn went from Gun Bow to Bold Lad and Buckpasser without missing a beat. Frankel bought his first horse from Allen Jerkens, and claimed his first stakes winner from MacKenzie Miller. Then, after spending the 1970s in California watching how Charlie Whittingham ran the table with a stable full of stakes horses, Bobby knew how it needed to be done.

"It's a whole different game going from training claimers to stakes horses," Frankel once said. "The good horses you have to live with and learn to like. They take more time, and you have to have the patience."

Frankel acquired like-minded clients, and with them ascended to the Hall of Fame in 1995. At that point in his career, he had yet to win a Breeders' Cup event or a Triple Crown race, or even a Santa Anita Handicap, an Arlington Million, or a Jockey Club Gold Cup.

"Maybe I don't belong," he told me at the time. "I've got to win a Derby and two or three Breeders' Cup races. Then I'll be all right. I've got more respect for a guy like Billy Mott than I do myself."

Frankel had to settle for a Belmont Stakes and six Breeders' Cups, but in the end, it was not the races that mattered as much as the horses who won them, or at least tried hard to win them.

"Money is paper," he said. "We're talking about horseflesh now. Live animals that go out every day and run their heart out. And you've got to do everything you can for that individual in all good conscience."

It has been a quiet six months at the track without Frankel holding forth, on any subject, at the drop of a hat. At home with his illness, a handful of close friends, and his Australian shepherds, Ginger and Punch, Bobby rode it out to the end, fighting hard when he could, relenting when there was no choice. He died in the house of his dreams, not far from the blue Pacific.

"Bonita was there with him, so much of the time," said Frank Lyons, a friend and former trainer. He was talking about Bonita Boniface Frankel, whose brief marriage to Bobby ended in 2006, but not their friendship.

"One night she thought he'd stopped breathing," Lyons went on. "She didn't want to panic, but when she checked him again, it was the same. Just as she was rushing to the telephone to call 911, she heard from the darkness, 'Hey, Bonita. Bring me that Saratoga condition book.' "

There are a few everlasting images that we decide upon for the iconic that walk among us. For Whittingham, it will be the sight of him baring his flat belly at a racetrack bar and daring a guy to punch him in the gut. For Jerkens, thankfully still going strong, it will be an early evening cruise across Saratoga Lake, him doing his Ed Norton impression from *The Honeymooners*, with nary a horse in sight.

Frankel, just 68, could have lived another 30 years, winning whatever he wanted to, saying whatever came into his mind, and still for me he would always be the Bobby I saw walking aimlessly through the Santa Anita Park paddock gardens late on the afternoon of March 18, 1984.

His fine filly Sweet Diane had just been killed on the first turn of the Santa Ana Handicap. She had fallen over High Haven, who broke her leg, and in falling she snapped her neck. Like that, she was gone, and for such occasions of random horror there can be no consolation. Frankel, tough guy, was alone, weeping like a child. After that, everything about him made sense.

~~~

## ORVIL HOVDEY

*July 28, 2006*

If you've been looking for someone to hold accountable for what you've been reading here, it's too late. Elvis has left the building.

The end came for my dad—the man who put the pen in my hand — early Tuesday evening, 83 years, four months, and a few days after he hit the ground running in a dry, cold corner of Montana prairieland that went by the name of Outlook.
~~~

At least, that's what it says on his birth certificate, only he told everyone he was from nearby Plentywood, a real town with a marching band and a high-school football team. He blew French horn and played both ways.

Dad did all the things you're supposed to do if you're raised on a hard-working Montana farm, which included getting off that farm as fast as he could, which he did, when he was barely 18. Before too long, he had the good sense to head straight for Southern California. And how about that—it fit him like a glove.

Except for this last bad patch with lung disease and those 18 months on a couple of godforsaken islands in the South Pacific, my dad had more than 80 good years. That's way more than anyone is ever guaranteed.

A whole bunch of them were spent at Del Mar, close to home, when my dad would shift into festive mode with each racing season, and I'd start getting it from all sides. He didn't miss a dance.

"Hey, Hovdey, met your dad Orvil last night at Scalini's. Man, he's nothing like you. He really knows how to have a good time."

The truth stings, but there it is. I had somehow suppressed my father's raucous gene—the one that made him both a peerless land salesman and the life of any party—rendering his oldest son a wet blanket by comparison. But that was okay. He was here first. And let's face it—no Orv Hovdey, no horse racing for his boy.

The first time he took me to the races, it wasn't even with me in mind. My grandfather was in town—we lived in a St. Louis suburb called Webster Groves at the time—and Grandpa was a voracious sports hound. When informed there was a racetrack across the river, we loaded all hands into the station wagon and lit out for Cahokia Downs, in East St. Louis. I remember only the lights, and horses like ghosts in the distance.

Back in California, where we really belonged, the romance of racing took hold. My dad tried hard to round out my sporting life with things like Game 3 of the 1963 World Series at Chavez Ravine, when we sat in the sun-fried first-base side of the second deck and watched Don Drysdale shut out Jim Bouton and the Yanks, 1-0, or the 1964 USC–Notre Dame game at the L. A. Coliseum, the day the refs robbed my Fighting Irish of both the game and the national title.

It was racing, though, that lit the real fire, and it was my dad who made sure we were at Hollywood Park to watch Native Diver beat Hill Rise and Colorado King in the 1965 Gold Cup, and at Santa Anita for three straight runnings of the Strub, beginning with Bold Bidder's mile and a quarter track record and ending with Most Host's unconscionable upset of Damascus. I remember being very quiet all the way home.

The night before our racing excursions, my dad would drive me to this seedy flophouse of a hotel in downtown Anaheim and keep the motor running while I darted inside to buy a *Racing Form.*

Eventually, my dad got the bug real bad and bought a few horses of his own. It wasn't the actual racing that jazzed him, though. It was being around the horses and the people who were drawn to the game. Anyway, his horses were mostly slow, but he managed to win a race, enough evidence alone to make a case for trainers Lewis Cenicola and Bill Delia to be given a special place in the Hall of Fame.

My dad was never getting to the Kentucky Derby as an owner. But he finally made it as a fan, in May of 2000.

Arriving on Thursday evening, he rubbed elbows at the barns Friday morning, and by Friday afternoon he was visiting John Henry and Cigar in Lexington. That night, back in Louisville, he dined with Joe Hirsch at the Brown Hotel, then around midnight excused himself to attend a party he just happened to hear about somewhere.

Returning at dawn, he napped, snacked, then took a cab to the track around 4 o'clock, in plenty of time for the Derby post parade. His choice was Fusaichi Pegasus, but he added Aptitude to the mix on a recommendation from Hirsch. He bet the winning exacta cold, celebrated in the Derby Museum, and went home the next morning a satisfied man. Now that is how you do the Kentucky Derby.

At the end, when my dad's lungs were shot and his kidneys were on their way to ruined, the only thing left to do was give him the reports from Del Mar's opening week and relay the sights and sounds of his favorite track.

I rigged him up with a set of headphones and played him "Rhapsody in Blue" and Hawaiian ballads—like Iz singing "Kaulana Kawaihae"—then read him some of his favorite Hemingway. Not "My Old Man," a racing story that ends badly, but "Big Two-Hearted River: Part I" instead, because it ends with Nick Adams cozy in his tent under the pine trees near the stream, his belly full of coffee and spaghetti and beans, curled up under his blanket and ready to sleep.

Ten

# HERSELF

*This is the way Joe Hirsch began a column about a near-mythical creature who reigned for five years as the finest Thoroughbred in the land:*

*"Once upon a time there was a horse named Kelso, but only once."*

*So that line was taken.*

*During the intoxicating run of her first 19 starts without a defeat, Zenyatta taxed the imagination. There was a point at which words began to fail, simply because there were only so many ways to describe her incredible physical dimensions, her idiosyncratic behaviors, her operatic style of running as if exploding at the end of a long, smoldering fuse, time after time after time.*

*Thank goodness then for the people in her corner. They were grounded by the reality that anything could always go wrong. They knew there was nothing as unpredictable as a horse race. When the inevitable happened, and she would win again, they would shrug, smile, and say, "What did you expect? She's Zenyatta."*

*"I was asked about the idea of a horse going through a career undefeated," said her trainer, the Vietnam vet John Shirreffs. "Come on. It would be very presumptuous to consider such a thing. Fortunately, we don't read the paper every day."*

*Zenyatta was six-for-six at the time and just 4-years-old. Two and a half years later, when she arrived at the end of her career on a cold, damp night in Kentucky, even Shirreffs had to concede he might have been aiming low.*

*Zenyatta had become nothing less than a vessel into which was poured the hopes and dreams of fans longing for that rare glimpse of Thoroughbred perfection.*

*I watched her last race standing on a folding chair in a trackside box at Churchill Downs along with David Flores, Zenyatta's first jockey.*

*"I had to be here for my girl," Flores said.*

*In the end, when her ferocious finish came up short for the one and only time in her life, Flores stared into the Kentucky darkness and declared:*

*"She's still the best. The best there ever was."*

# WORTH THE WAIT

*May 25, 2009*

Those seven months between starts for Zenyatta passed quickly, didn't they? Perhaps it was all the distractions that helped dull the pain. To kill time, Americans elected their first African-American president. Not long after that the economy was destroyed, Guantanamo was ordered closed, and the Steelers won another Super Bowl. When Tiger Woods came back from his long absence, we knew Zenyatta would soon follow. Then suddenly, it was last Saturday, and her light shone across the land once more.

They were nervous, the Zenyatta crew, and rightfully so. Perfection is an awful burden. Of all the things that can go wrong in horse racing, at least one of them usually does. As they waited to take Zenyatta to Hollywood Park's backstretch receiving barn, trainer John Shirreffs paced like a caged tiger, while exercise rider Steve Willard pawed the ground in anticipation.

"I just love her," Willard said, in a voice familiar to any father who has ever stared down at his sleeping child. "She's been training better than she ever has in her life. But I just want her to come back okay."

By that Willard did not mean come back to the races in a blaze of glory, which she certainly did with her domination of the Milady Handicap. He meant that she should go do her thing, and then come back to him and the others in the Shirreffs world as healthy and strong as she was right now, an hour before post time, as assistant trainer Felipe Rivera knelt in her stall and applied back wraps and rundowns.

Awful things will happen—as they did that same afternoon at Arlington Park when Rene Douglas and his mount suffered such tragic damage—but Zenyatta's chances are always better than most, for a holistic combination of reasons that mark the character of the Shirreffs operation.

For instance, Zenyatta was all dressed up and ready to roll on the morning of May 1, when she found herself at Churchill Downs and entered to make her return that afternoon in the Louisville Distaff. What a stage it would have been—Kentucky Oaks Day, featuring Rachel Alexandra, with Zenyatta as the warm-up act. But steady rains had played havoc with the Churchill Downs racing surface, and Shirreffs was in no mood to roll the dice.

"There were reasons to run or not to run," Shirreffs said, looking back at the brief Kentucky trip. "I decided to let it come down to one thing. I would make my decision based on what they did with the track after training that morning, whether they would harrow it or float it. When they floated it, I knew they were more concerned about the track for Derby Day, so I scratched."

In many ways, the checked swing in Kentucky was just what Zenyatta needed to clear any remaining cobwebs. She shipped like an old pro from her California safe house and galloped around the tight, tacky Churchill Downs surface with consummate ease. A horse race is different, though, and so she came home.

Now, an hour before going over for the Milady, both Zenyatta and stable-mate Life Is Sweet were standing calmly in ice boots and ice buckets, a couple of snow queens getting ready for the dance. Shirreffs was asked about this stuff called "ice." An exotic new treatment?

"No, we can make it right here," Shirreffs said.

So, it is a synthetic substance. Legal, though?

"Yes," Shirreffs replied, playing along. "But they'll probably develop a test for it and then ban it."

The ice was pulled, and both Zenyatta and Life Is Sweet put on their matching shadow rolls, D-bits, snaffles, and tongue ties. Life Is Sweet, on a roll of three major wins at Santa Anita, is a handsome athlete in her own right, but even Rachel Alexandra would look a little drab next to Zenyatta's 17-plus hands' worth of dark mahogany carving. After an uneventful walk through the breezeways of several barns, the Shirreffs mares arrived at the receiving facility, where supervisor Larry Damore—a respected exercise rider in the mornings—flipped their lips and checked their shoes.

"That's her," Damore deadpanned, as he waved Zenyatta in.

The race itself was memorable mostly because of how hard Garrett Gomez and Life Is Sweet tried to beat Zenyatta, and how easy it was for Zenyatta to swat them away. The crowd in attendance was small—barely 6,000—but they were tightly bunched. When Mike Smith asked Zenyatta to make that warp-speed burst around the turn (I swear little trails of light flicker out of her tail when she does it), there could be heard from the stands gasps and giggles of delight and gratitude.

Zenyatta was back. It had been a long seven months after all.

~~~

# PURE PLATINUM

*August 8, 2009*

Jerry Moss compares each appearance of Zenyatta to the debut of a new album by The Police, and he should know, since he has owned them both—or at least, in the case of The Police, owned the company that produced their records.

"We actually released only five albums, and after the first one, each time was huge," Moss said. The third of the five was *Zenyatta Mondatta.*

For their fans, The Police are one of those musical gifts that keeps on giving—their reunion tour last year broke the bank—just as Zenyatta has never failed to please the crowd.

The difference, and it is significant in the current climate, is that The Police were never required to validate their work by going one-on-one with the Eurythmics or Duran Duran, although a Sting–Annie Lennox smackdown would have packed the house.

That is what Moss is up against this year. The story line is no longer Zenyatta's flawless career—currently at 11 wins—nor her ability to win without serious bother, nor her breathtaking physical presence. For all her stature,
~~~

Zenyatta is now being judged in the court of Rachel Alexandra, a 3-year-old filly who was barely weaned when Zenyatta won her first race.

Jack Nicholson, meet Zac Efron.

Unfortunately, Zenyatta has been trading this year primarily on the capital of last season's glory. It is the second week in August, and she has run exactly twice, descending from the mountaintop to win the Milady and the Vanity at Hollywood Park. Both of those races, widely rumored to be fantastic, might as well have taken place at midnight in Bakersfield for all the attention they received. In terms of bodies at the track, the swap meet at the local drive-in gets more action than a Saturday afternoon at Hollywood. There was no live broadcast outside simulcast and TVG. Zenyatta's races were covered widely on the Internet, but so what? As of Friday morning, there were 55,900 Google hits for "Zenyatta horse" and 2.7 million hits for "Lohan drunk."

Zenyatta's appearance on Sunday at Del Mar in the $300,000 Clement Hirsch Stakes will draw her most energetic crowd since she won the Ladies' Classic on Breeders' Cup Friday last October. There is still no broadcast television following the Zenyatta story, nor even ESPN, the network of the Breeders' Cup. But at least they'll be talking about her at Red Tracton's and the Brigantine that night.

The point of Thoroughbred horse racing is to find out which horse is faster, better, stronger, tougher—use any of these as a measuring stick. In the end, there is only one way to find out, and that is to race them against each other over a period of time, observe them in a variety of conditions, and wait until the dust settles to decide.

On Sunday, it will be up to Zenyatta and Mike Smith to make the most of the opportunity presented by the Hirsch. Even then, a loud statement would only go so far. By Monday morning, if Zenyatta walks her beat, the clamor will rise afresh for a race against Rachel, even though Moss has already told everyone where Zenyatta will be on either November 6 or 7 and means it.

"As a fan, I was sorry the Breeders' Cup was coming to Santa Anita two consecutive years," Moss said. "I love going to other tracks, other restaurants, meeting other horsemen. Florida, Churchill Downs. I loved Monmouth Park, a beautiful little track, even if it did rain for four days.

"It does seem, though, that the racing press has excused the owner who doesn't want to run in the Breeders' Cup, saying that's his prerogative. And it is. But isn't that the place where champions are supposedly crowned?"

It is laughable to think that men like Jess Jackson and Jerry Moss can be browbeaten by press and public opinion to run their best horses someplace they don't want to run. Jackson says he will not run Rachel Alexandra in the Breeders' Cup this year at Santa Anita. Moss and his trainer, John Shirreffs, see no point in an East Coast invasion when that very same Breeders' Cup is their main target. If anything, fans should be angry at the way the sport has failed to make a meeting between the filly and the mare inevitable.

"For starters, there's been no chance to run against Rachel Alexandra even if we wanted to," Moss said. "We don't qualify to run against 3-year-olds. I still think it could happen somehow. But all I can concentrate on is Sunday. And she's not scaring anybody away."

No, but she should. It remains to be seen how many of the nine entered against Zenyatta end up in the gate. Second is not bad in a Grade 1 event, but Zenyatta's stablemate Life Is Sweet is in there, so third might be all that's left.

Moss takes nothing for granted, which is wise. This is an owner who had his first world-class 2-year-old filly, Delicate Vine, break down before she could run in the 1986 Breeders' Cup. This is an owner who had to watch his 1994 Kentucky Oaks winner, Sardula, suffer through a long illness and finally succumb. Moss is too competitive to duck and dodge just to keep Zenyatta unbeaten, but he will do what he can to keep her as safe and sound as this rough game will allow. There should not be any confusion between the two.

"To have a horse of this nature, this stature, is a dream come true," Moss said. "So I don't care. I'll take it all. Ask me anything. I'll talk to anybody. I just love her. I just hope she's happy and healthy and goes on to be all she's supposed to be. And I do love watching her run."

Good. It's Sunday. Time to give Big Mama the ball.

~~~
~~~

# CLASSIC SERENADE

*November 9, 2009*

A week before the Breeders' Cup Classic, while on the way to the track at Hollywood Park for their final work, Mike Smith could be heard softly singing to Zenyatta in Spanish as they walked along the backstretch road.

"It's a song called 'Antes de Que Te Vayas,' " Smith said, "by Marco Antonio Solis. It means 'Before You Go,' and it's sort of about saying good-bye to someone you love and hoping they come back to you safe. I sing it to her every time I get on her. She keeps time to it when she walks."

Not that anyone in the house of more than 58,000 could hear it, but Smith was serenading his mare what he thought would be one last time on Saturday afternoon at Santa Anita Park as he walked Zenyatta slowly up the stretch toward the starting gate for the $5 million Breeders' Cup Classic.

The others in the field of 12 were strewn around the turn and down the backside, going through their conventional warm-ups, while Zenyatta lagged behind, not because of some dramatic disposition to single herself out, but because Smith, in consultation with trainer John Shirreffs over the years, figured it was better not to light the physical fires under the big mare before you needed them. After all, she was the younger half-sister of Balance, a Santa Anita Oaks winner of notorious temper, and as a young filly, Zenyatta suffered from hives and bouts of bleeding, both related to stress.

"She can get a little stirred up," Smith said. "It's always right there, beneath the surface. It's best not to give her a reason."

Still, one would think a $2.7 million first prize and an indelible place in racing history would be justification enough to at least break into a little prerace trot. But no. Zenyatta walked. Smith crooned. And the fans went wild at the sight of their majestic serenity in the face of such a moment in time.

*"Antes de que te vayas/*
*Dejame mirar/*
*Una vez mas ese rostro/*
*Que nunca he de olvidar."*

It can be frustrating at first blush to hear Smith say that Zenyatta won the Classic in hand, with plenty in the tank, and for Shirreffs to report that she bounced out of the race looking for more. Such an image runs contrary to the way horse racing usually treats its greatest stars, who are asked to run until it is either physically impossible or economically impractical to continue.

Fans and media tend to admire above all those professional athletes who play hurt, get bloody, and leave it all out there on the field. Sports, after all, are elaborate metaphors for war, and for the metaphor to work there must be casualties. Thoroughbreds, though, can go terribly wrong when they are exhausted, a cold fact every trainer lives with every day.

As impressive as she was in splendid isolation in the Mother Goose or the Kentucky Oaks, or in her graceful dismissal of young males in the Haskell, it will always be Rachel Alexandra's narrow escape from the Preakness against Mine That Bird, or her desperate struggle at the end of the Woodward against flummoxed older horses that are held in highest esteem.

Zenyatta always played against that theme. Except for a couple of close calls in timing her exuberant move, Smith always tended to have his hands in his lap as her races came to an end. In that sense, as Shirreffs once said of the mare in so many words, we were watching an artist at work, who just happened to be painting with an athlete's brush.

Which is why it really never mattered where Zenyatta ran, or against whom, or in what kind of race. As a racehorse, she has been unconventional in every sense of the word, very much in a world of her own. Her career has been 14 visits to the Louvre, 14 performances by the New York Philharmonic, 14 trips to the edge of the Grand Canyon. How did you like the view?

"The greatest mare I ever rode was Bayakoa," said Laffit Pincay at the end of last Saturday, surrounded by fans in the Santa Anita paddock. "And before Zenyatta, the greatest mare I probably ever saw was Ruffian. But you know what, I never got the chills watching a race. This race today gave me the chills."

"All the things I've seen," said Kent Desormeaux, who rode Summer Bird to a noble fourth in the Classic, "I'm glad I witnessed this. And my colt was running."

"It was inside the sixteenth pole," said Ramon Dominguez, who beat them all but Zenyatta with Gio Ponti. "That's when I heard the commotion from the public. I looked over and saw her, and thought, 'Okay.' There was nothing I could do."

It was also Dominguez aboard reigning champion Ginger Punch in April of 2008 when they met the emerging Zenyatta in the Apple Blossom Handicap at Oaklawn Park. The experience left its mark.

"She was wide the whole race and blew by us with her ears like this," Dominguez said, giving his fingers the now famous Zenyatta waggle. "I knew that day, she was something very special."

To quibble at this point about something so mundane as the voting for 2009 Horse of the Year seems far beneath the significance of what Zenyatta represents. For those closest to her embrace, she will always be the horse of a lifetime. For the media, a story without peer. For horseplayers and fans, just imagine—a free spot and a happy ending every time she ran. To the end, she did it without fuss and without physical strife, dodging the evident dangers of the game to give life to the words of the song her jockey sang:

*"Once again before you go/*
*Allow me to look/*
*Once more into the face/*
*That I will never forget."*

*(It was expected that Zenyatta would be retired after winning the 2009 Breeders' Cup Classic. Then her owners, Ann and Jerry Moss, did the unexpected and announced that she would race for one more season. This qualified as very good news.)*

~~~

## ENCORE

*March 11, 2010*

One day between races at Santa Anita, Mike Smith was sitting on the bench in front of his jocks' room cubicle. His eyes were closed, and his head was swaying, side to side, keeping time to the tune of some internal rhapsody. His valet, former jockey Raul Ramirez, was more amused than concerned.

"What are you doing?" asked Ramirez.

Smith came back to earth.

"I'm riding Zenyatta," he said.
~~~

The good ones will do that to even the most seasoned riders. Moments spent in their company are lived in vivid Technicolor, the memories intense beyond words.

Smith awoke last November 8, having just won the Breeders' Cup Classic aboard his remarkable mare. The view from the top of the racing world was fine. But then, after a splash of cold water, he was asked to say good-bye.

Things change. Two months later, Ann and Jerry Moss decided that Zenyatta belonged not in a grassy pasture, laden with foal, but between the lines, doing her true thing. Now, that promise is on the verge of fulfillment, and on Saturday at Santa Anita, in the $250,000 Santa Margarita Handicap, Zenyatta and Smith will try to pick up where they left off last fall.

"Watching the Olympics the other day, I noticed the skiers, before they competed, would go through the course in their mind," Smith said earlier this week. "They'd be waving back and forth with their head and hands, visualizing. I do that with her all the time, sometimes even when I'm driving, and I've got to stop myself. Enough already. What's gonna happen is gonna happen. Let her rest. Put her back in the stall."

After a string of 11 perfect outcomes aboard the 14-0 Zenyatta, Smith, 44, has become indelibly connected to the fortunes of the champion mare, just as Eddie Arcaro was with Citation, Bill Shoemaker with Swaps, or Milo Valenzuela with the reign of Kelso.

Smith and Zenyatta first collaborated in April of 2008 to win the Apple Blossom Handicap at Oaklawn Park. Over the past 23 months, both mornings and afternoons, the rider has thrilled to Zenyatta's evolution, from an oversized, absurdly talented ingénue to a breathtaking creature of regal poise.

"We used to work her with two horses," Smith recalled. "When she'd go by the first one, she'd think, 'Eh, this is boring,' and just go through the motions. Now, you break one off three, four in front of her, and zoom! She's locked in, in a good way. And when I ask her to finish up, she's all business."

Zenyatta's style of coming from far afield tends to create its own drama.

"There are naturally more decisions to make, just because she has to pass the whole field almost every time she runs," Smith noted. "The great thing about her is that she's like a light switch. I can turn her off and on any time, which is amazing for such a big horse."

Smith learned about Zenyatta's gears the hard way, in that first Apple Blossom together.

"The communication wasn't a hundred percent yet," Smith said. "I wasn't even turning for home, and I thought I'd left her way too much to do. I went from picking her up to going 'Hyahhh!' and slapping her on the shoulder. Whoa! The next thing I'm thinking is that I hit the front way too soon. I learned then that it's baby steps with her.

"So the first part of the race, I'll put my hands way down and keep them way back, palms down, and let her get into that big rhythm," Smith went on. "If she wants to pick it up a little sooner than I think we should, I can just lean back without moving my hands. When I want her to pick it up, I sit way up on her so I can look over her head. I'll kind of lean forward, bow over her a little, and she'll just run underneath me.

"After that, if I'm looking for somewhere to go, or go around, I'll reach up and gather her a little bit, and there she goes again," Smith continued. "If I need more, I'll pick it up a little higher. If I need more than that, I show her the stick, and man, there's another gear. They just keep coming. If I hit her a time or two, she'll jump right then and there. Then up come the ears and she's loping on home again."

And again, and again and again. The racing fan in Mike Smith never tires of Zenyatta highlights.

"Watching most big races afterwards, you always kind of watch yourself," Smith said. "You might even think, yeah, I rode a pretty good race. With her, it's like I'm not even on her. I'm going, wow, all the time. Somebody will say, 'Hey, great ride,' and I'll say, 'Me? Did you see what *she* did?' "

Before Zenyatta came along, Smith's Hall of Fame résumé was already crammed full of stars like Holy Bull, Azeri, Sky Beauty, Devil His Due, Lure, Inside Information, Spook Express, and Coronado's Quest, going back in a career of 28 years that began in his native New Mexico. As good as they were, they were all beaten, at one time or another, a fact that keeps Smith from taking anything for granted, or looking ahead to the anticipated showdown with Rachel Alexandra at Oaklawn on April 9.

"You still have to go out there and run, so you worry about the little things," he said. "A lot of things can happen and do happen in a race. So let's just take it one race at a time and get through Saturday. I do believe, though, that her first race back could be pretty impressive.

"I hate to say it, but it is what it is," Smith added. "If I didn't know no better, I'd say she's coming back even bigger, stronger, even better. She's more forward, more intelligent as each day goes by. Really, it's kind of scary. When you get a 6-year-old mare as healthy and happy as she is, there's nothing like it."

~~~

## Z-TOWN

*June 6, 2010*

With the exception of that flamboyant victory in the 2009 Breeders' Cup Classic at Santa Anita Park, Zenyatta has made her history in small, relatively conventional pieces. Another one of those pieces comes along Sunday at Hollywood Park, when Zenyatta faces five in the $250,000 Vanity Handicap, a race she has won the past two seasons.

For kicks, just to keep the troops on edge, she makes some of those pieces look tougher than others, like the 2009 Clement Hirsch, when she ran her final quarter in 22 and change to win by a head, or the 2008 version of the Vanity, when she washed out and won by just a half-length, while running 1-1/8 miles for the first time. (For the record, and fond memory, runner-up Tough Tiz's Sis went on to win Belmont's Ruffian Handicap later that year by 12-1/4 lengths.)

Still, for the most part, Zenyatta's impact has been that of a steadily rising tide, with no ebb in sight. Her fans have come to terms with the fact that there is no splashy Triple Crown appearance decorating her record, no daring trip to Dubai, no significant shifts in surface, distance, or, for that matter, weather. In some ways, Zenyatta's career has been a controlled experiment, or at least as controlled an experiment as possible when dealing with the chaos inherent in the handling of a Thoroughbred racehorse.

John Shirreffs, Zenyatta's trainer, is the control freak at the center of the storm. He was asked one morning this week if maybe things weren't getting
~~~

a little boring, after running the mare 16 times and having the same old thing happen each and every time. Obviously, training Zenyatta has become no more challenging than turning on the barn lights.

"Are you kidding?" Shirreffs shot back. "A big mare like her, there have been things to deal with. The mental challenges alone have been considerable."

Citing trainer-trainee privilege, Shirreffs declined to expand on any physical hurdles Zenyatta may have faced during her 31 months in competition, although it is broadly known that her summers at Del Mar have not been exactly a day at the beach. There is a reason Zenyatta will remain at Hollywood Park this year after the meet closes, even though the Hirsch at Del Mar is tentatively on her schedule.

As for Zenyatta's psychological baggage, she has reached the midpoint of her 6-year-old season still preferring to run sideways in the mornings rather than straight ahead. She will protest, in various ways, even the slightest departures from established procedures. In the afternoons, her goose-stepping post parades are a physical transference of bottled anxieties, which are eventually soothed by her unhurried but carefully orchestrated stroll to the post, while the others gallop and jog. For the crowd, it's just good theater.

"We learned that absolutely everything with her has to be part of a strict routine," Shirreffs said. "We found that she'd get too worked up if you warmed her up, so we decided to pick a spot where she could walk and then stand and be calm and relaxed. We chose the quarter pole."

And there Zenyatta will stand Sunday, in isolated splendor, before wandering back to the gate and entering stall No. 5. After 16 races and 16 wins, the conclusion would seem to be foregone, even though she has faced none of her Vanity opponents before.

Owners and trainers anxious not to end up Zenyatta roadkill have gone to some lengths to avoid a confrontation. Earlier this year, Santa Maria winner St Trinians sought refuge by running against males in the Santa Anita Handicap. Zardana, the Bayakoa Handicap winner also trained by Shirreffs, found sanctuary running instead against Horse of the Year Rachel Alexandra in New Orleans and beating her in the bargain. On Sunday, both Zardana and St Trinians finally face the music.

Arnold Zetcher, Zardana's owner, still recalls the sound of stunned silence greeting the shocker at the Fair Grounds. His mare tried to beat Rachel Alexandra again in the La Troienne at Churchill Downs but threw in a stinker. Then, as recently as a week ago, Zardana was headed to New York for the Ogden Phipps, but an excessively fast workout scrapped those shipping plans and kept her home.

"We're not deluding ourselves," Zetcher said when the possibility of another upset was suggested. "It would be nothing short of amazing if it happened. But when people say, 'How can you run against Zenyatta?' I say, 'It's horse racing!' I don't think anyone would want to see her out there by herself just running an exhibition. I'm a racing fan, and fans want competitive races. At the weights, and with St Trinians in there, I think it could be a pretty good race."

With her style, no matter what the competition or the challenge, Zenyatta is always entertaining. Each appearance is a tale for the grandkids. It is a shame, though, that once again her appearance has not inspired some kind of national network coverage. TVG, which gets a Hollywood Park exclusive, is the only live televised source for the Vanity. There also is something now called NTRA Live!, which is streaming video, and makes its debut with the Vanity featuring Randy Moss in a studio in Oklahoma and remote coverage from the scene. Good luck to them, and their exclamation point.

I'm guessing, though, that more people will see Zenyatta just driving by that L.A. Dodgers billboard towering over the corner of 106th Street and Hawthorne Boulevard, a couple miles from the track. "This Is My Town" is the message, and the image of Zenyatta is larger than life. If that's possible.

~~~

## LOUD AND CLEAR

*June 15, 2010*

Last Friday night at Dodger Stadium, Ozzy Osbourne led a ballpark full of unsuspecting fans in a one-minute scream to raise money for the Think Cure! Weekend for cancer research. They called it "Scream for a Cure," which of
~~~

course had nothing to do with Osbourne's upcoming album, *Scream*, but the fans did get themselves into the *Guinness Book of World Records* for "loudest and longest scream" while raising $50,000 in the process. I know what you're thinking: "They let Ozzy Osbourne do another album?"

The scream let loose from a densely packed 12,000 or so folks at Hollywood Park Sunday afternoon could have been a contender. It didn't last as long, but it was aimed in a single direction, and when it hit its peak it was one of those paint-peeling screams that shakes the building and leaves the ears ringing for a long, long time. More Black Sabbath than Dodger Blue.

John Shirreffs stood on the guinea stand next to the grandstand crowd, smack in the maw of the sound, wearing a painfully dated cap ("Zenyatta 14-14") and holding his breath for the few eternal seconds it took Zenyatta to take St Trinians seriously enough to flop those big ears back for a few strides and reel her in to win the Vanity Handicap, her 17th without defeat. It was her third Vanity, which is great, but does not mean as much as the fact that a Grade 1 horse—any Grade 1 horse—is around long enough to run in a race like the Vanity three times.

The scream at Hollywood Park, echoing the cheers at Churchill Downs the day before for Rachel Alexandra's romp in the Fleur de Lis, effectively quieted all that moaning and groaning about a sub-standard 2010 Triple Crown series. Both races were handicaps, love 'em or not, and Rachel did her work under 124 pounds and won by 10-1/2, while Zenyatta packed 129 and won by half a length, which sort of tells you which racing secretary did his job. Who they beat and how they did it will supply red meat for a week's worth of comments. Let's just say there were no surprises and considerable relief, since there was every bit as much pressure surrounding Rachel Alexandra's 0-for-2 record this year as there was on Zenyatta's 16-and-0 lifetime.

Of course, a showdown between the two would be great, and every racetrack with either a marketing budget or a sliver of imagination should be scrambling for a way to make it happen. If that day comes, we'll all be there. Promise.

Until then, it is fun to wonder. The Rachel Alexandra camp likes to keep the troops guessing as to her appearances right up to the brink. This mitigates against buying cheap airfares, but as long as she continues to run in the big houses on big days, which is her style, she usually ends up where she belongs.

As for Zenyatta, there remains an intense longing to see her race far and wide. Even the Mona Lisa toured the world. A couple days before the Vanity, owner Jerry Moss was asked about statements made earlier this year that seemed to leave little doubt Zenyatta would be pointed toward more engagements outside California. But now, the realities of campaigning a huge, 6-year-old beast, who has been in fairly steady training nearly three solid years, appears to be coming into play. Last week, Shirreffs was quoted by Steve Andersen in the *Daily Racing Form* suggesting that the Clement Hirsch at Del Mar was on Zenyatta's dance card after the Vanity. In that event, Zenyatta likely would have room for just one more race before heading to Churchill Downs for the Breeders' Cup Classic in November.

"I'm not going to go chasing Horse of the Year," Shirreffs told me. "Just being Zenyatta should be enough."

You would think. Moss, clearly the more adventurous of the two, was floored by the rock-star reception Zenyatta received at Oaklawn Park, where she won the Apple Blossom in April, as well as enlightened by its physical effects on his mare.

"I didn't realize how much trips take out of the horse," Moss said. "And it's not just preparing for the race. It's the crowd, and the people that gather around her all the time. We saw that at Oaklawn Park, and we really hadn't thought about it before. You can put up a screen, like John does. But she's still aware there's something going on. There's a lot of energy generated. As far as racing elsewhere, we did think about trying to do other things, and we still might. There's options. I wouldn't pay too much attention to Del Mar being a solid item. There's no commitments there."

The Zenyatta team always ends up very much on the same page, and the big mare always comes through to tie things up with a bright ribbon. Anyone who thinks Zenyatta beat a bunch of patsies on Sunday needed to put a clock on St Trinians—who handled Life Is Sweet earlier in the year—through that final quarter mile. Her front legs going all directions, the British mare gave as much as you can give to a race and still be upright at the end. Standing there afterwards, being unsaddled in the backwash of the Zenyatta din, she was spent, dizzy, and noble. I hope she knew some of that noise was for her.

~~~
~~~

# REALITY CHECK

*October 3, 2010*

Alonso Quinonez, welcome to the club. Jumping off Hollywood Oaks winner Switch after the Lady's Secret on Saturday at Hollywood, Quinonez uttered those words now becoming familiar.

"I thought I had her beat," he said, figuring everyone would know who "her" was.

There was an echo, though, variations on a theme, from the lips of jockeys who, for an intoxicating few moments, deep in the stretches of Santa Anita, Hollywood, or Del Mar, thought they would be the one to deliver the blow that knocked Zenyatta off her pedestal.

"I thought I won it," said Tyler Baze, sick with disappointment, after Zenyatta caught Anabaa's Creation at the wire in the 2009 Clement Hirsch at Del Mar. "I didn't know where she was, but I knew she was coming. She came and just got us."

"I don't know what to say," said a disheartened Martin Garcia last summer, after St Trinians emptied her tank in the Vanity Handicap. "I can't say anything right now. I couldn't have asked her for any more. The other mare is just too much horse."

Rafael Bejarano was more circumspect after his near miss aboard Rinterval in the 2010 version of the Hirsch, when Zenyatta beat them by a neck. Bejarano noted that he inherited a pace he did not necessarily want that day, and had he been able to sit behind horses early, the result may have been different. This speaks highly of Bejarano's self-confidence, and in his belief that nothing is ordained. For a slightly more reality-based point of view, he needed only to consult with Garcia, Baze, or the rest of the riders on the list who have been aboard the last horse passed by Zenyatta in each of her 19 wins.

Bejarano, sorry to say, did not get a chance to fine-tune his tactics with Rinterval on Saturday. A message of sorts was sent the race before, when his mount, Boxeur des Rues, bolted so badly on the final turn of the Norfolk Stakes that Bejarano hit the deck. The colt took off in the direction of the chute at the head of the homestretch and, undaunted by the securely locked gate guarding the path from the backstretch to the paddock gardens, wedged his way through a narrow gap at the railing and fled toward the grandstand. Boxeur des Rues left a few tufts of horsehair on a bent piece of metal extending from the gate hinge and was caught before he could be claimed as a door prize by someone in the reported crowd of more than 25,000. But the 2-year-old did not look the least bit embarrassed as he circled with his relieved groom off to the side of the path while Zenyatta, Rinterval, and the rest of the Lady's Secret field passed by, on their way to be saddled.

Bejarano shook it off and was ready to go again when he got word from the paddock that Rinterval had reared in her stall and tried to flip with such ferocity that the stewards had no choice but to remove her from the race. It is tempting to suggest, giving full voice to an anthropomorphic angle, that Rinterval wanted nothing to do with the monster being saddled two stalls down, especially after what had happened at Del Mar. But these odd things happen, and after giving Informed Decision and Zenyatta good fights in her last two starts, it is hoped Rinterval recovers to fight again.

That left Quinonez and Switch to play the part of the Washington Generals to Zenyatta's Globetrotters, and they did it well, actually making it appear as if Big Mama Z raised her pulse rate a notch. Mike Smith even smacked her a couple of times—must have been a nervous tic—to finish the job. And that was that. Zenyatta's 17th and final California appearance, dating back to her maiden win on November 22, 2007, was in the books with another check mark.

These last few races from Zenyatta have had a ceremonial element that distracts from the intrinsic challenges of simple competition. The signs, the hats, the T-shirts, the people who come to town with tales of pilgrimage and inspiration—this is entertaining, up to a point. But it has nothing to do with horse racing. These are people finding reason to invest in a Thoroughbred horse as a reliable hero—thin times indeed—just as Secretariat gave rise to unreasonable hopes that he could heal the sick and make the lame to walk, or at least provide a distraction from the headlines of Watergate and Vietnam.

Unfortunately, horse racing has disappeared so far into a niche of its own making that Zenyatta remains largely unknown beyond the game's most devout followers. As such, she is far from a Secretariat-style cure-all for the Iraq-Afghanistan blues, or a soothing balm on the recession-ravaged middle class of a nation back on its heels. Still, it was nice that Penny Chenery, better known as Secretariat's mom and in town for the *Secretariat* movie premiere, could be alongside Ann and Jerry Moss for the winner's circle presentation Saturday. Fine birds of a feather.

What was left properly unsaid in the flurry of another Zenyatta-palooza was the fact that it took place just four days after Rachel Alexandra had been retired. As it turned out, their only real rivalry was in the polling of those Eclipse Award voters last year who went for Rachel for Horse of the Year. Otherwise, they existed in universes that weren't even particularly parallel—just a couple of very good horses competing at the same time in different parts of this very large country.

It is an everlasting shame that Rachel Alexandra never recovered from the effort it took to beat older males in the 2009 Woodward Stakes. But that is the nature of the beast.

Now the ball is cleanly in Zenyatta's court. Stepping up at Churchill Downs on November 6 in the Breeders' Cup Classic, she has that rare chance afforded only the greatest, most romantic of athletes who arrive at their final hour with a chance to make it their finest.

~~~

## THE LAST HURRAH

*November 10, 2010*

Chris McCarron, who won the 1988 Breeders' Cup Classic with Alysheba under considerably less illumination than was provided last Saturday at Churchill Downs, saw what was happening from ground level, standing as he was about a hundred yards past the finish.

"Everyone's asking me why he let her drop back so far," said McCarron, figuring the listener would know the "he" was Mike Smith and the "her" was Zenyatta, who had just lost, by the length of Blame's head, for the first time in her 20-race career.

"I don't think it was his idea," McCarron went on. "When he went by me he was niggling on her, trying to get her to pick it up a little. She must not
~~~

have been all that comfortable with the surface, and that can happen. Then look what she did."

In order to do what she did—to close from so far back that fish stories seem tame by comparative exaggeration and still finish alongside the tenacious Blame—Zenyatta had to do what John Henry did in the 1981 Arlington Million, when the turf was so deep, his flawless, ground-clipping stride was sinking with every step until, with Bill Shoemaker's patience, he found enough rhythm to gain purchase on the ground and move steadily toward The Bart to catch him with a head bob at the wire.

She had to do what Forego did in the 1976 Marlboro Cup when the big gelding loathed every step of the mile and a quarter on a slop-ridden Belmont main track and still, again with Shoemaker aboard, managed somehow to get his 137-pound burden up just in time to catch Honest Pleasure and beat him a head.

Zenyatta had to take inspiration from the way Dr. Fager dealt with his only race on grass, in the 1968 United Nations at Atlantic City, when he went slipping and sliding, never really able to extend, through a fierce pace duel with Advocator, who carried 22 fewer pounds. Somehow, Dr. Fager prevailed to win by a neck.

"It had rained, and the grass was wet on top," said John Nerud, the man in Dr. Fager's corner. "I could have put stickers on him, but didn't, and he was sliding all over the place around the turns. But then when he got to the eighth pole, he found his stride and was able to come back on and beat that horse. The great ones find a way to get it done."

The fact that Zenyatta—like Dr. Fager, Forego, and John Henry—was able to compensate for the unfamiliar terrain and still run her race was of little comfort to the friends and family who gathered at the barn after her return from the backstretch testing facility. There were tears and quiet mumblings, guys with badges barking "get back" and "no flash" to pressing fans, and feeble words of consolation passed around like leftovers from a stale buffet.

"We really wanted it for her," Jerry Moss said. "We know she's perfect, but we really wanted it for her."

After a few turns with barn foreman Frank Leal, Zenyatta started to stride out, hardly the picture of defeat. John Shirreffs took the shank and led her out back, and there, silhouetted against the headlights of cars and busses heading down Longfield Avenue, Zenyatta nibbled at the sparse grass behind Barn 41, the headlights illuminating "Zenyatta" on the creamy white blanket she wore.

"Would you know it was her anyway?" one of the dozen or so fans gathered on the street side of the chain-link fence was asked.

"Of course I would," she replied. "I'd know her anywhere."

The others were staring, talking softly, while another group of at least 50 stood behind a line of sawhorses adjacent to the barn itself. The honk of a horn was followed by a cry from the dark, "You're the queen!" and fans, on the street side of the chain-link fence and standing behind the sawhorses, began to applaud, tentatively at first, as if not to disturb the sobriety of the moment, then louder, until Zenyatta picked up her head in acknowledgement. Shirreffs led her to the fence to sniff at her fans through the links, then guided her along the line of sawhorses before finally taking her back inside.

Inside, Jerry Moss sat with his 6-foot-4 frame folded onto the cot where groom Mario Espinoza had slept through the nights leading up to the Classic, in a tack room overheated against the cold. Taking out a pen and a folded scrap of paper, Moss set about composing a statement for the media. He had done this sort of thing before, running companies, boosting charity drives, so the language of colorless, odorless public statement was hardly foreign. This was different, though, since the subject matter was so unusual.

The statement began with "We're very proud . . ." and ended with ". . . he beat a superstar," and that was more than enough for the purpose. Ann Moss, clutching a sheet of Zenyatta photos, thought the less said the better, worrying more about how Zenyatta was taking it.

"I hope she doesn't know she lost," Ann said, and then, as Zenyatta walked past, "There's my girl—you're the best, the greatest."

There appeared then, without warning, Freddie Johnson, dressed in denim and fleece, standing in the crowd at the mouth of the barn, quietly insistent that he wanted to congratulate John Shirreffs and everybody in the Zenyatta camp for the fantastic job they had done with the mare.

"I told Al I wanted to come over here and do this," said Johnson, referring to his boss, Al Stall, Jr. "He said, 'Freddie, I think that's a real good idea.' I know how hard these people worked to keep this mare so good for so long. She ran her heart out. She deserved that win. But I got hoarse hollering for Blame, 'cause I knew once he took the lead it's hard to pass him, and she was coming like a freight train."

Shirreffs was busy bedding Zenyatta down, so Johnson approached Moss and extended his hand, and in the moment their hands clasped the disparate worlds embraced by the power and glory of the Thoroughbred racehorse came vividly alive in the chill of the Louisville night.

Johnson, 37, first went to work for trainer Frankie Brothers at the Fair Grounds as a 10-year-old kid before joining Al Stall. Johnson's father, who maintained vending machines, was murdered on the job. His family home where his mother still lived, near the University of New Orleans, was wiped off the map when the nearby levee was breeched in the storm surge of that terrible August of 2005.

That same year, Jerry Moss—the kid from Brooklyn who made his fortune in the music business, married a model, and considers himself as lucky as a man could be—won the Kentucky Derby with Giacomo. But now it was Johnson, who'd been around Blame from the moment he arrived in the Stall barn, offering words of consolation and praise to the man who owned Zenyatta.

"The day I knew he was good was the day he beat Gone Astray at Saratoga in the Curlin," Johnson said of Blame. "After that, Al said, 'What do you think I should do?' and I said, 'Try the Super Derby.' That's what we did, and Regal Ransom got out there, nobody pressing him, and he just walked around there. So we gave him time off, let him come back as a 4-year-old, and look what he's done."

What Blame has done is as much as any older horse in recent history, winning the Fayette on a synthetic Keeneland surface, the Stephen Foster at Churchill Downs, and the Whitney at Saratoga in addition to the Classic. The only mark against him this year was the Jockey Club Gold Cup, when Haynesfield freaked on the lead and Blame could not catch him.

"The only reason Haynesfield got us," Johnson said, "was we got up there the day before the race and he just stood at the back of the stall, just lookin' lookin' lookin'. I told Al something ain't right. He's not the horse I know."

The horse Johnson knew put the Gold Cup loss behind him and showed up like a champion for the Classic.

"That just shows you," Johnson said. "They can all have a day like that.

"Except her," he added. "She never had a day like that."

Ever.